## BOOKS BY B. KLIBAN

CAT
CATCALENDAR CATS

NEVER EAT ANYTHING BIGGER THAN YOUR HEAD & OTHER DRAWINGS
WHACK YOUR PORCUPINE
TINY FOOTPRINTS
TWO GUYS FOOLING AROUND WITH THE MOON

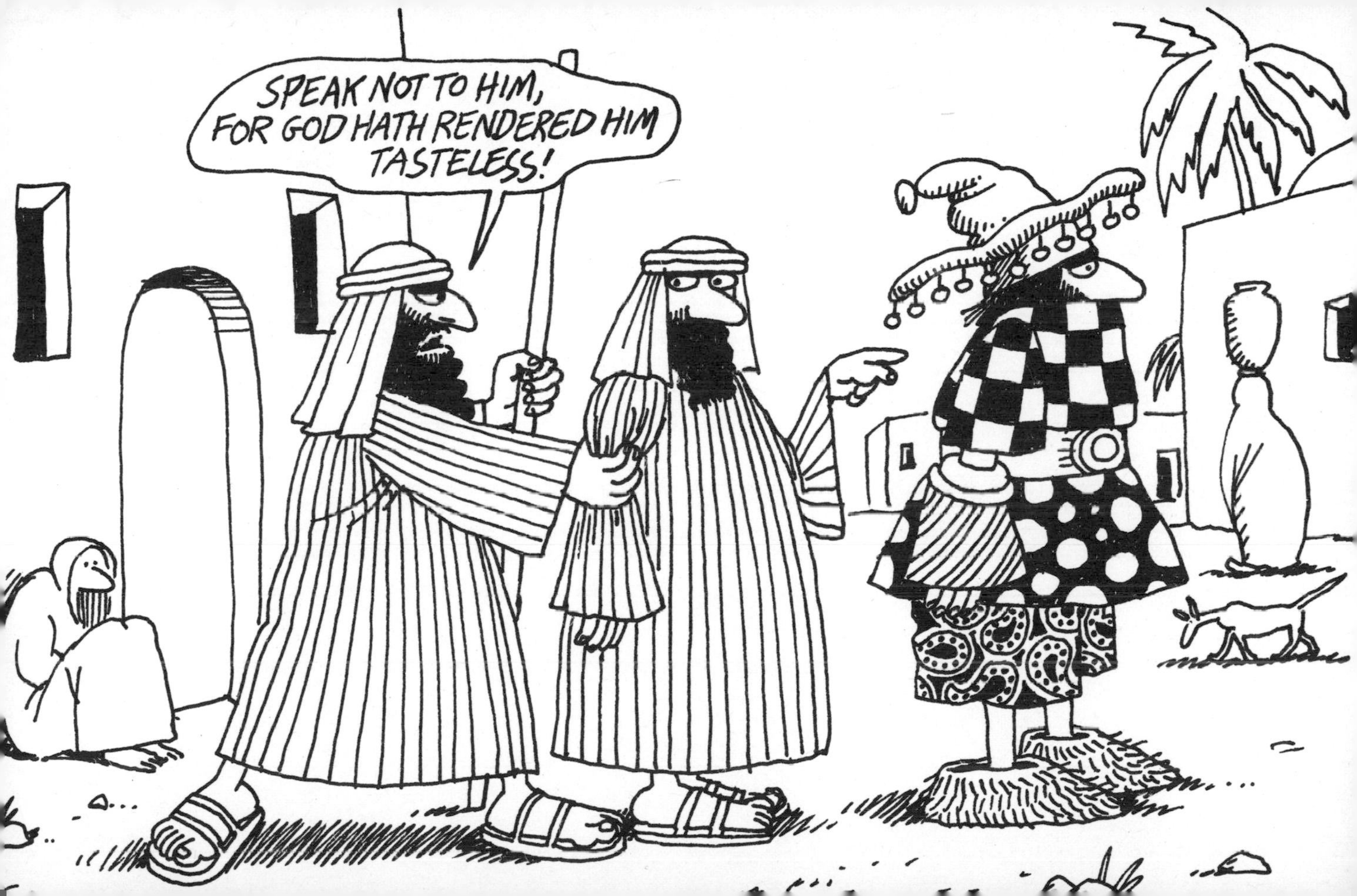
SPEAK NOT TO HIM, FOR GOD HATH RENDERED HIM TASTELESS!

# TWO GUYS FOOLING AROUND WITH THE MOON
## AND OTHER DRAWINGS

B Kliban

WORKMAN PUBLISHING, NEW YORK

PUBLISHED SIMULTANEOUSLY IN CANADA BY SAUNDERS OF TORONTO, INC.
LIBRARY OF CONGRESS CATALOGING IN PUBLICATION DATA
KLIBAN, B.
TWO GUYS FOOLING AROUND WITH THE MOON.
1. AMERICAN WIT AND HUMOR, PICTORIAL. 1. TITLE.
NC1429.K58A4 1982 741.5'973 81-43780
ISBN 0-89480-198-8 AACR2
BOOK DESIGN: JUDITH KAMMAN
WORKMAN PUBLISHING CO., INC.
1 WEST 39TH STREET
NEW YORK, NEW YORK 10018
MANUFACTURED IN THE UNITED STATES OF AMERICA
FIRST PRINTING MARCH 1982
10 9 8 7 6 5 4 3 2 1

What's good for Business is good for America

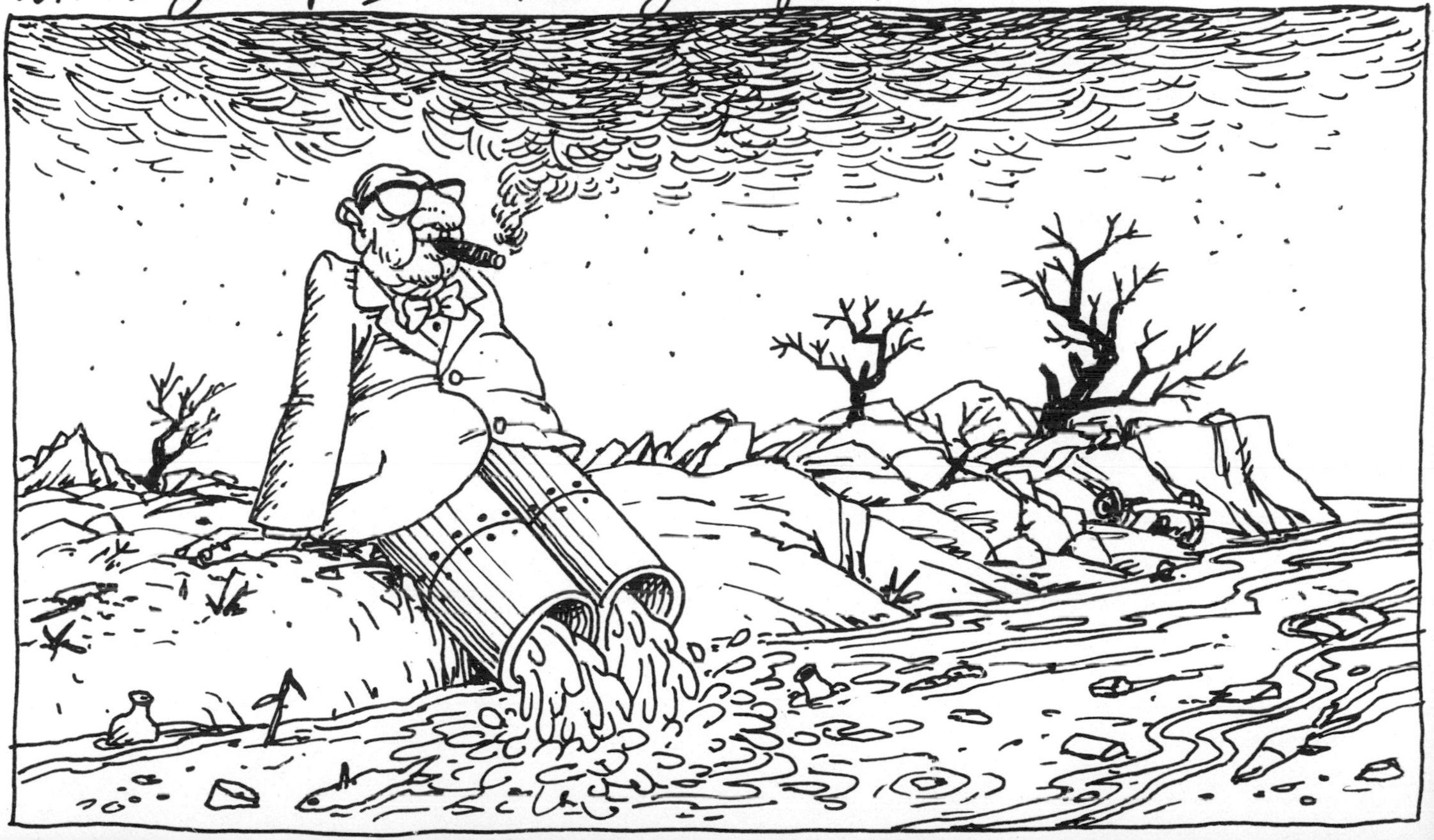

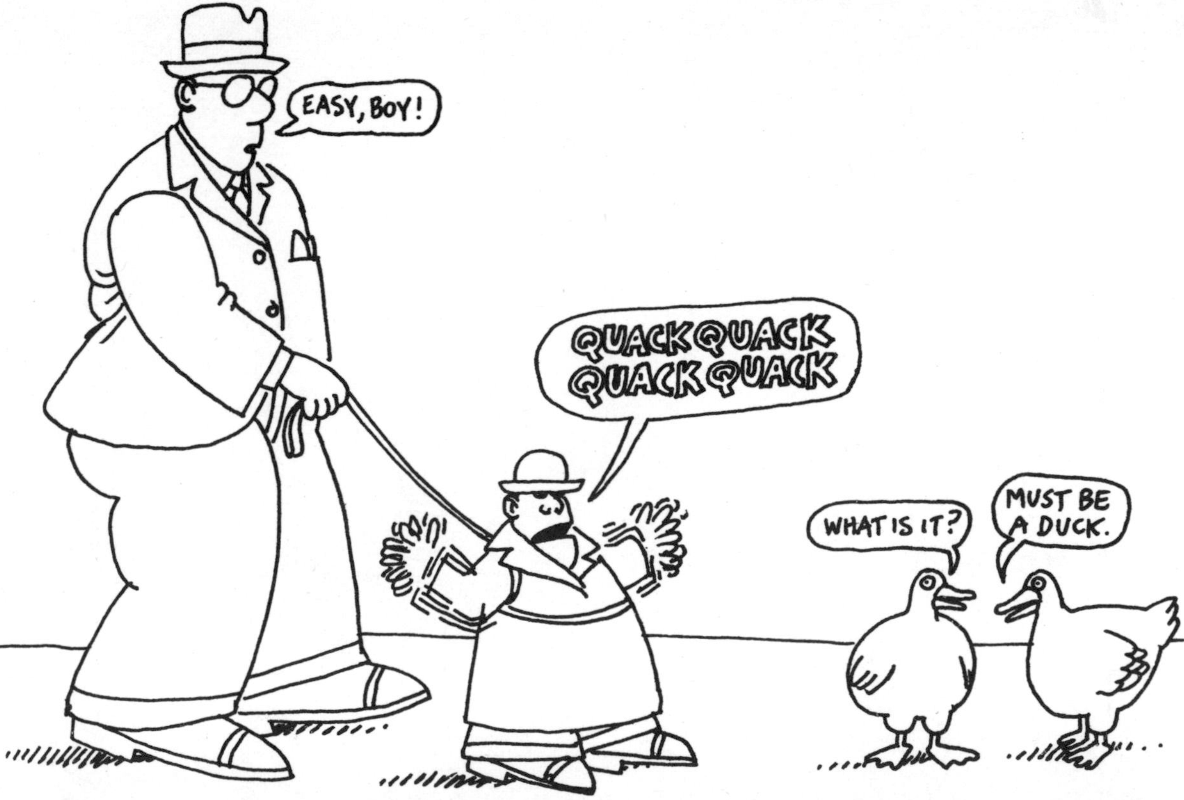
EASY, BOY!
QUACK QUACK QUACK QUACK
WHAT IS IT?
MUST BE A DUCK.

# Flimsy Dog Model

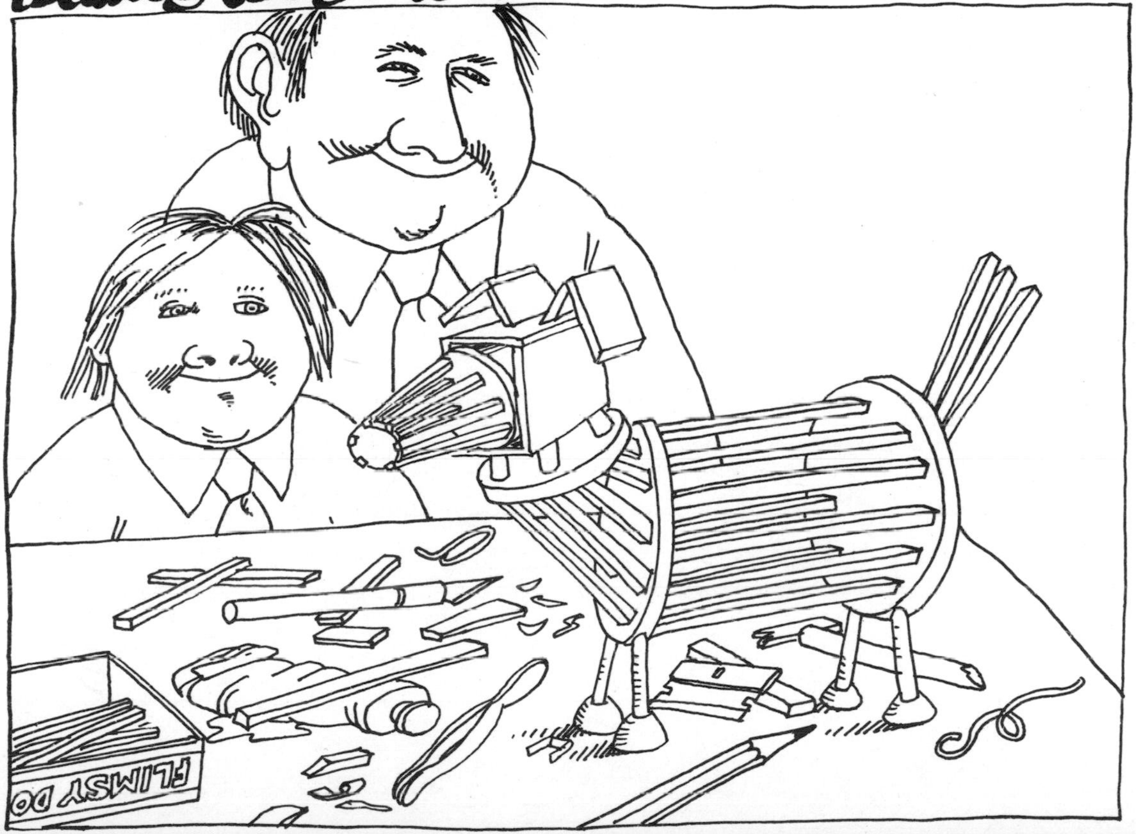

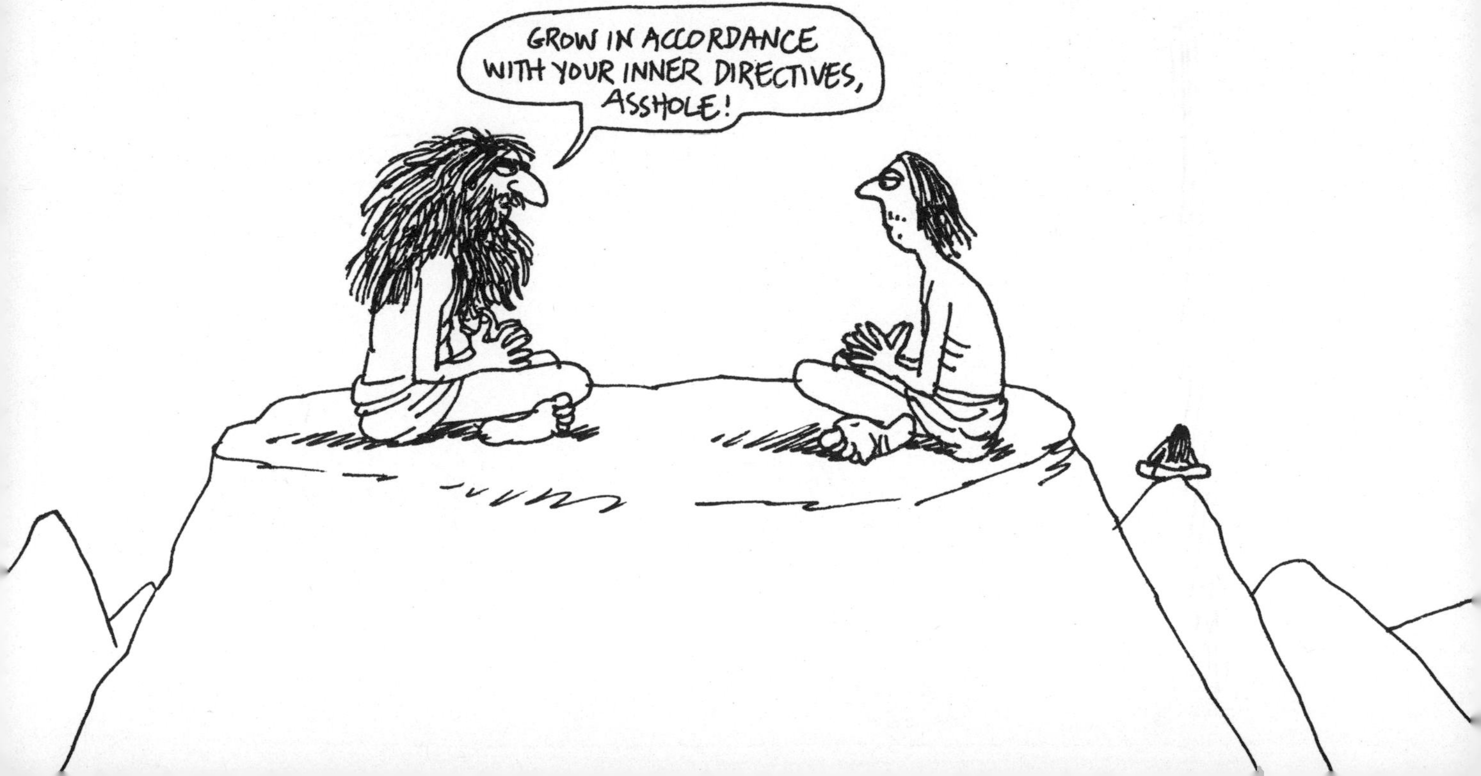
GROW IN ACCORDANCE WITH YOUR INNER DIRECTIVES, ASSHOLE!

BRASSIERE FULL OF NICKELS Los Angeles Museum of Science

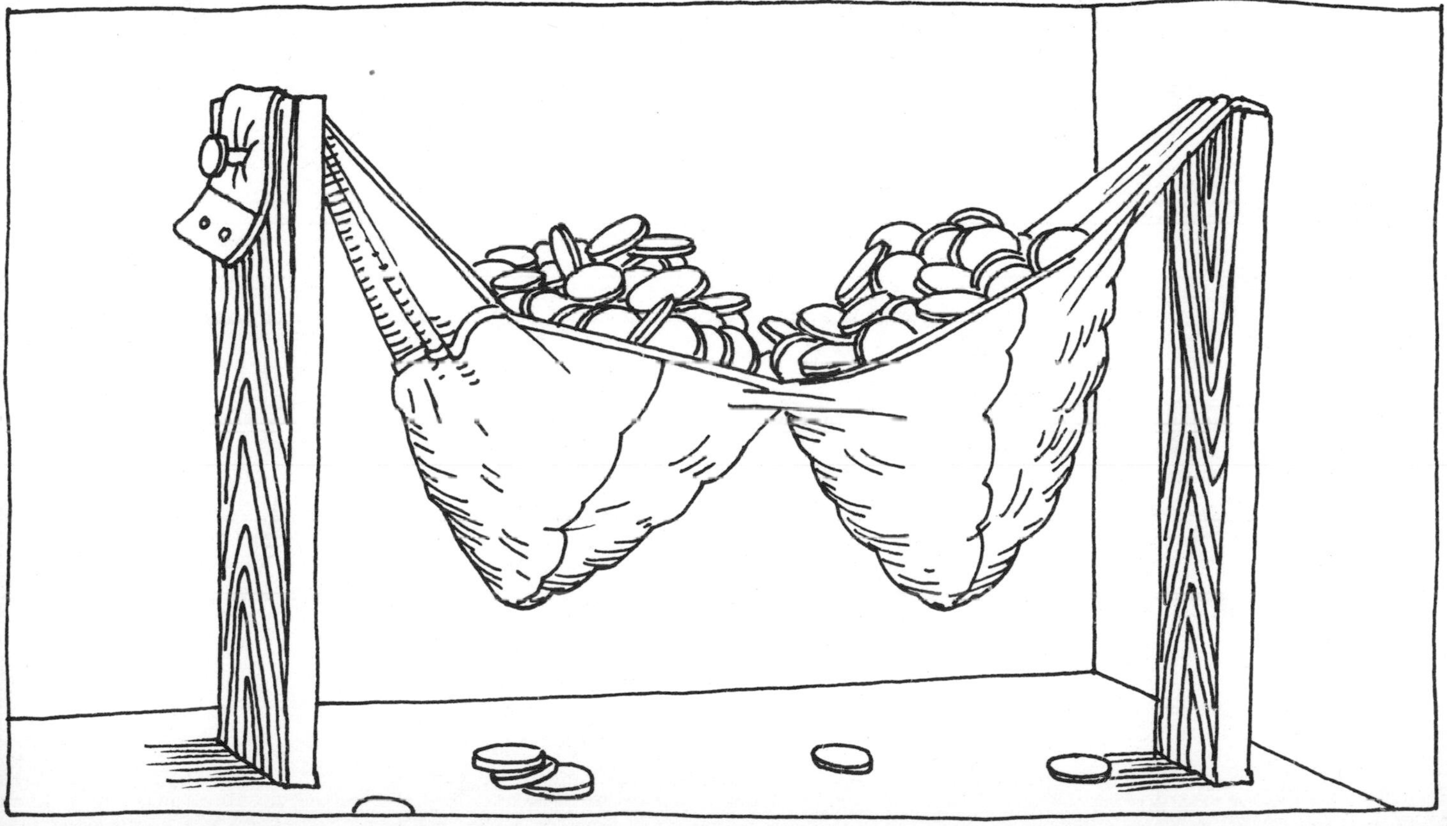

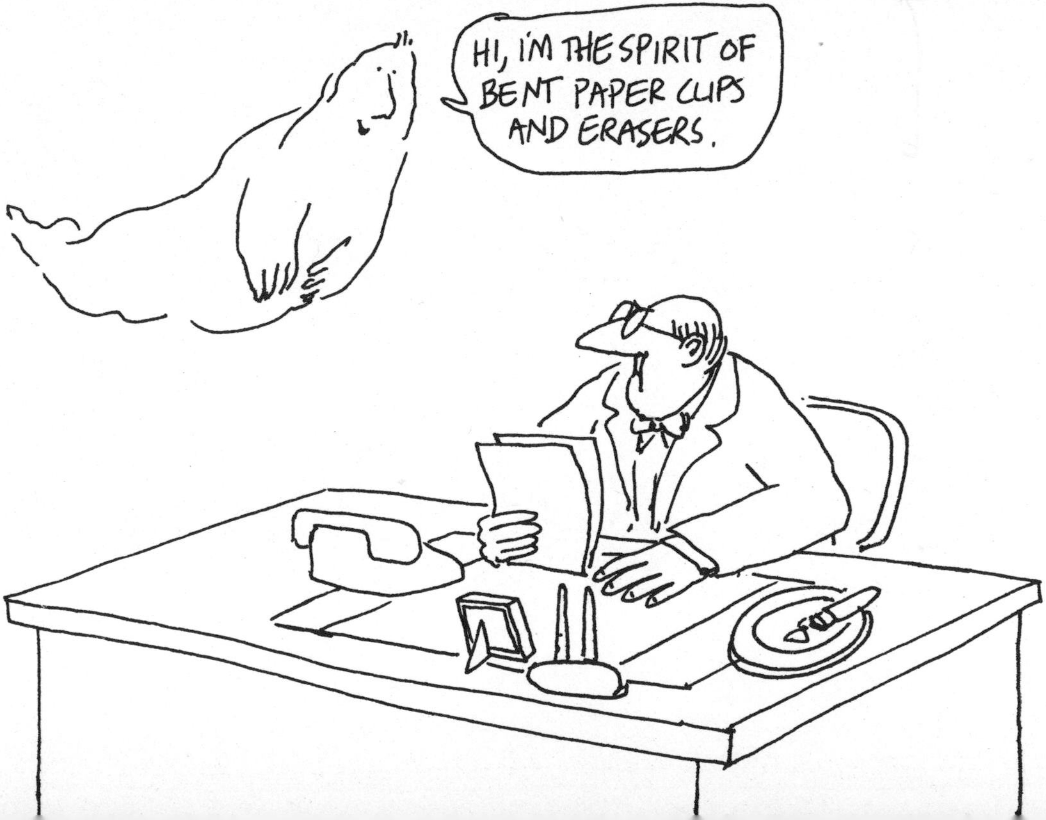
HI, I'M THE SPIRIT OF BENT PAPER CLIPS AND ERASERS.

# Lights Every Time

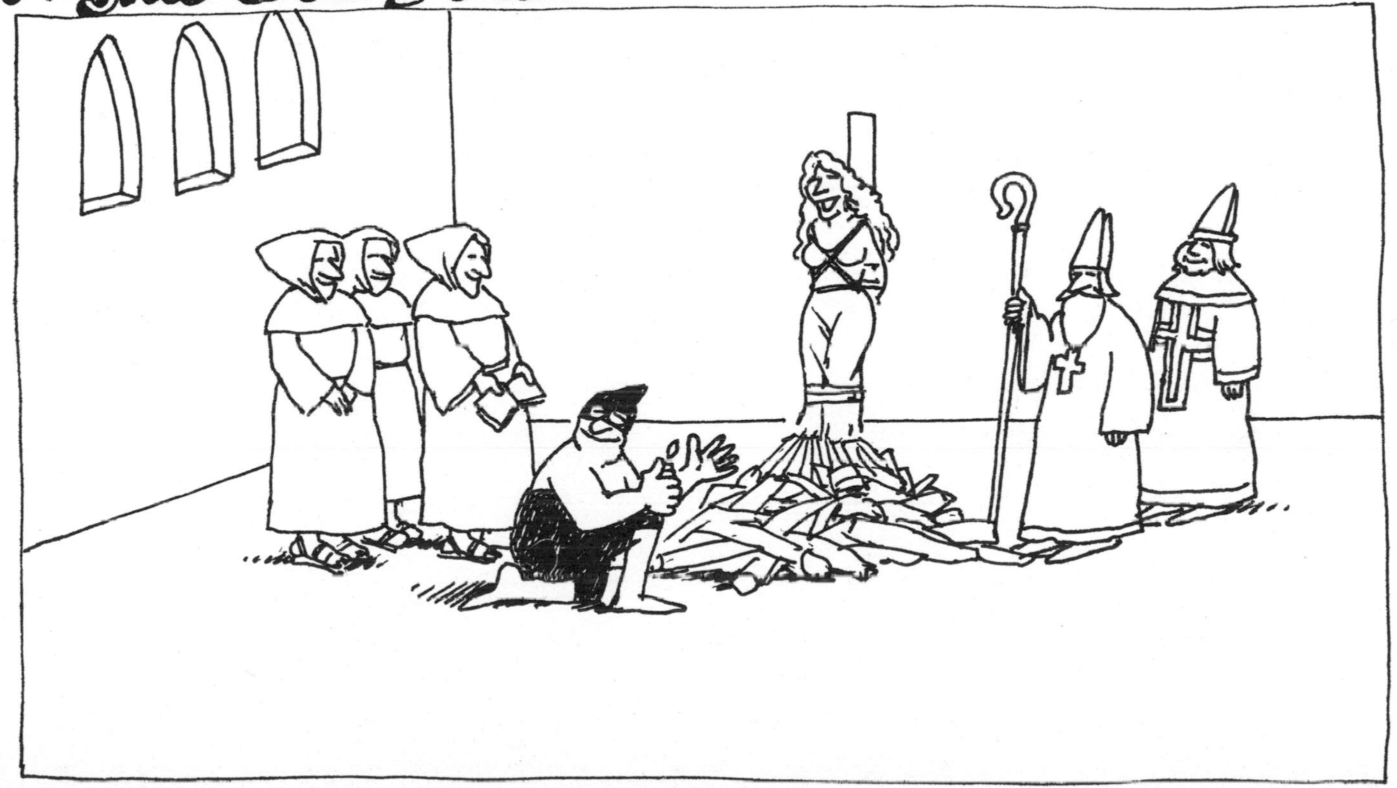

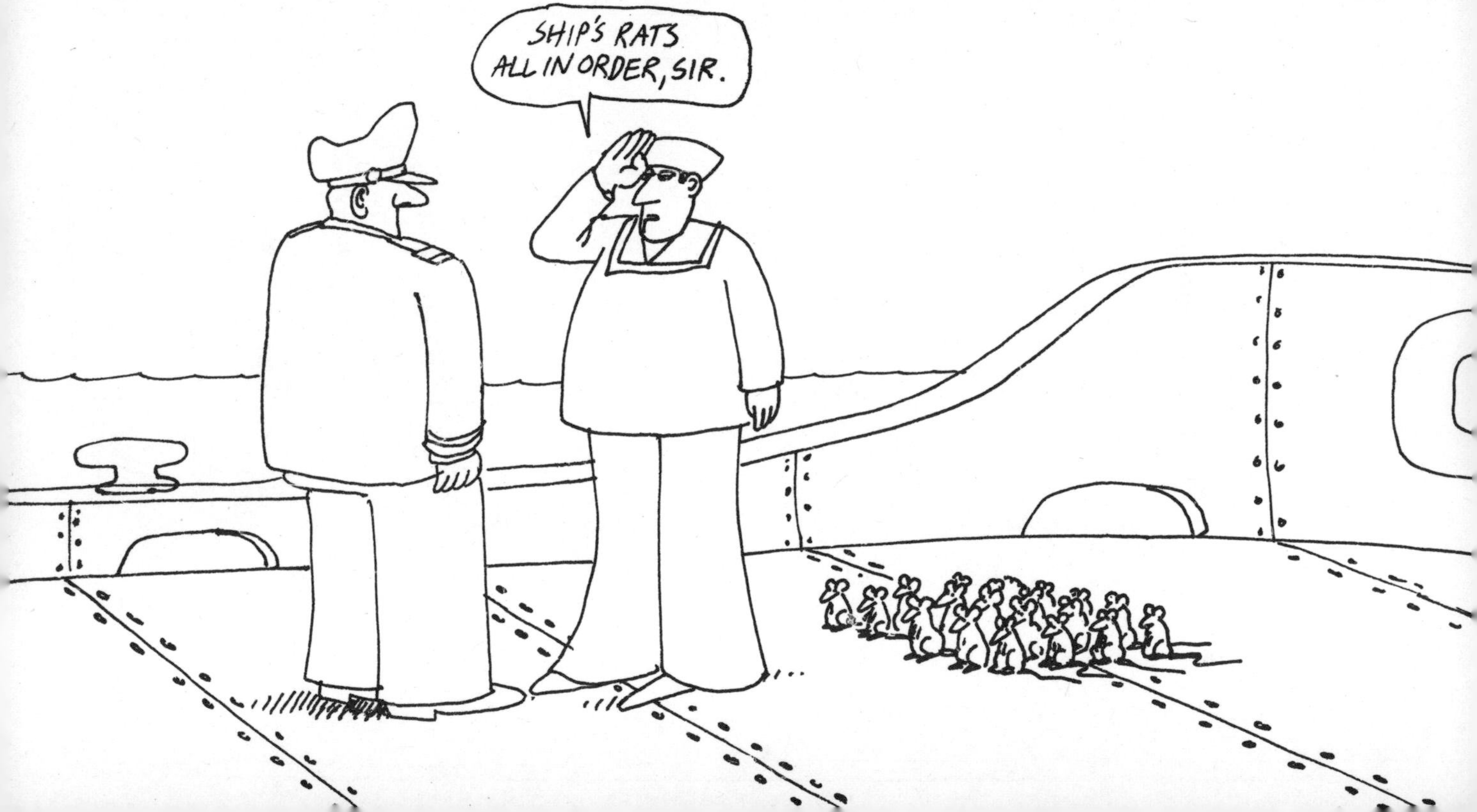
SHIP'S RATS ALL IN ORDER, SIR.

IN CALIFORNIA EVERYBODY SWIMS TO WORK

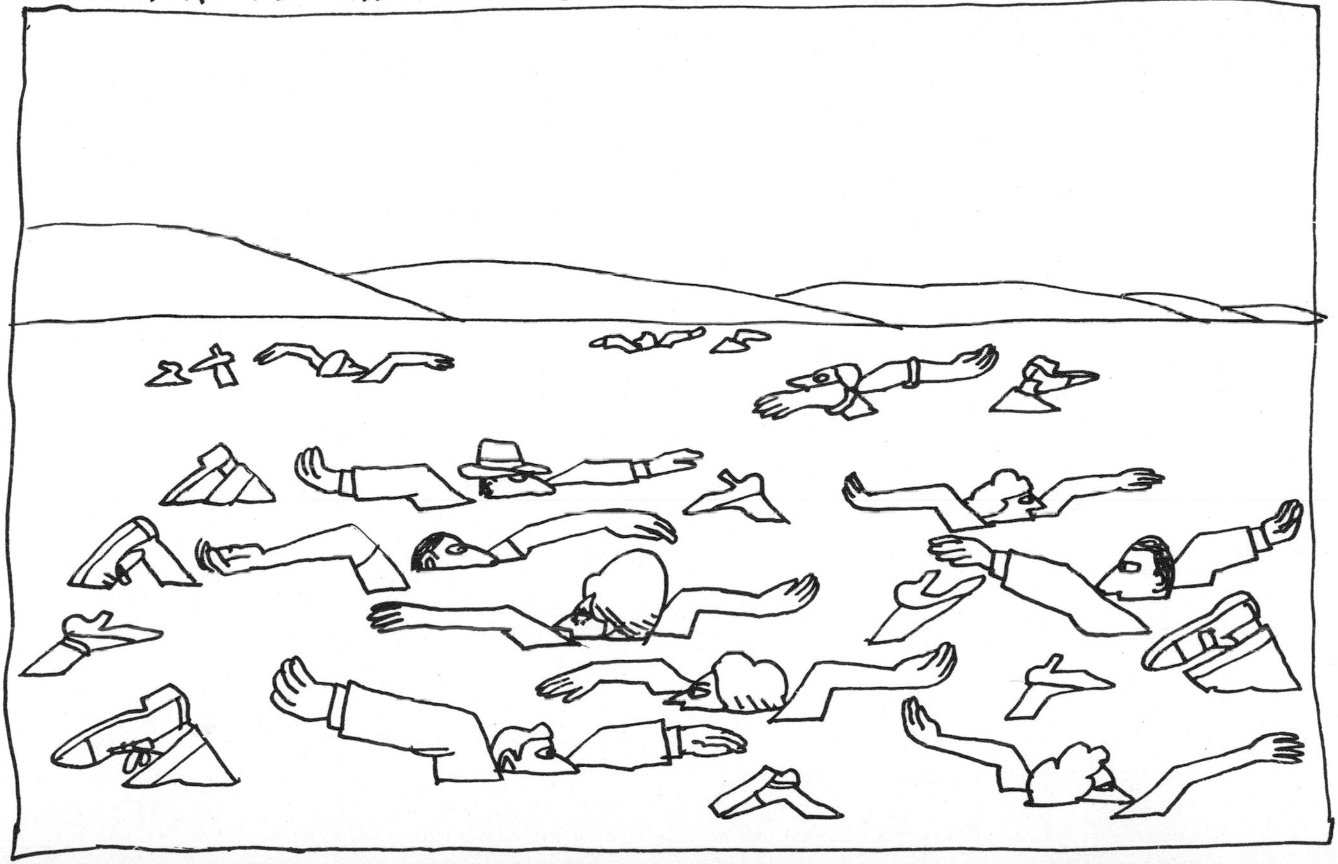

# The Meat Hat

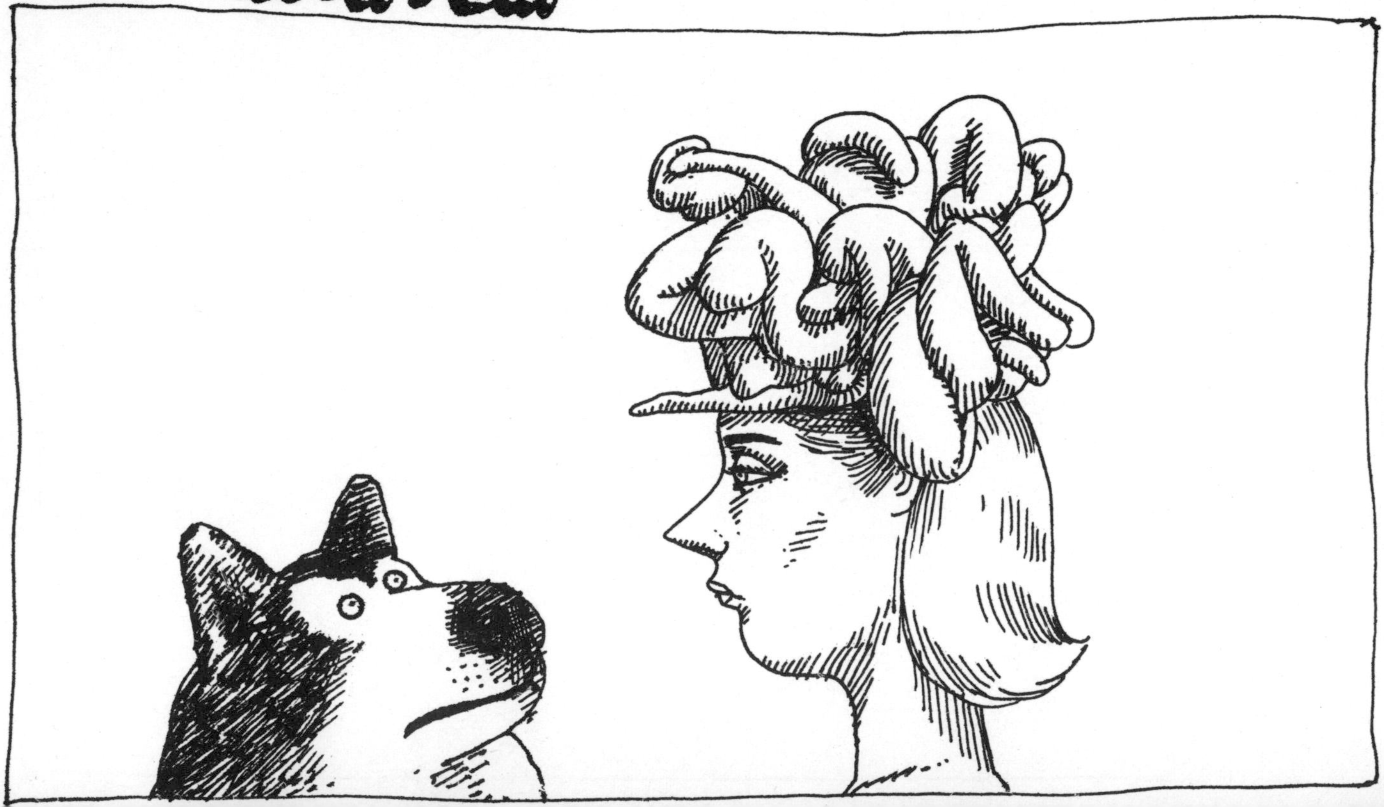

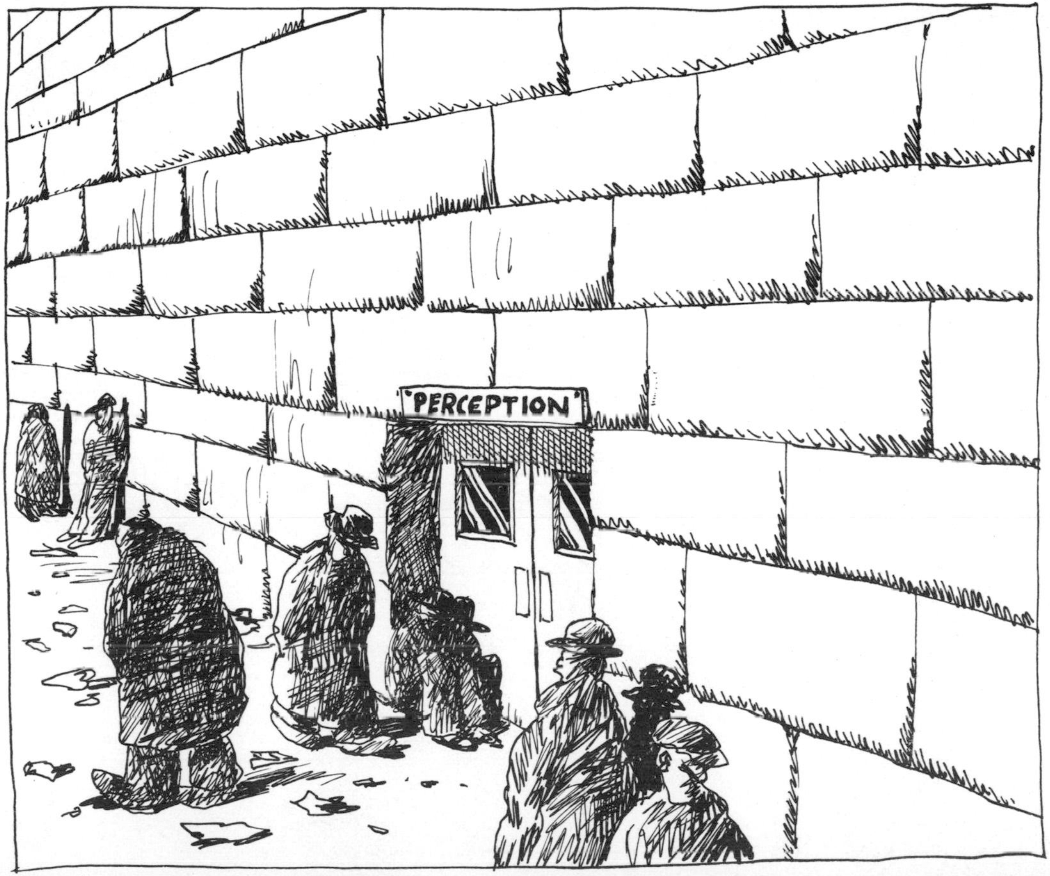
"PERCEPTION"

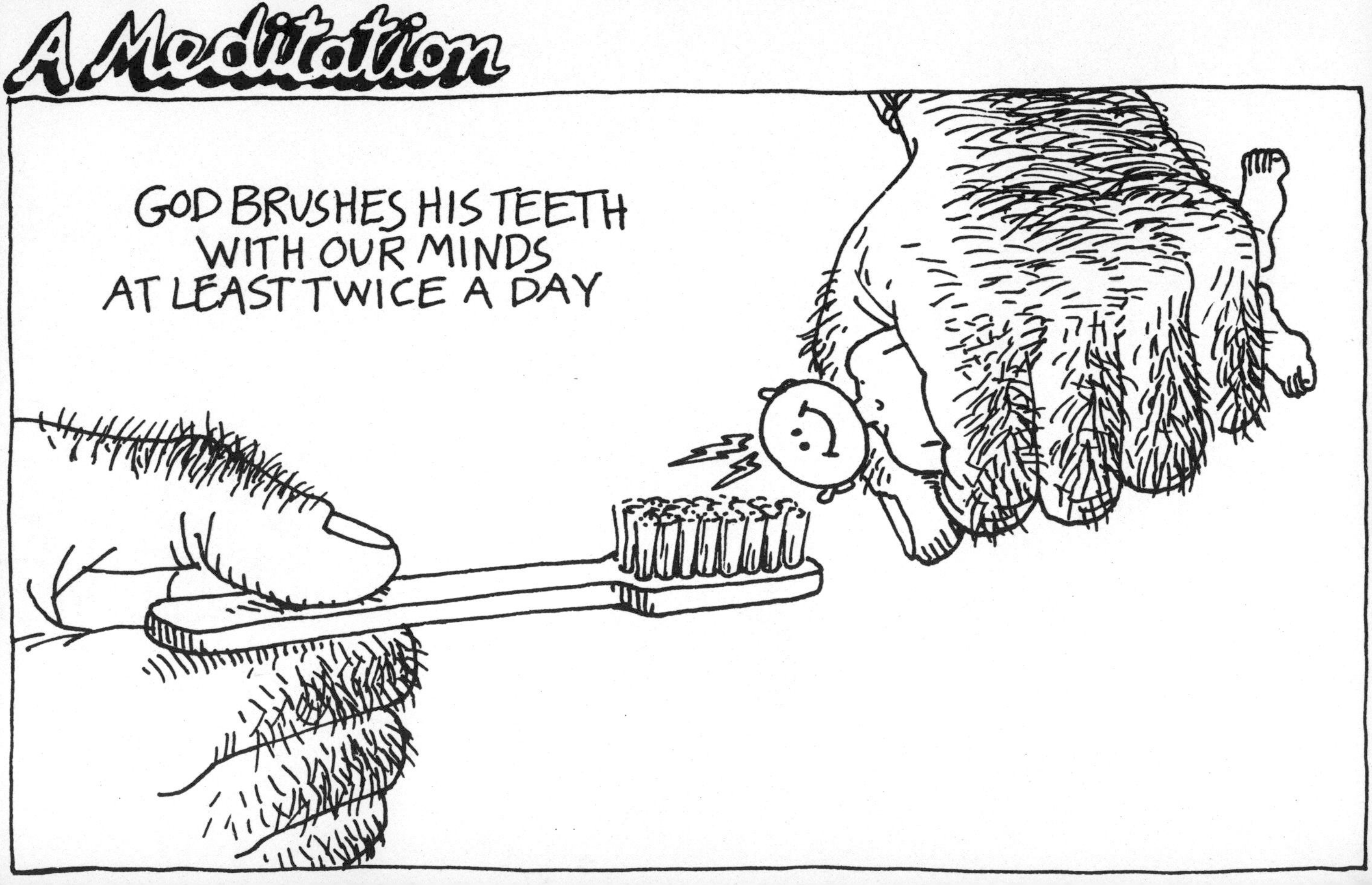
A Meditation
GOD BRUSHES HIS TEETH
WITH OUR MINDS
AT LEAST TWICE A DAY

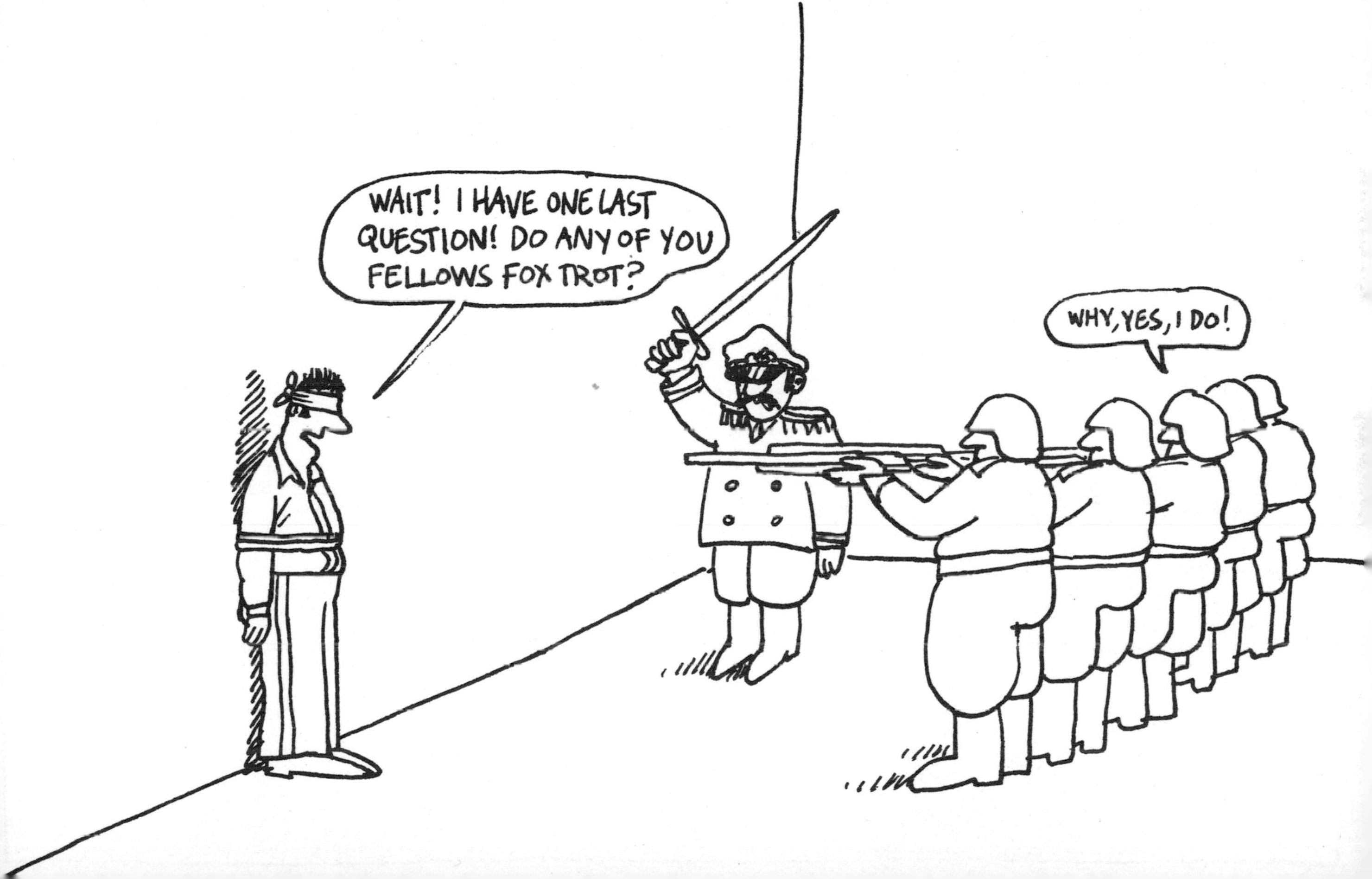
WAIT! I HAVE ONE LAST QUESTION! DO ANY OF YOU FELLOWS FOX TROT?
WHY, YES, I DO!

# Lizard Food

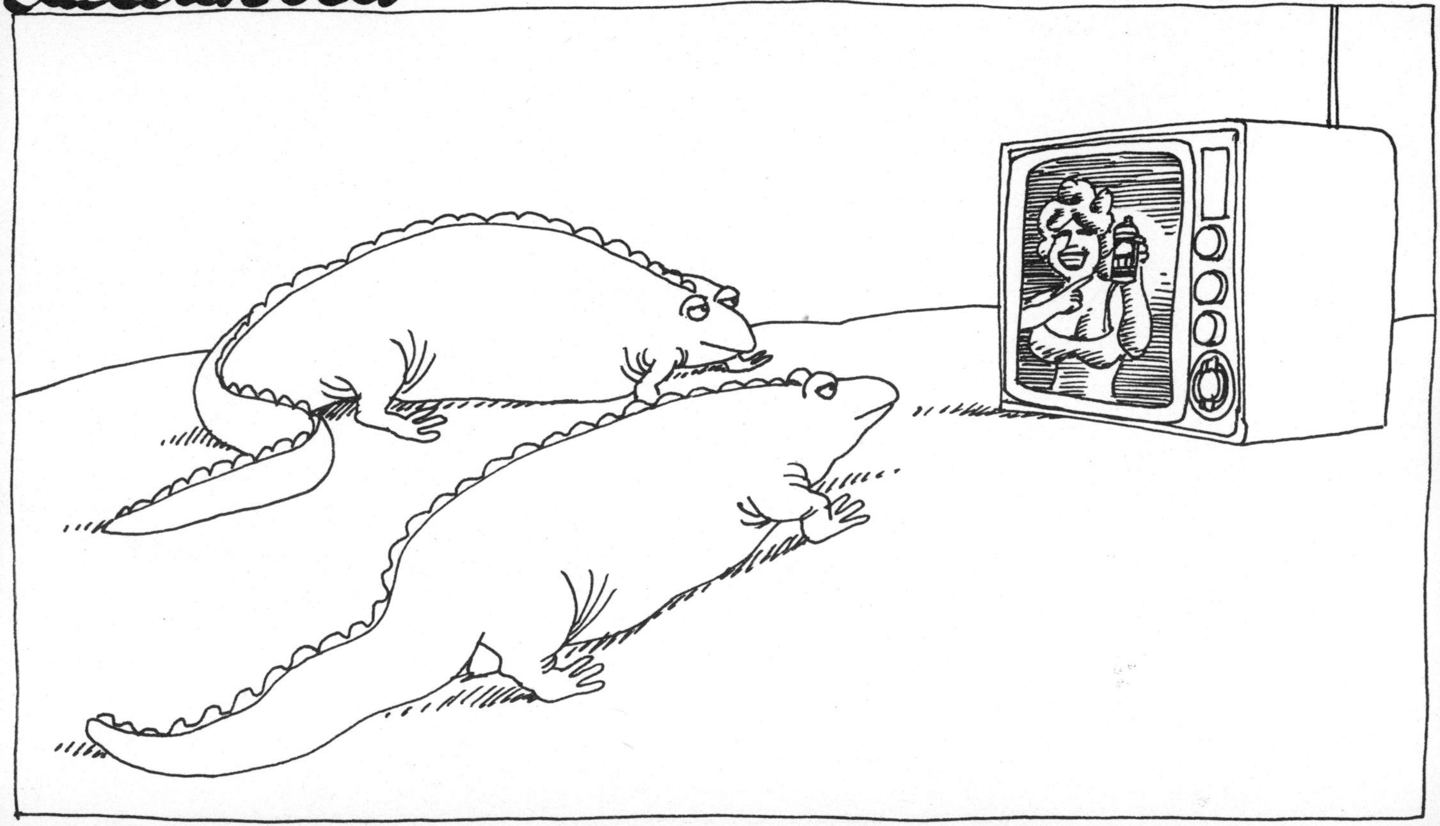

# Basic Sci-Fi

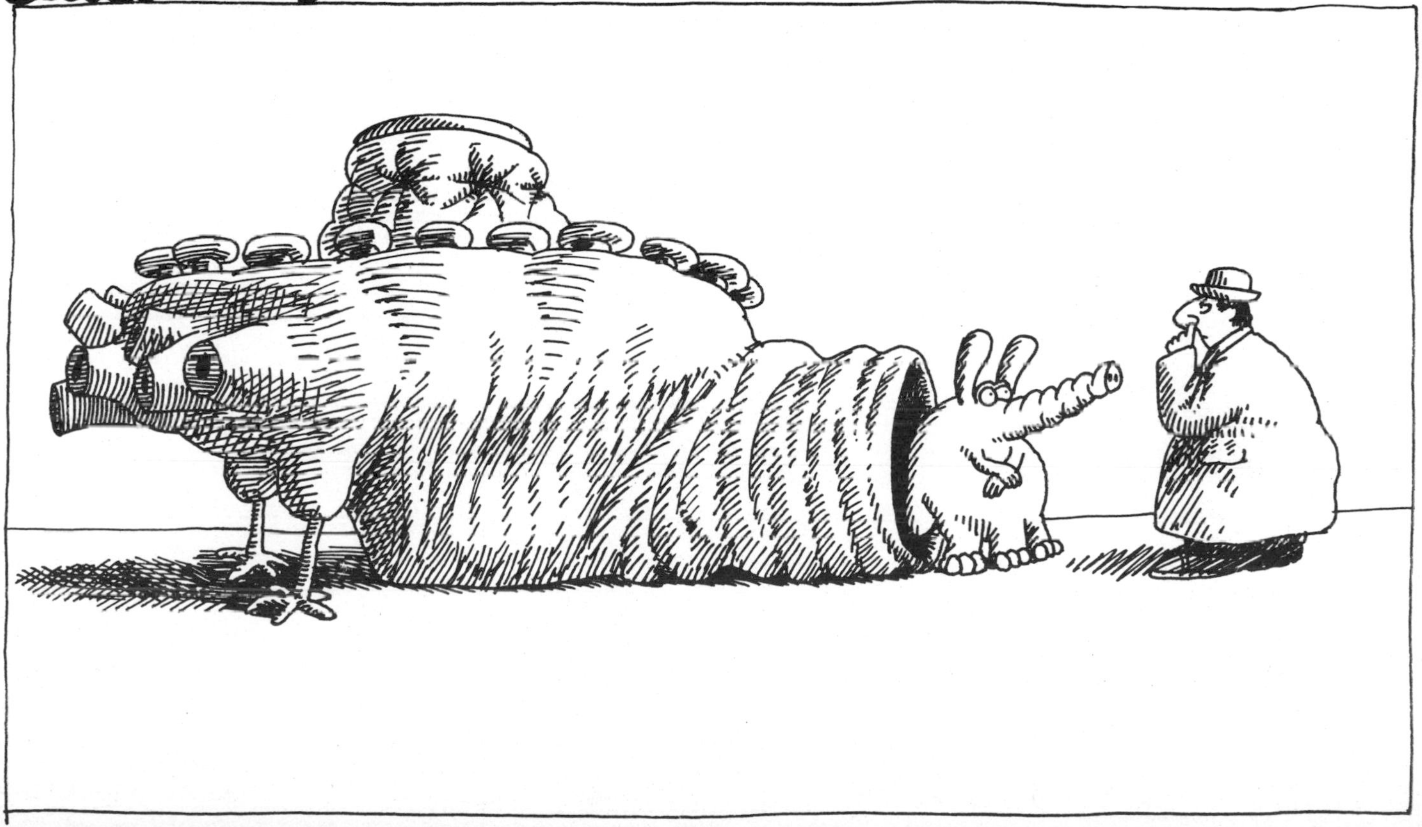

# Your Government in Action

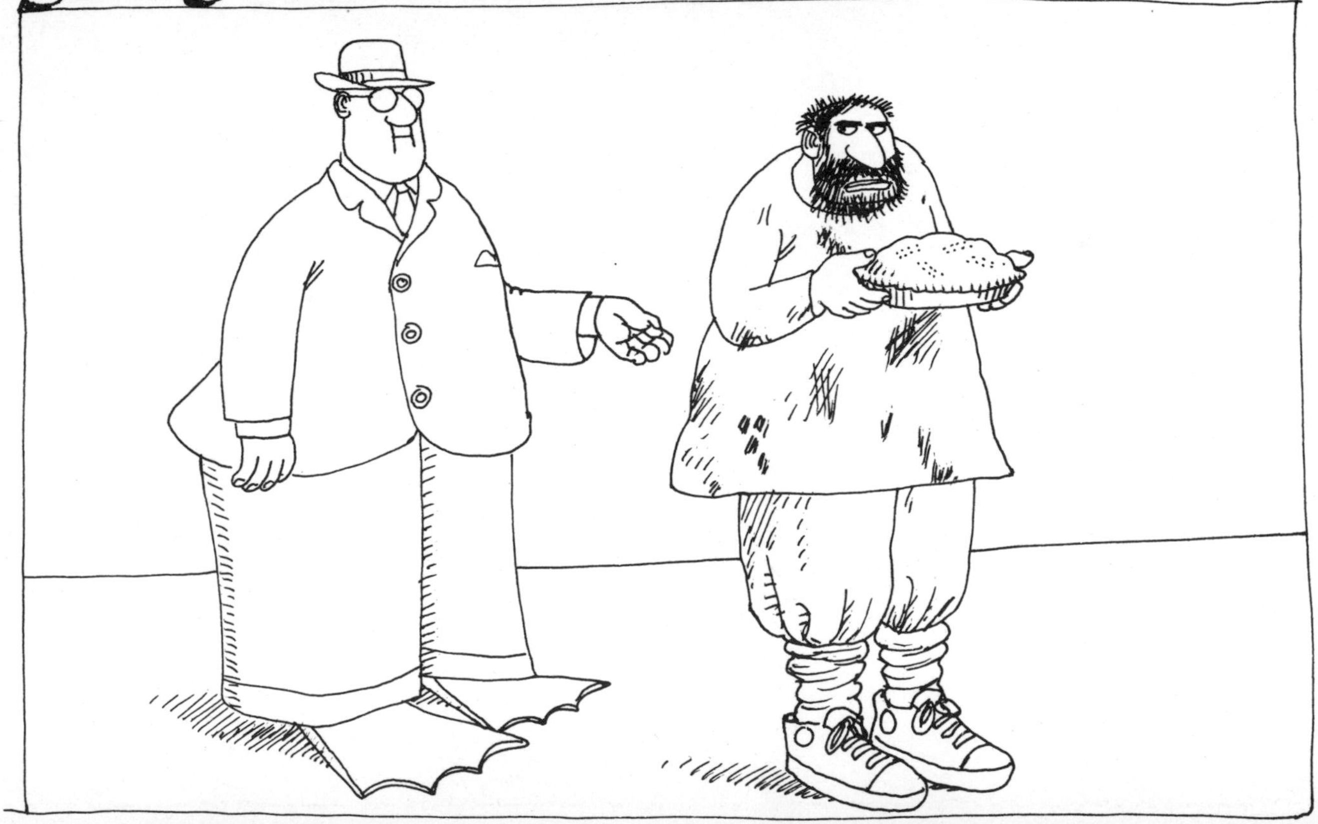

The Bridge of Considerable Difficulty

Venice - Italy

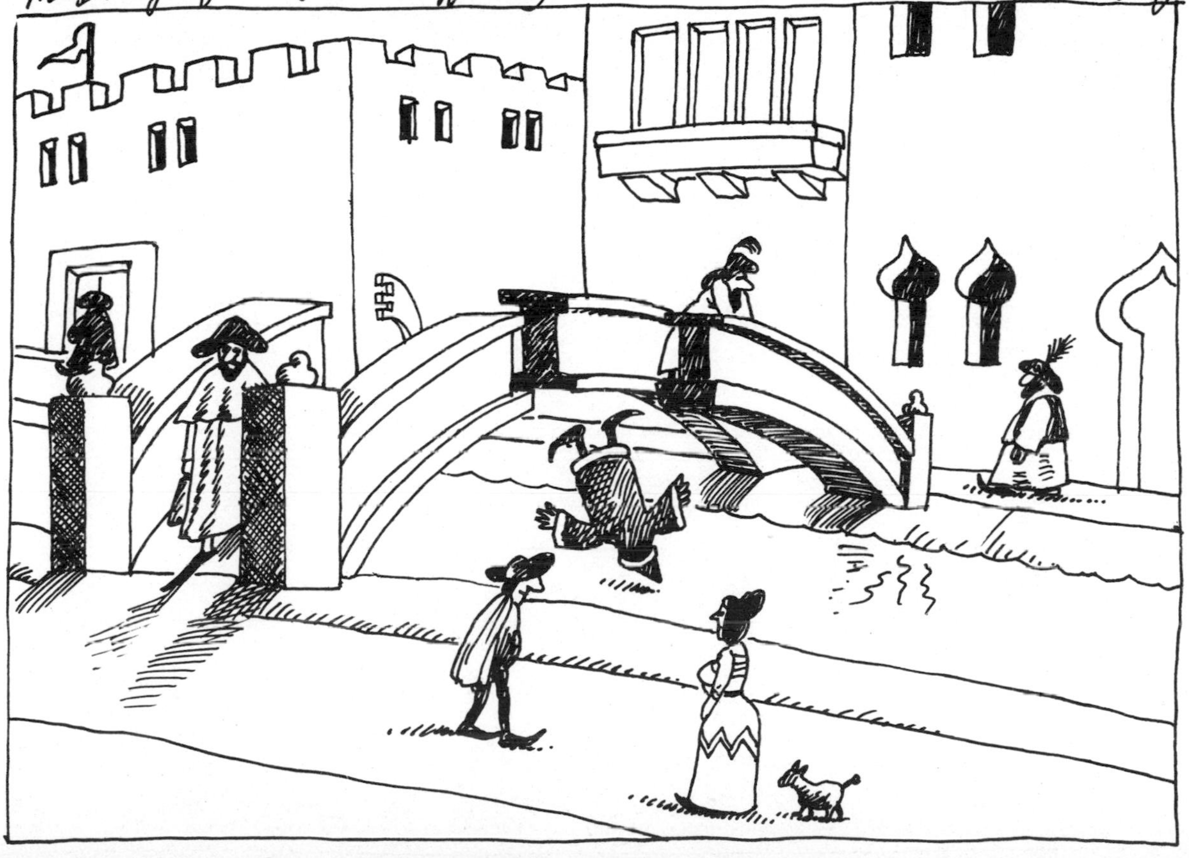

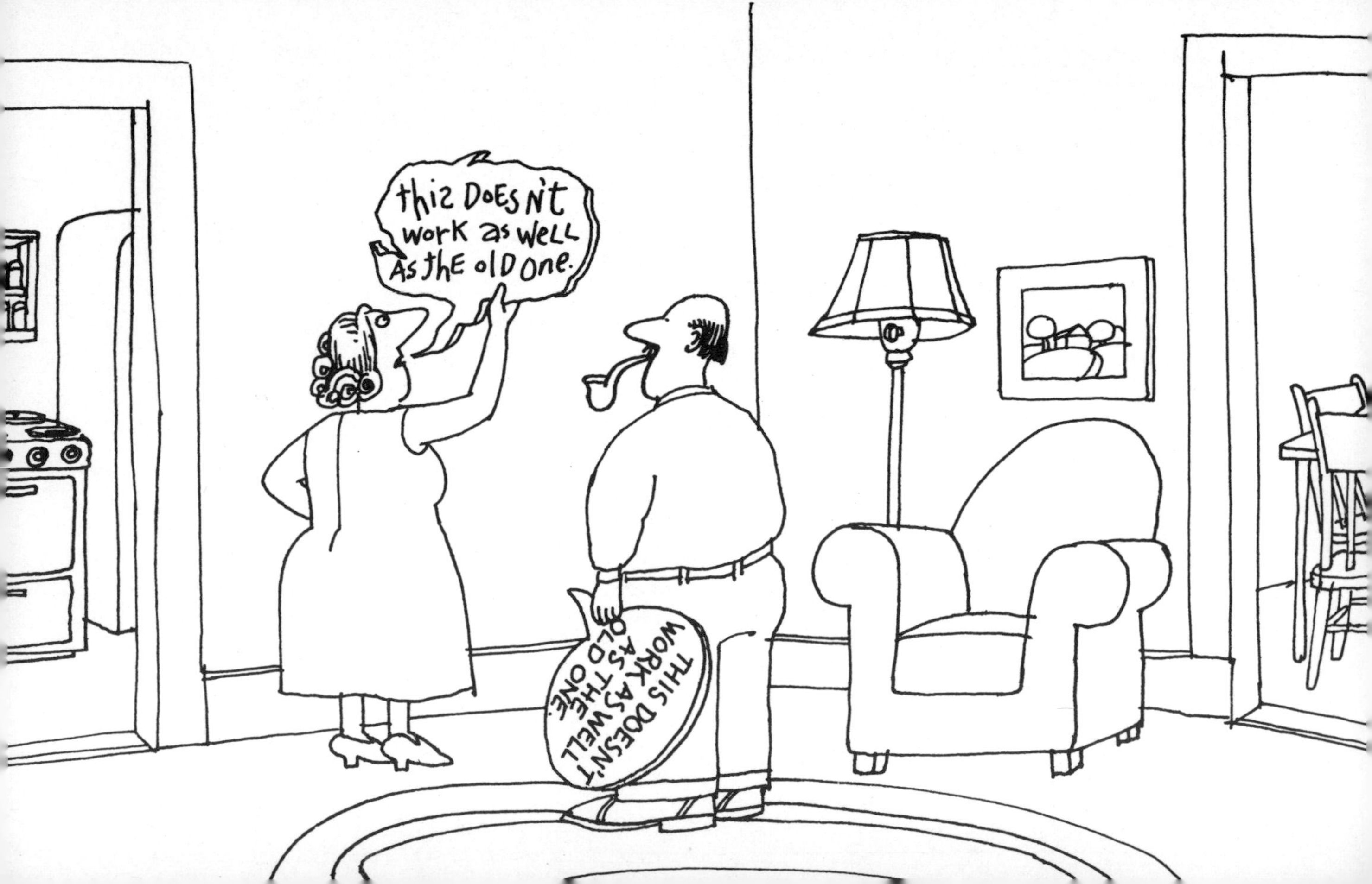
this DOESN't work as WELL AS the old one.
THIS DOESN'T WORK AS WELL AS THE OLD ONE.

# Chapter I- EVERYBODY KILLS EACH OTHER.

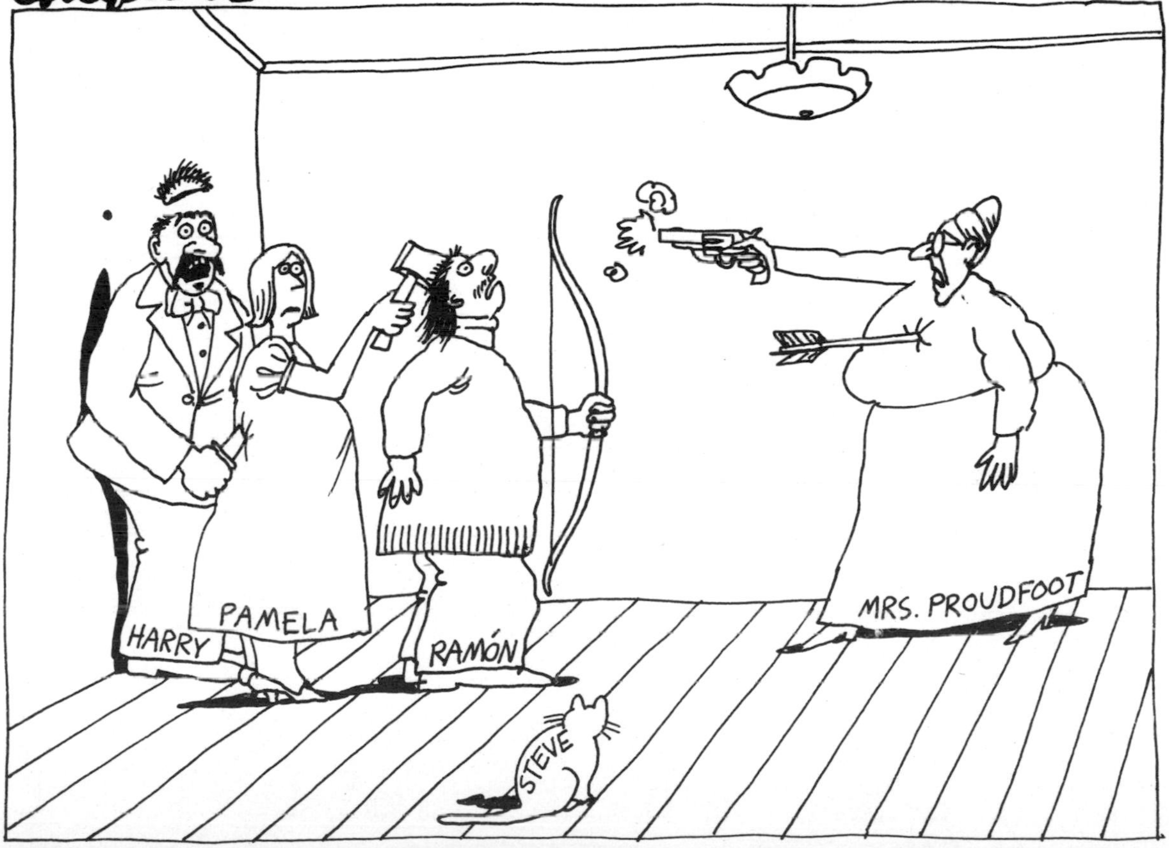

# The Art of Cartooning

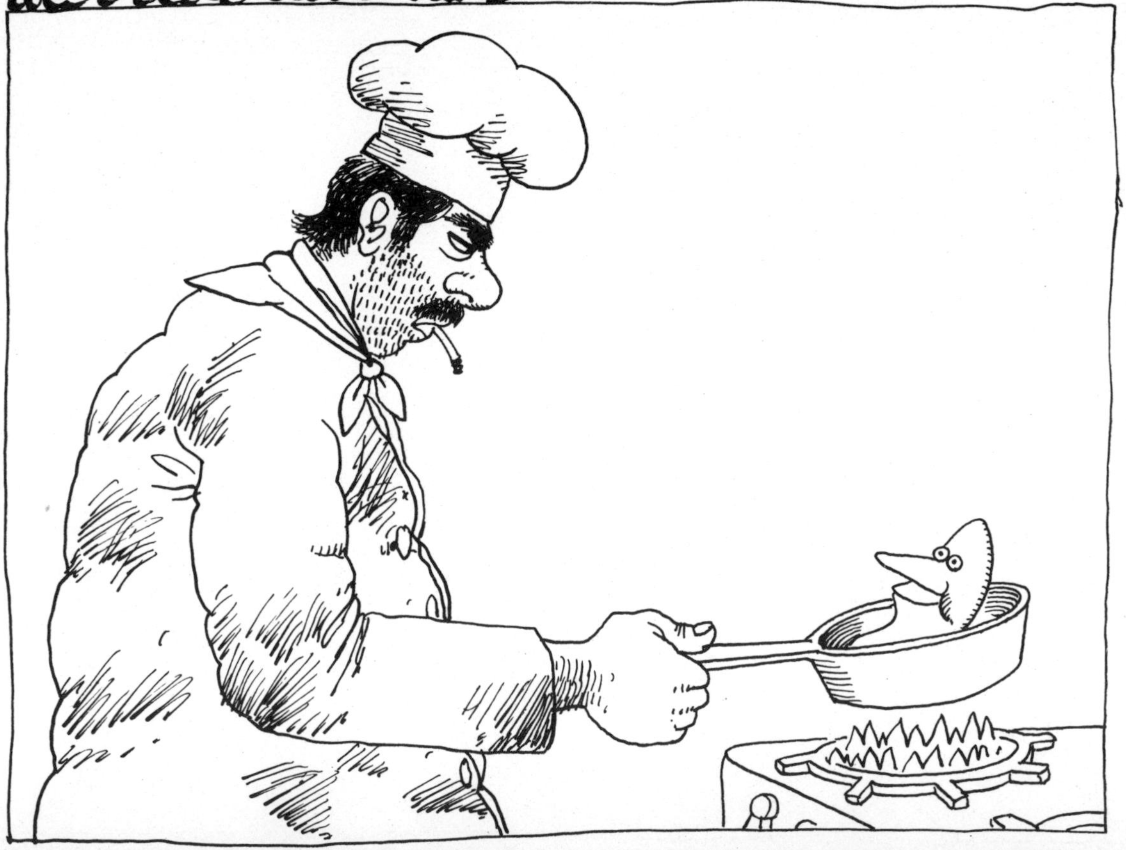

George Lived by an Ocean Which Proved to be Inaccessable.

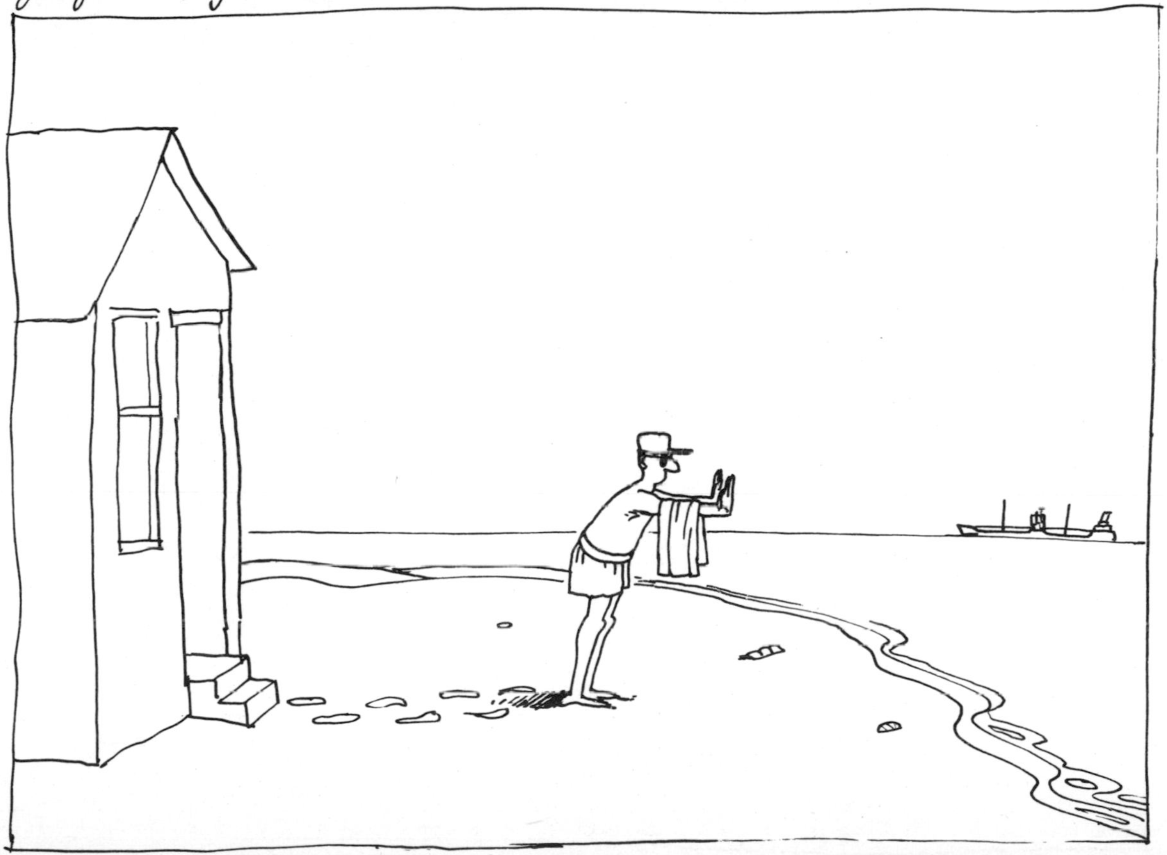

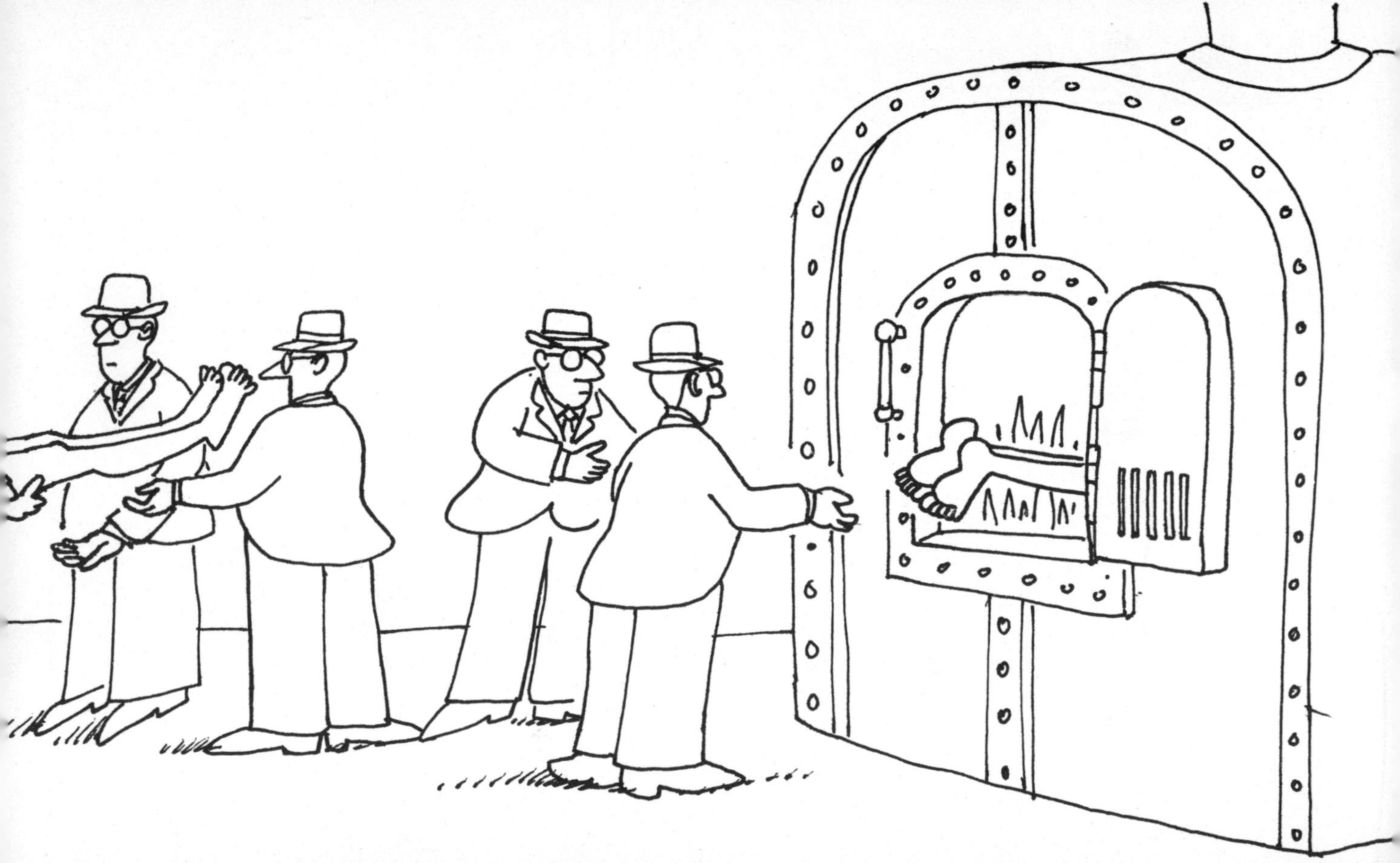

# Wasted Foreplay

## CHAPTER SEVEN

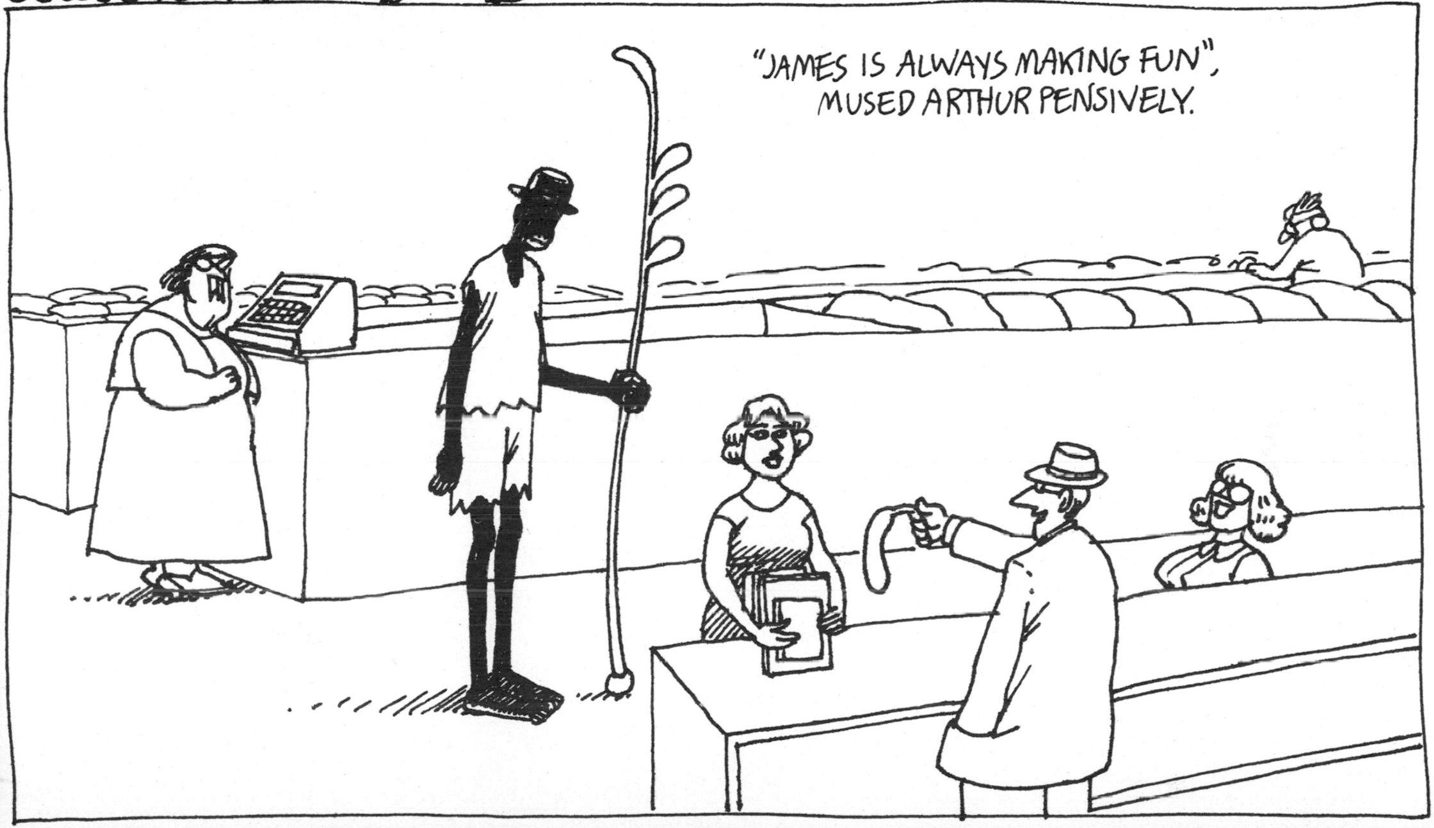
"JAMES IS ALWAYS MAKING FUN",
MUSED ARTHUR PENSIVELY.

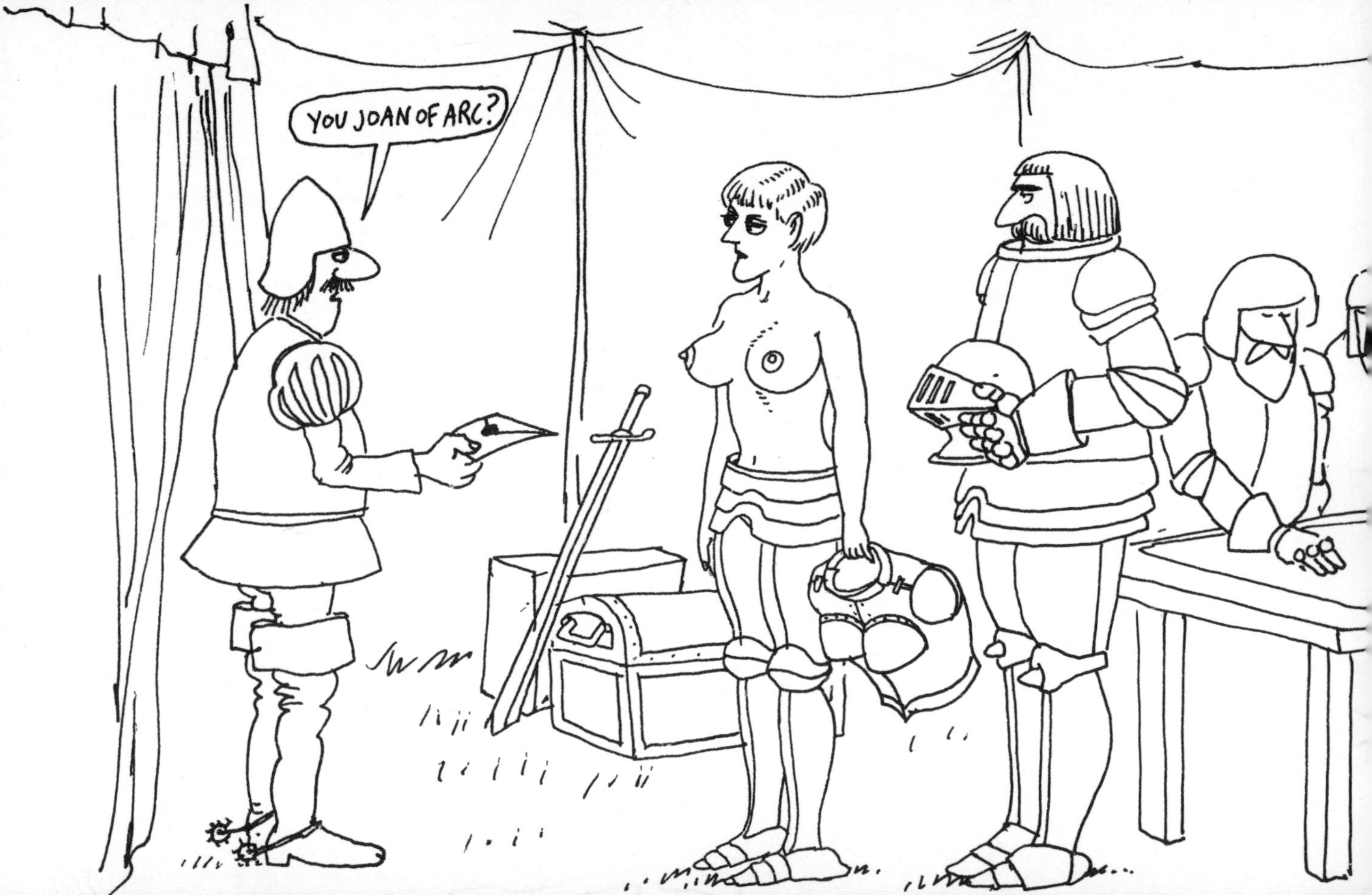
YOU JOAN OF ARC?

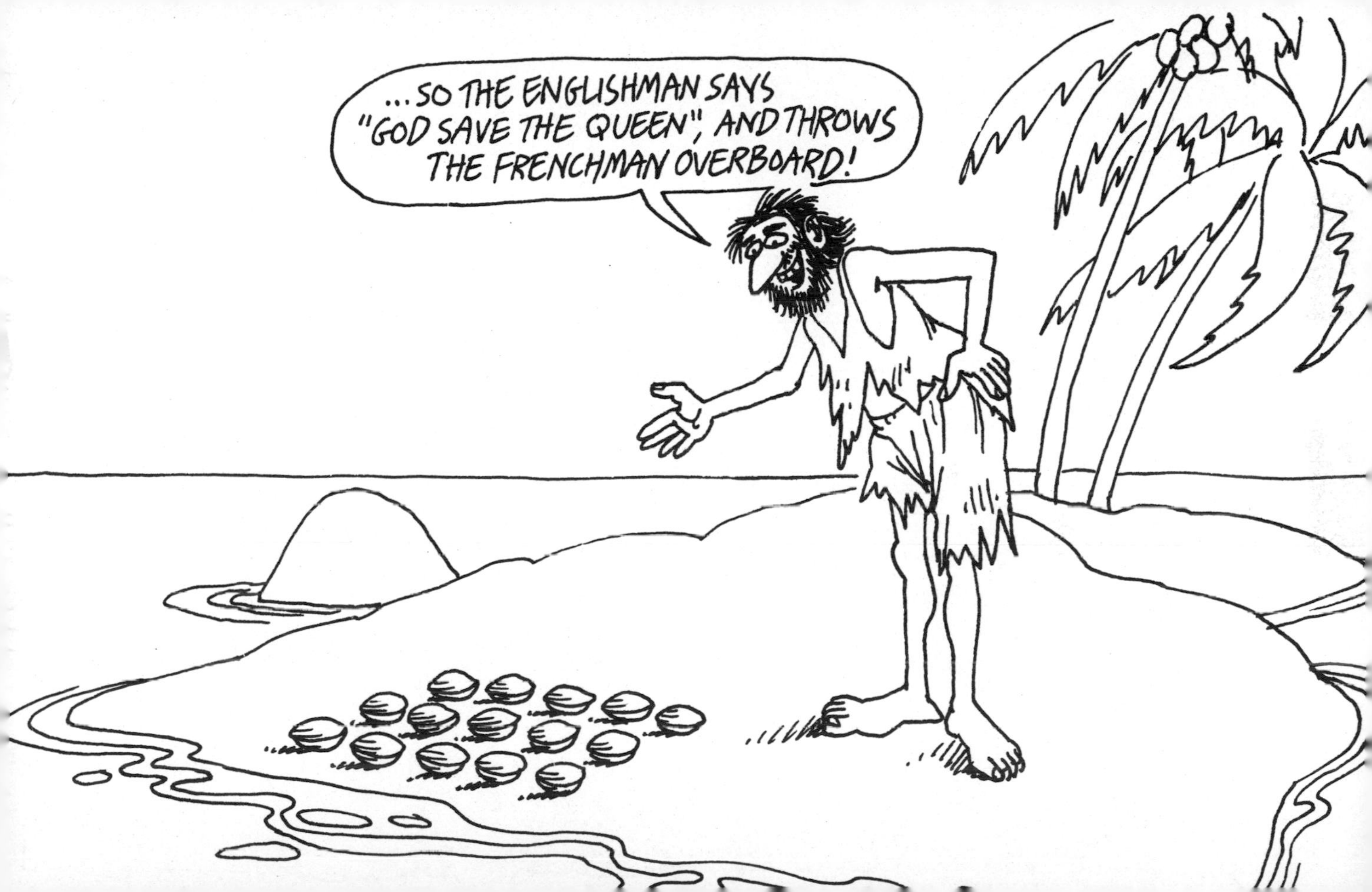
...SO THE ENGLISHMAN SAYS "GOD SAVE THE QUEEN", AND THROWS THE FRENCHMAN OVERBOARD!

# Itzhak Diddley

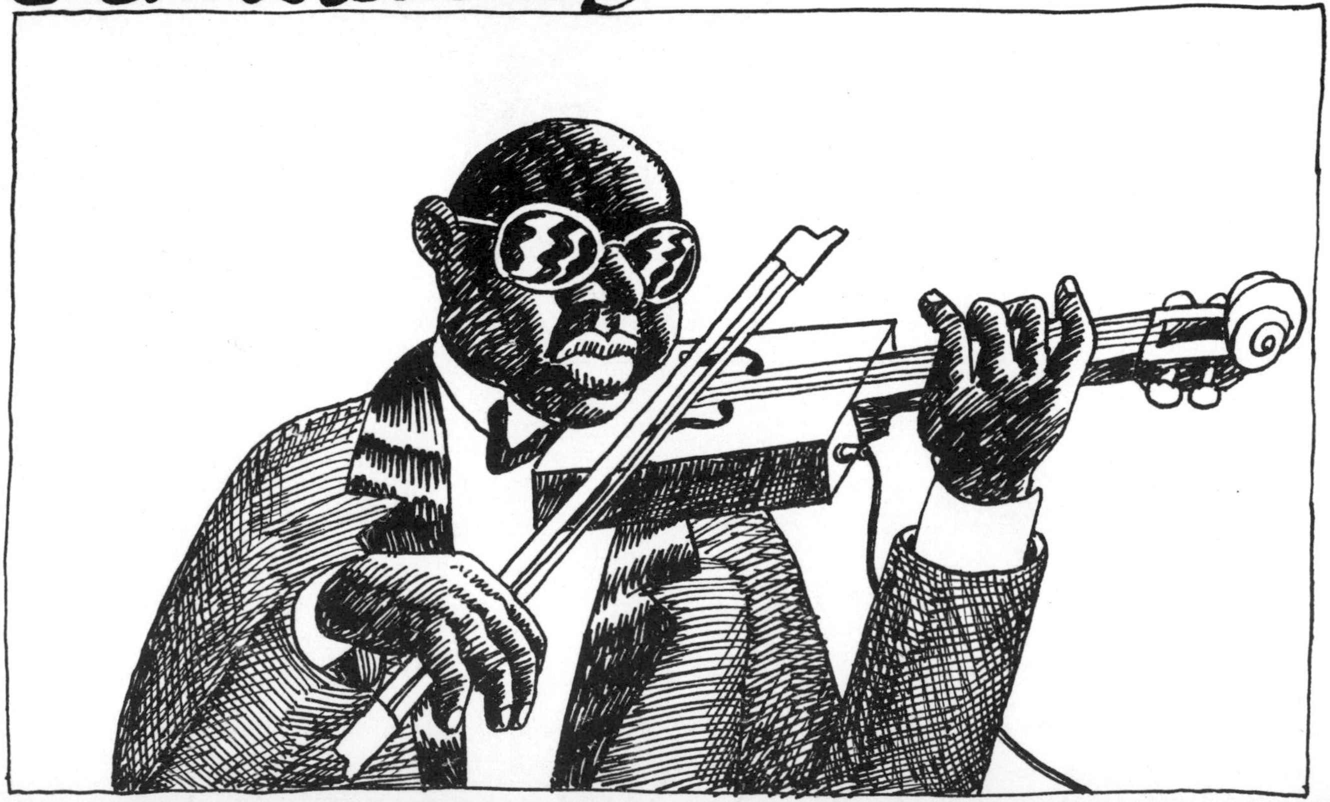

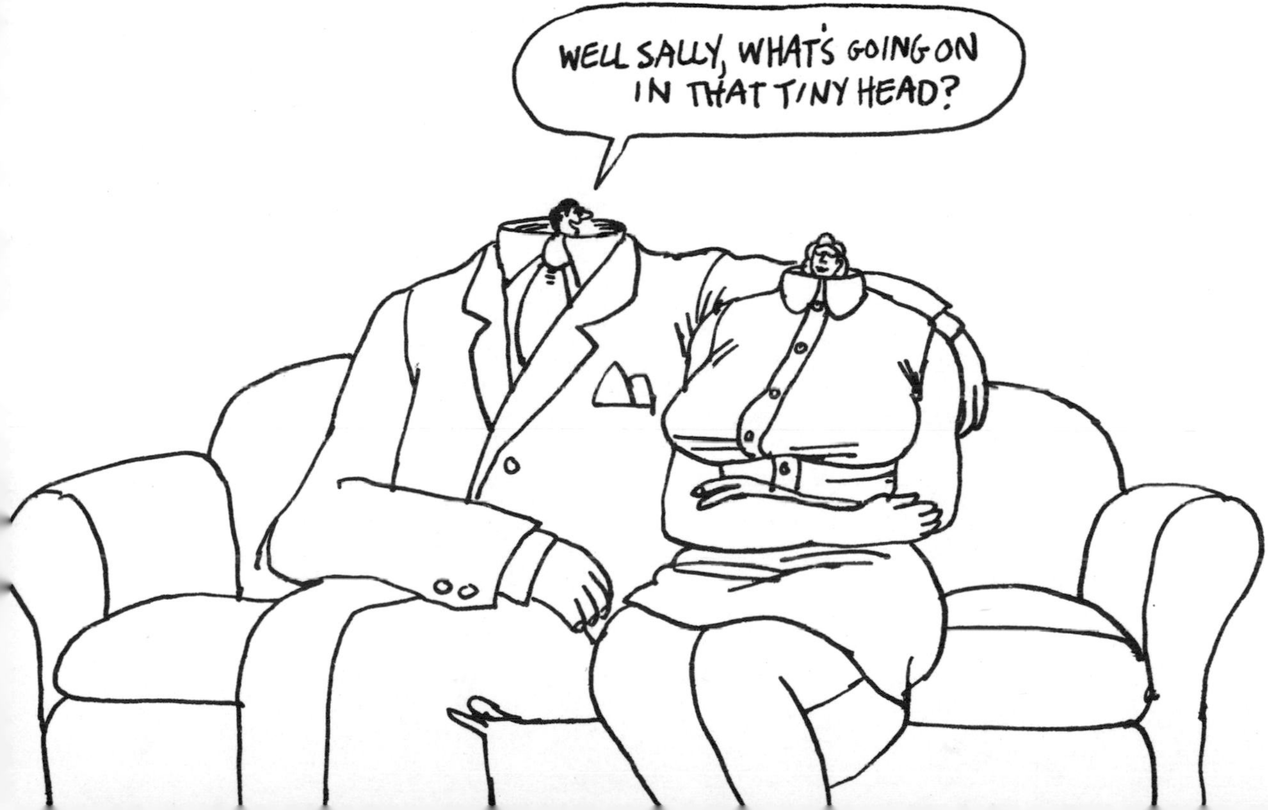
WELL SALLY, WHAT'S GOING ON IN THAT TINY HEAD?

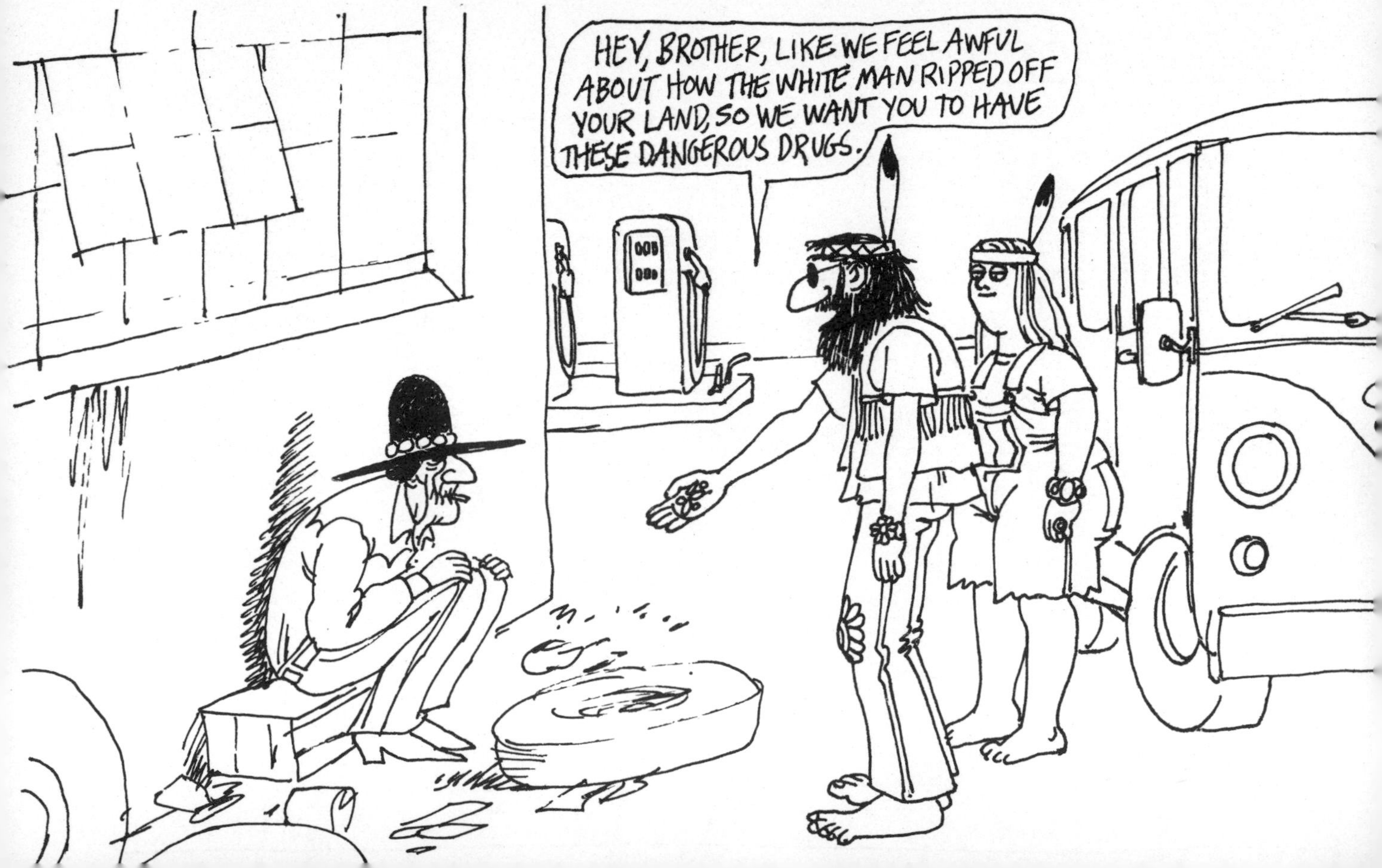
HEY, BROTHER, LIKE WE FEEL AWFUL ABOUT HOW THE WHITE MAN RIPPED OFF YOUR LAND, SO WE WANT YOU TO HAVE THESE DANGEROUS DRUGS.

On Cold Mornings it was Carl's Job to Start the Animals

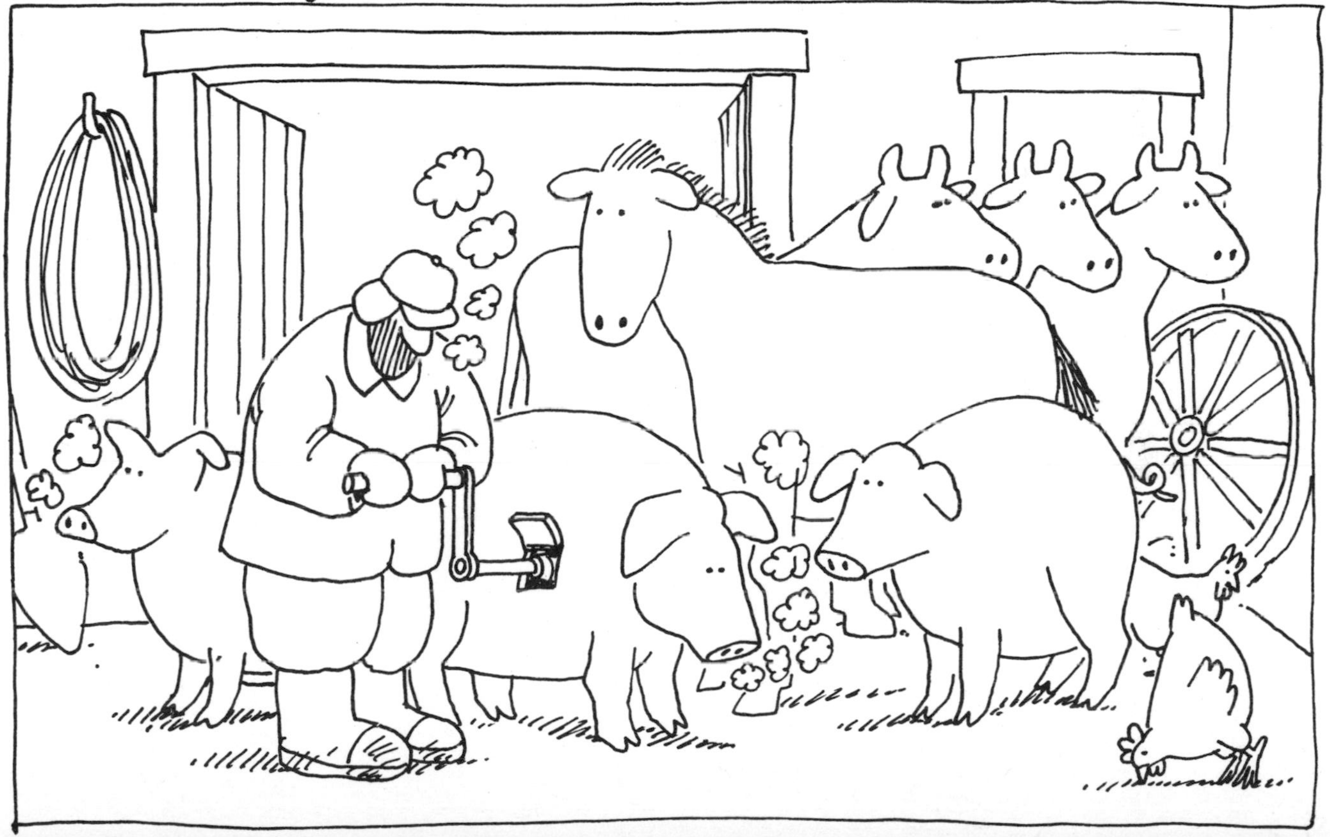

ONE OF MANY HONEST BONES IN MY BODY

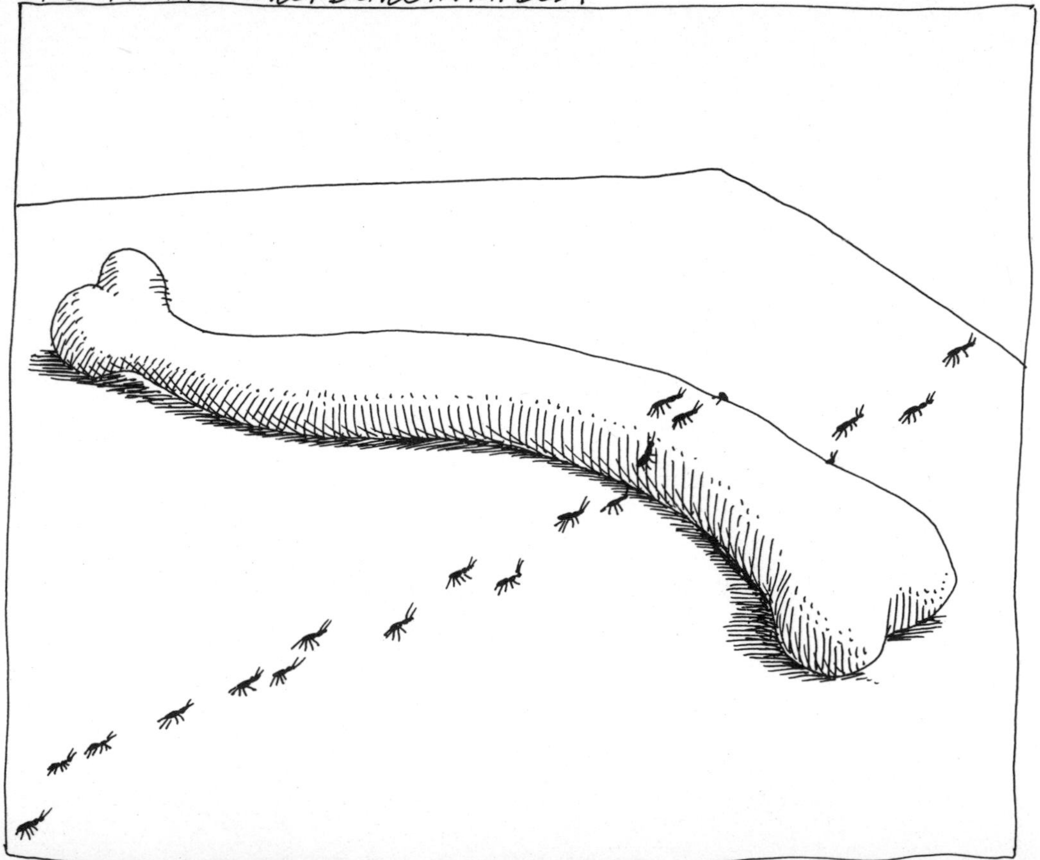

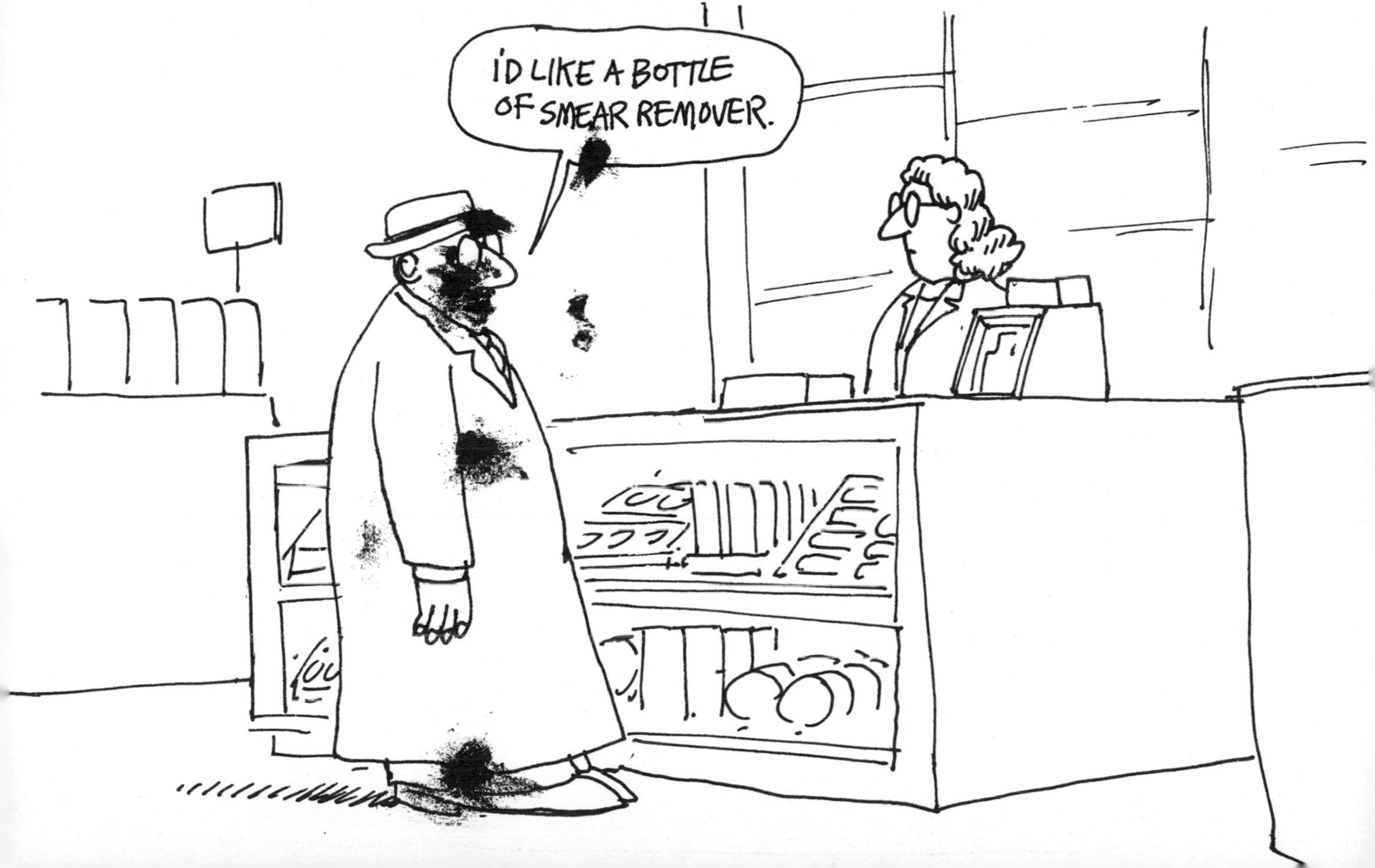
I'D LIKE A BOTTLE OF SMEAR REMOVER.

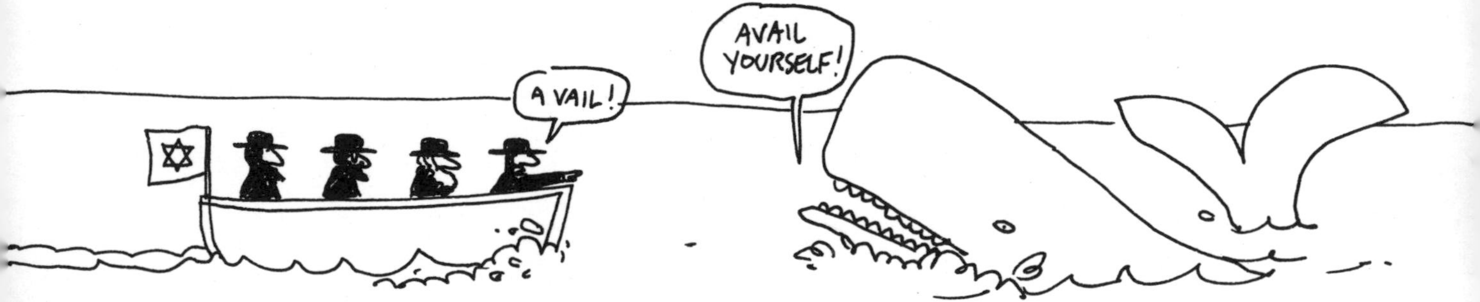
A VAIL!
AVAIL YOURSELF!

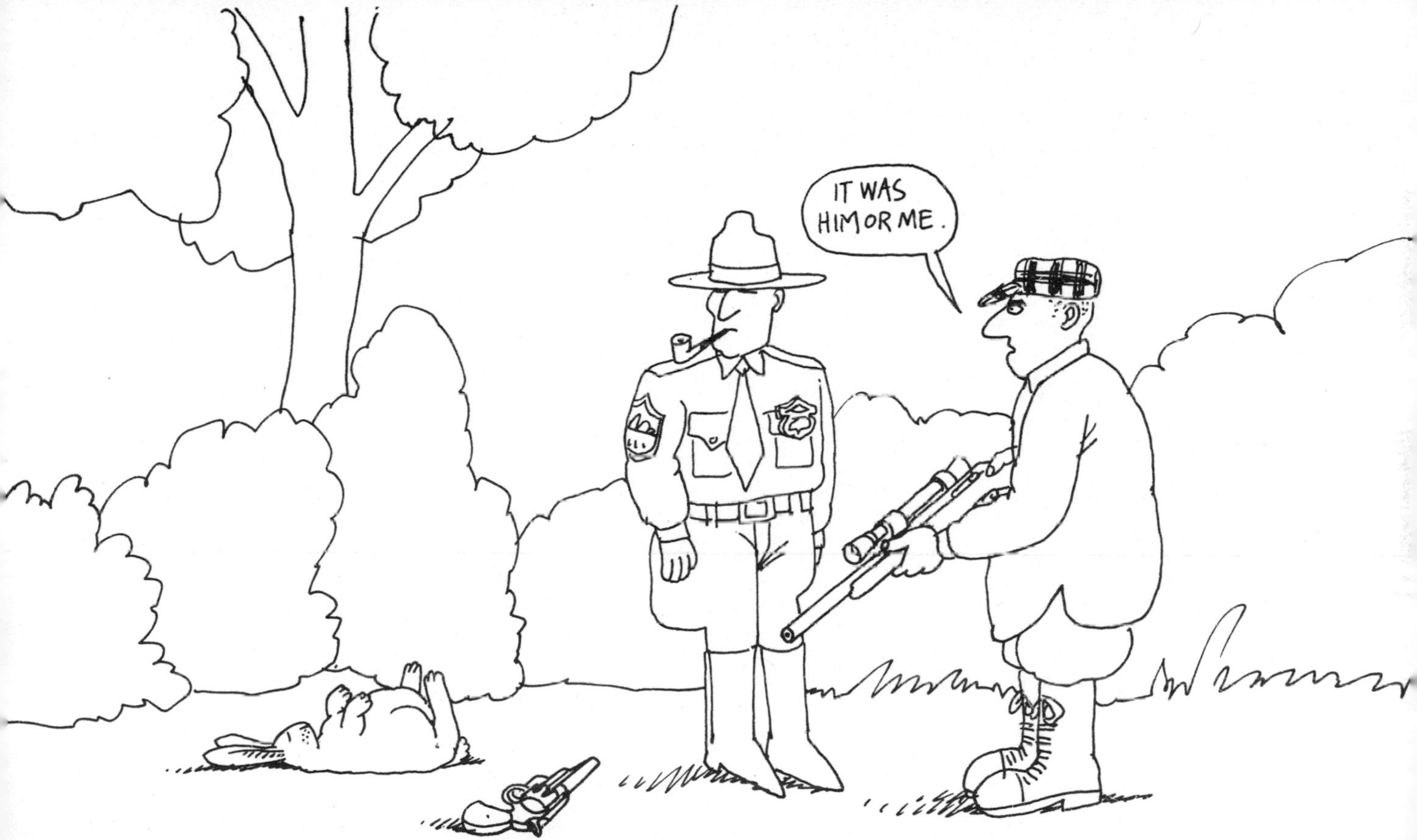
IT WAS
HIM OR ME.

## Trashing Johann

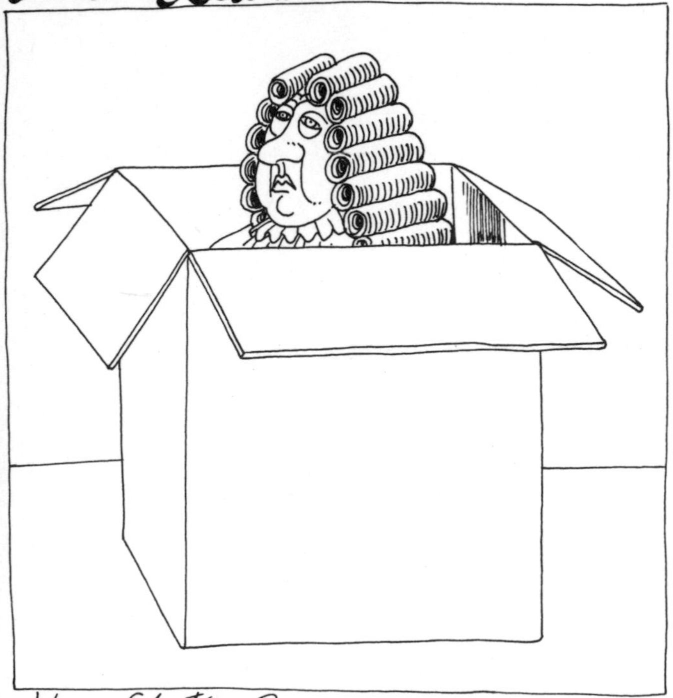

Johann Sebastian Box

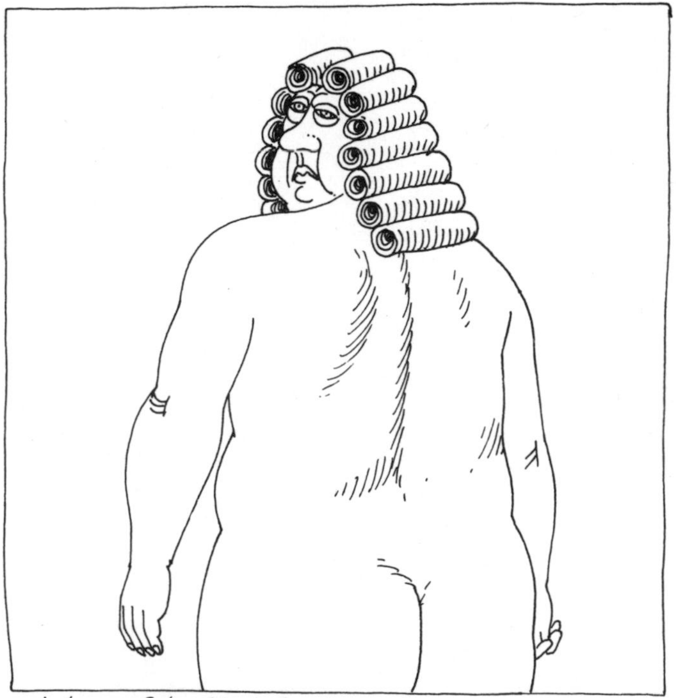

Johann Sebastian Back

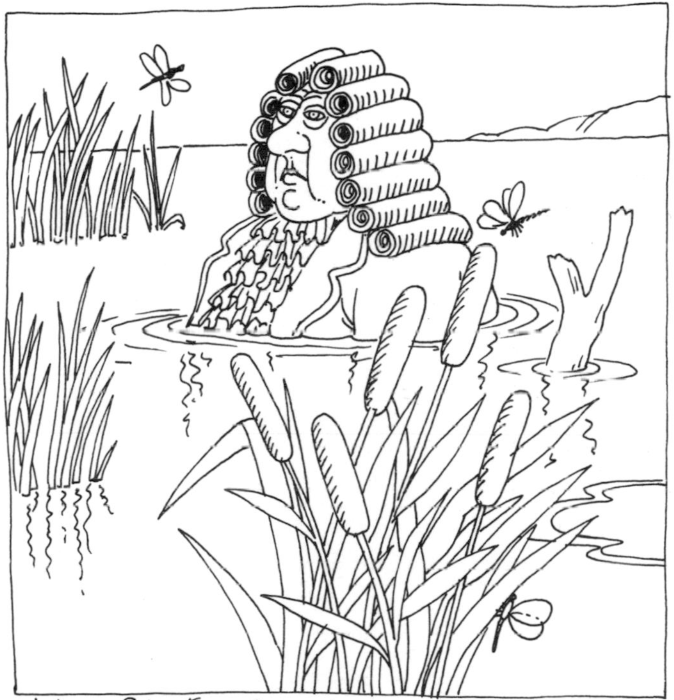

Johann Sebastian Bog

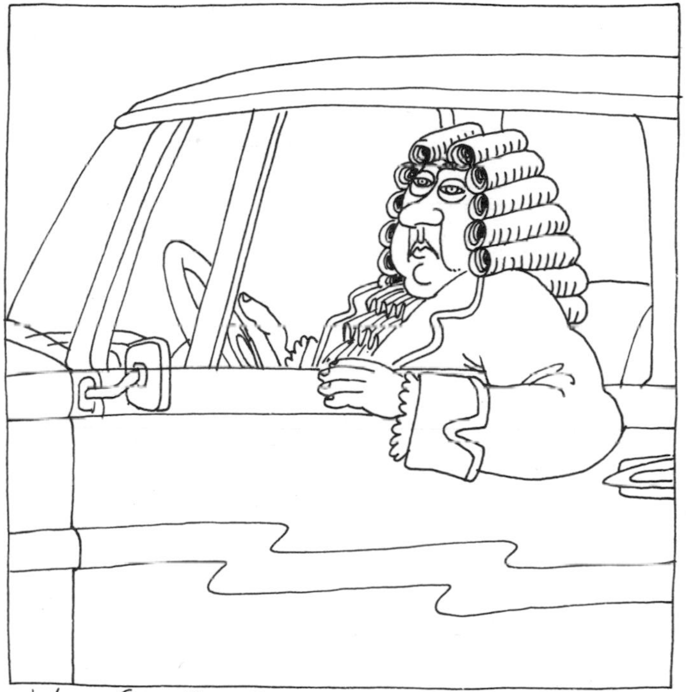

Johann Sebastian Buick

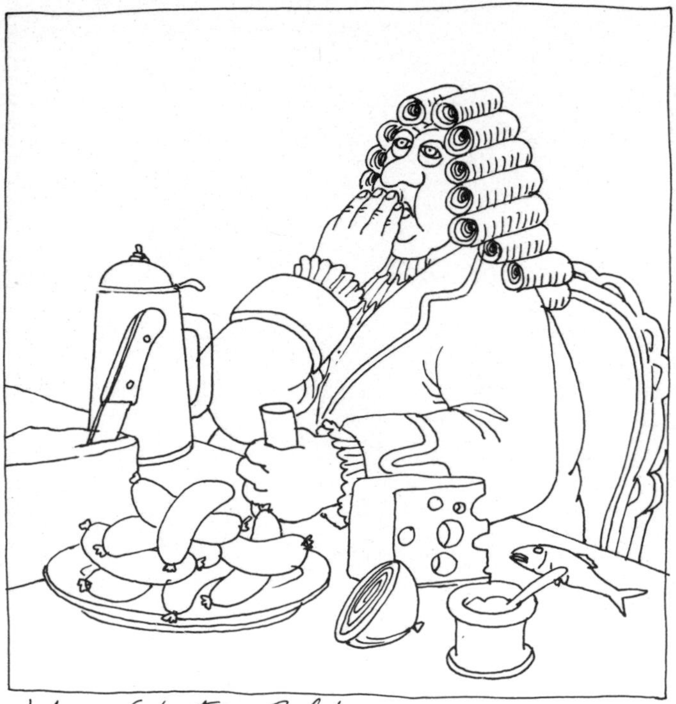

Johann Sebastian Belch

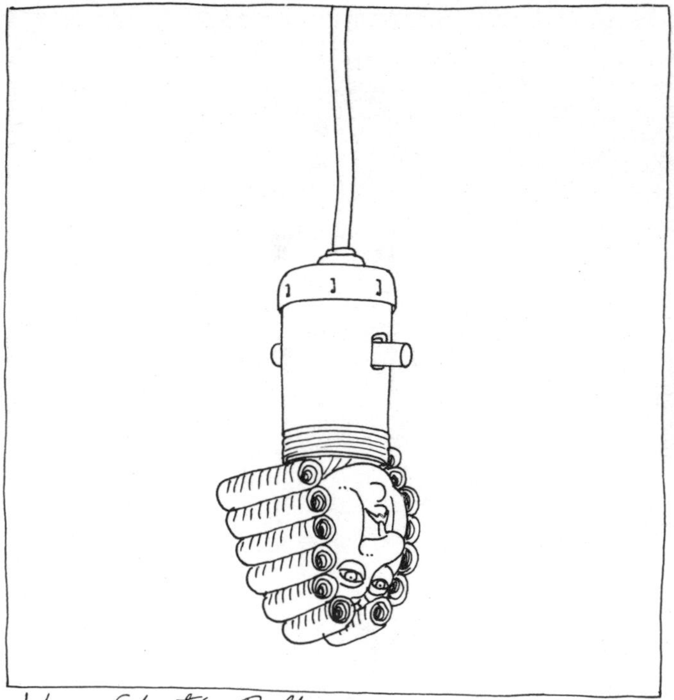

Johann Sebastian Bulb

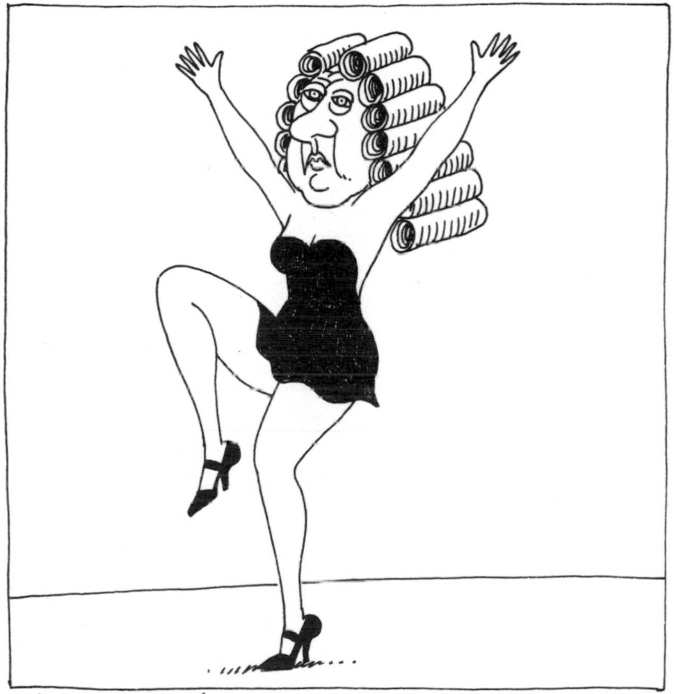

Johann Sebastian Boop

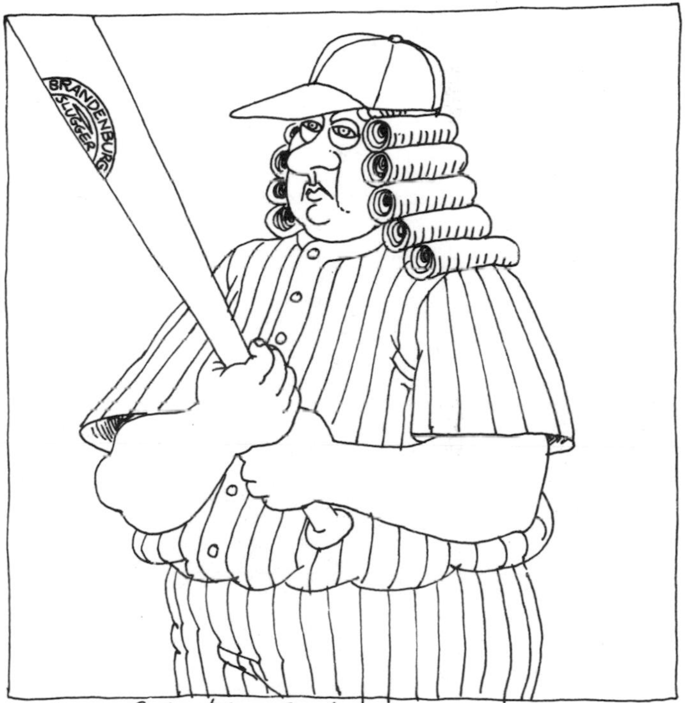
BRANDENBURG
SLUGGER

Johann Sebastian Di Maggio

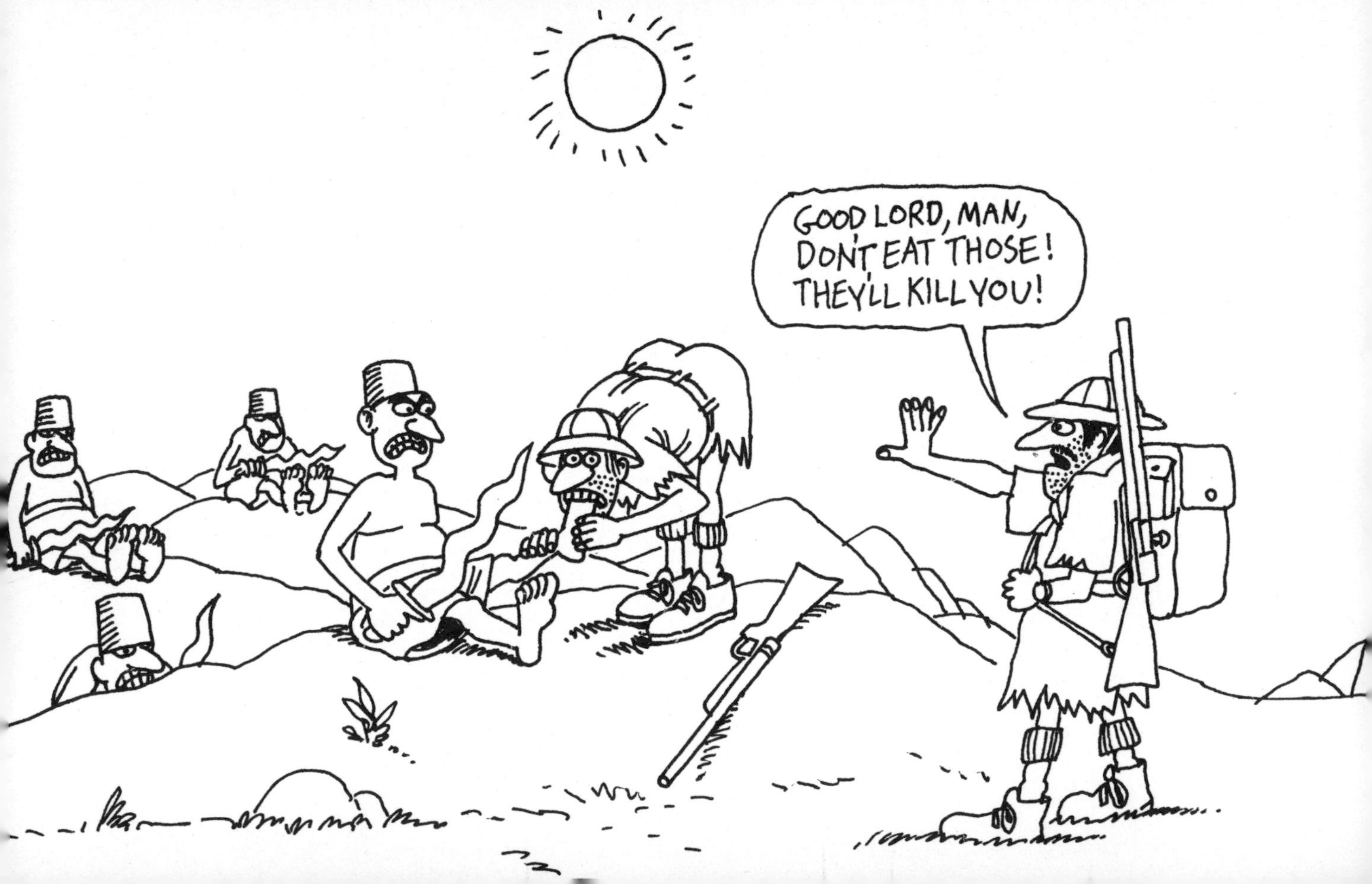
GOOD LORD, MAN, DON'T EAT THOSE! THEY'LL KILL YOU!

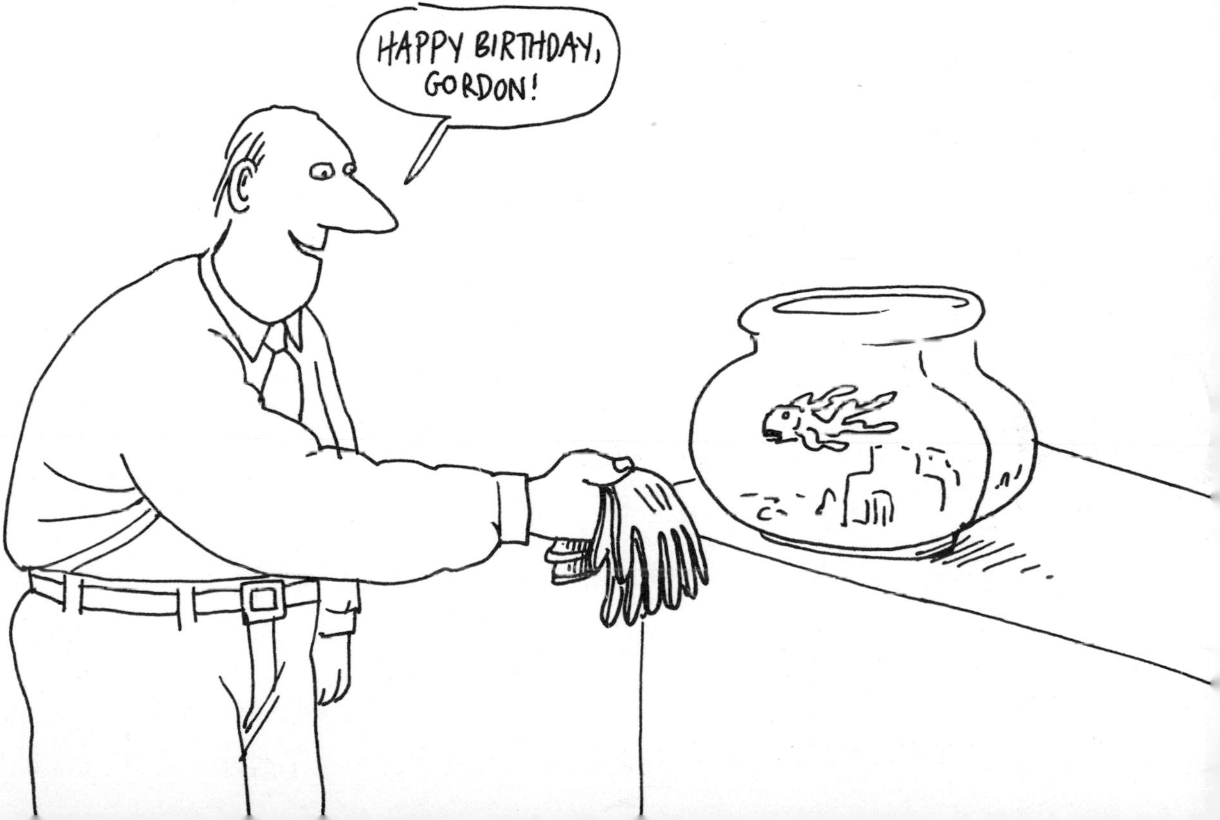
HAPPY BIRTHDAY,
GORDON!

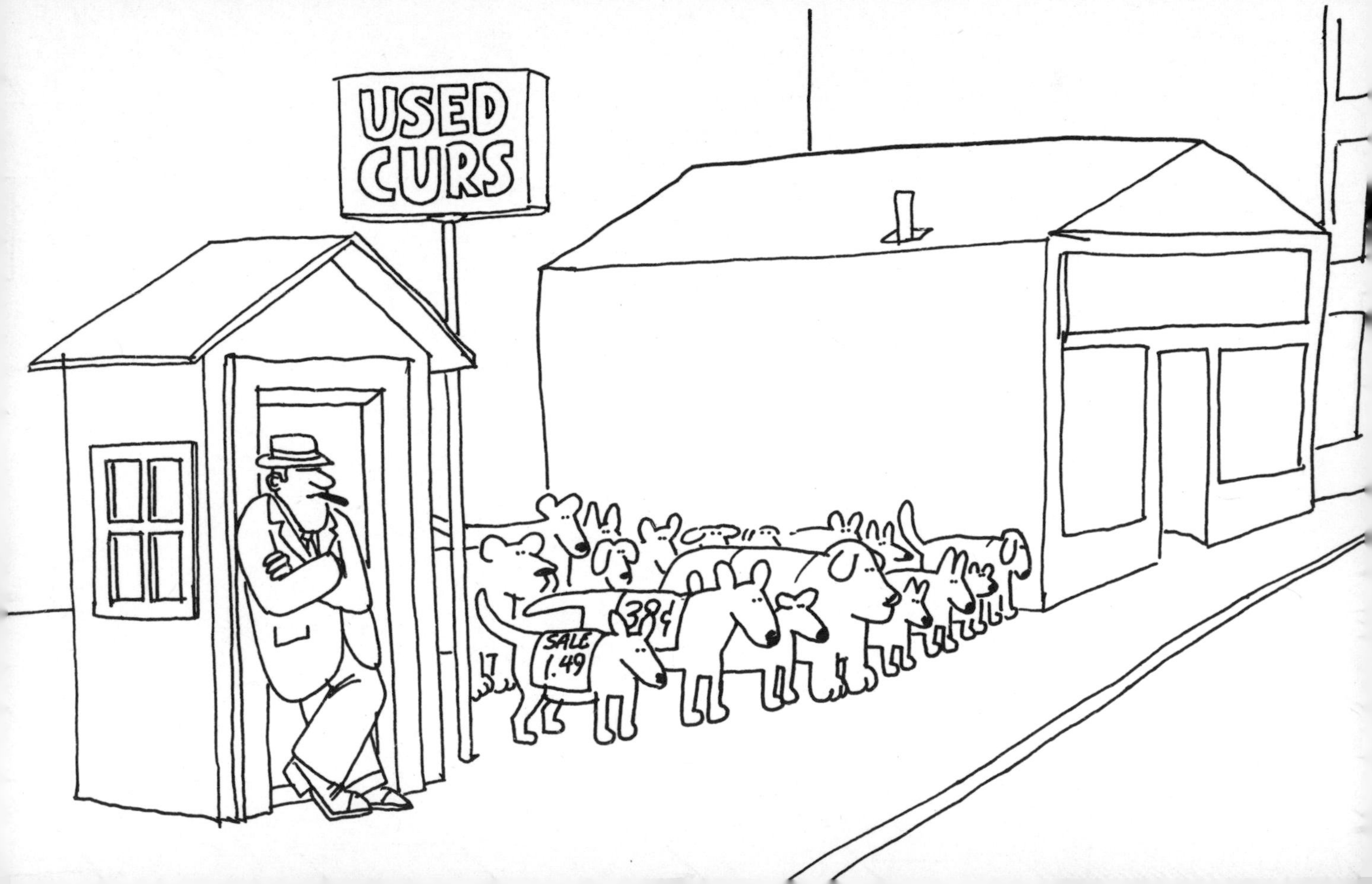

USED CURS
SALE 1.49
39¢

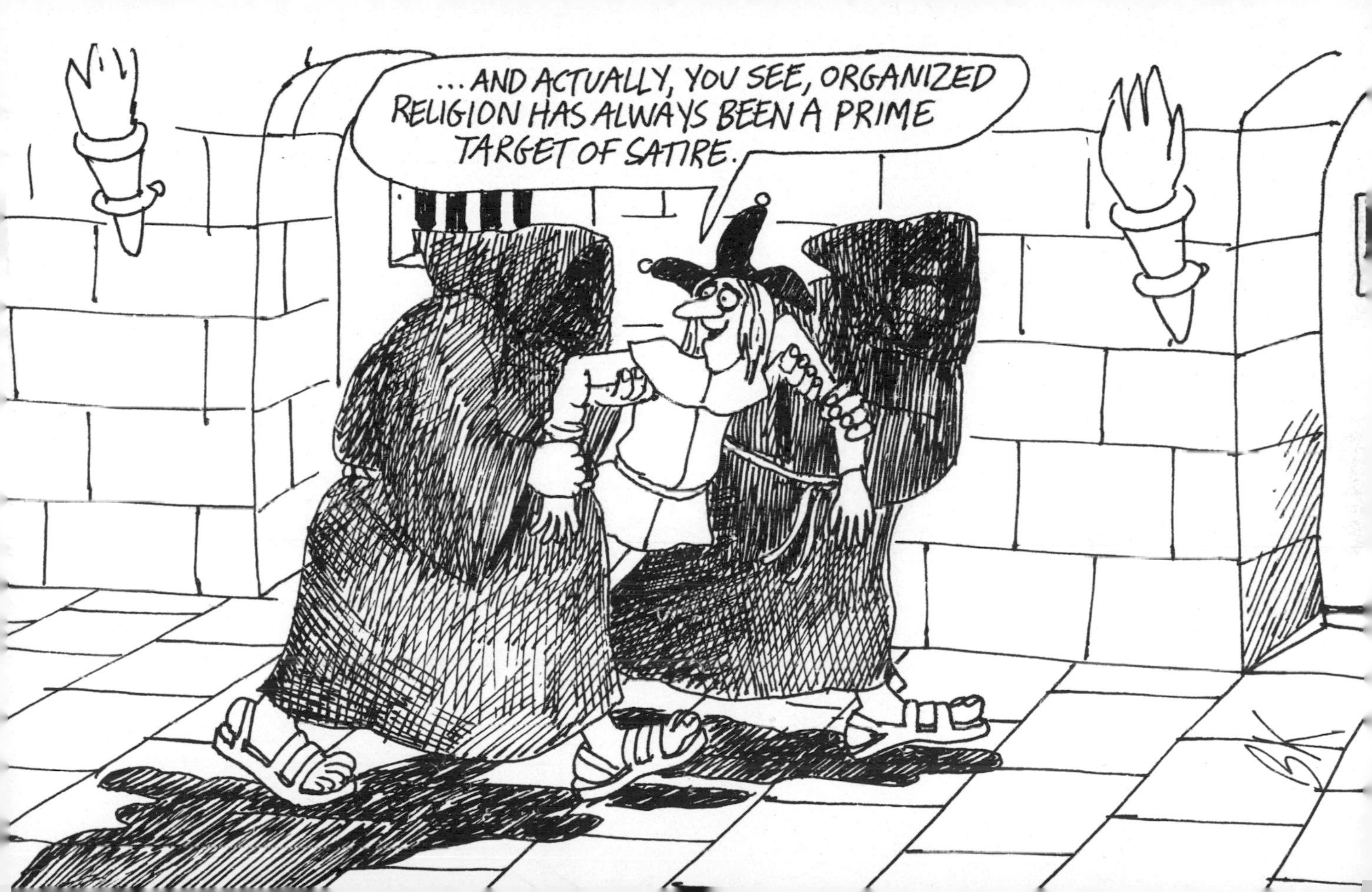
...AND ACTUALLY, YOU SEE, ORGANIZED RELIGION HAS ALWAYS BEEN A PRIME TARGET OF SATIRE.

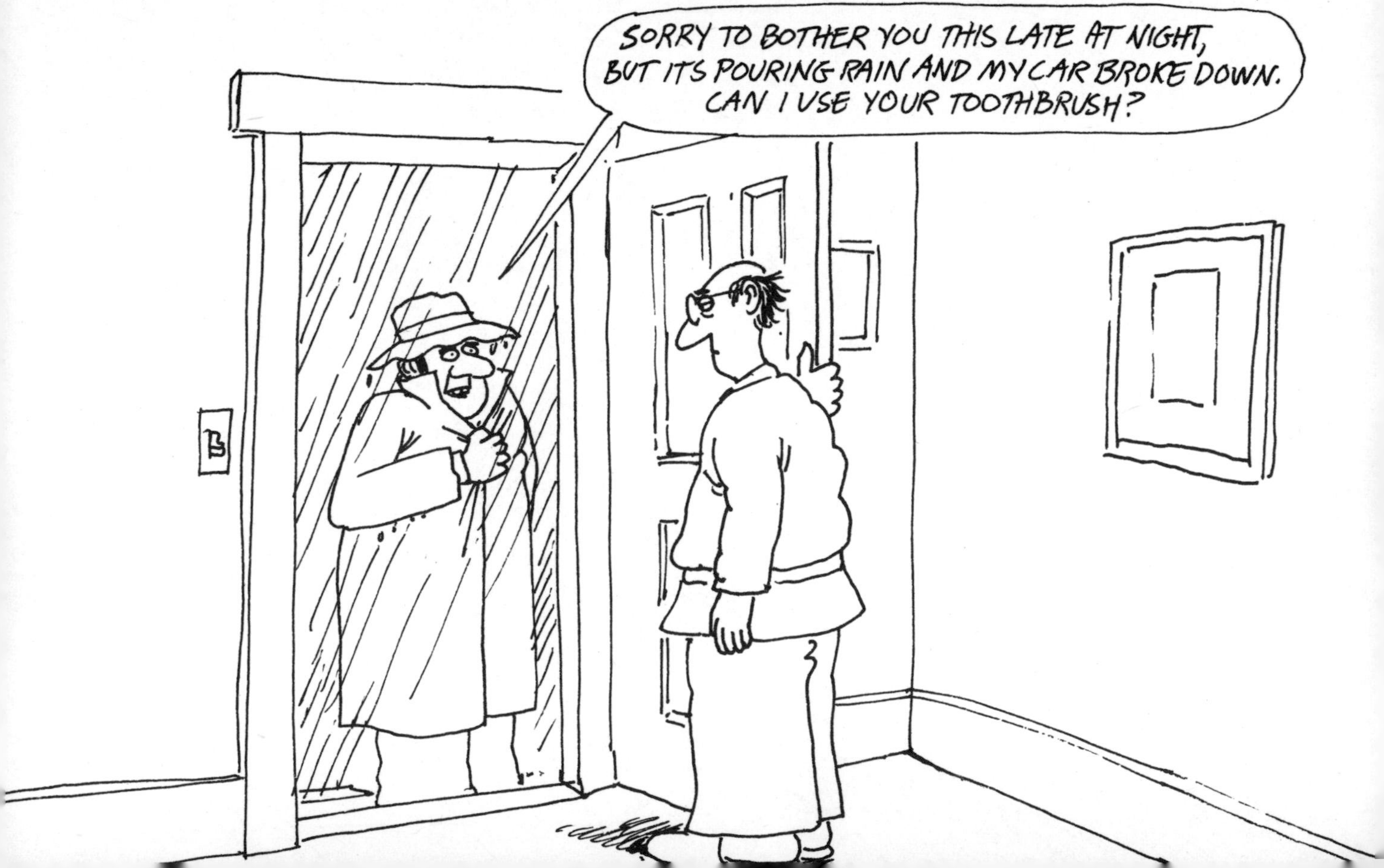
SORRY TO BOTHER YOU THIS LATE AT NIGHT, BUT ITS POURING RAIN AND MY CAR BROKE DOWN. CAN I USE YOUR TOOTHBRUSH?

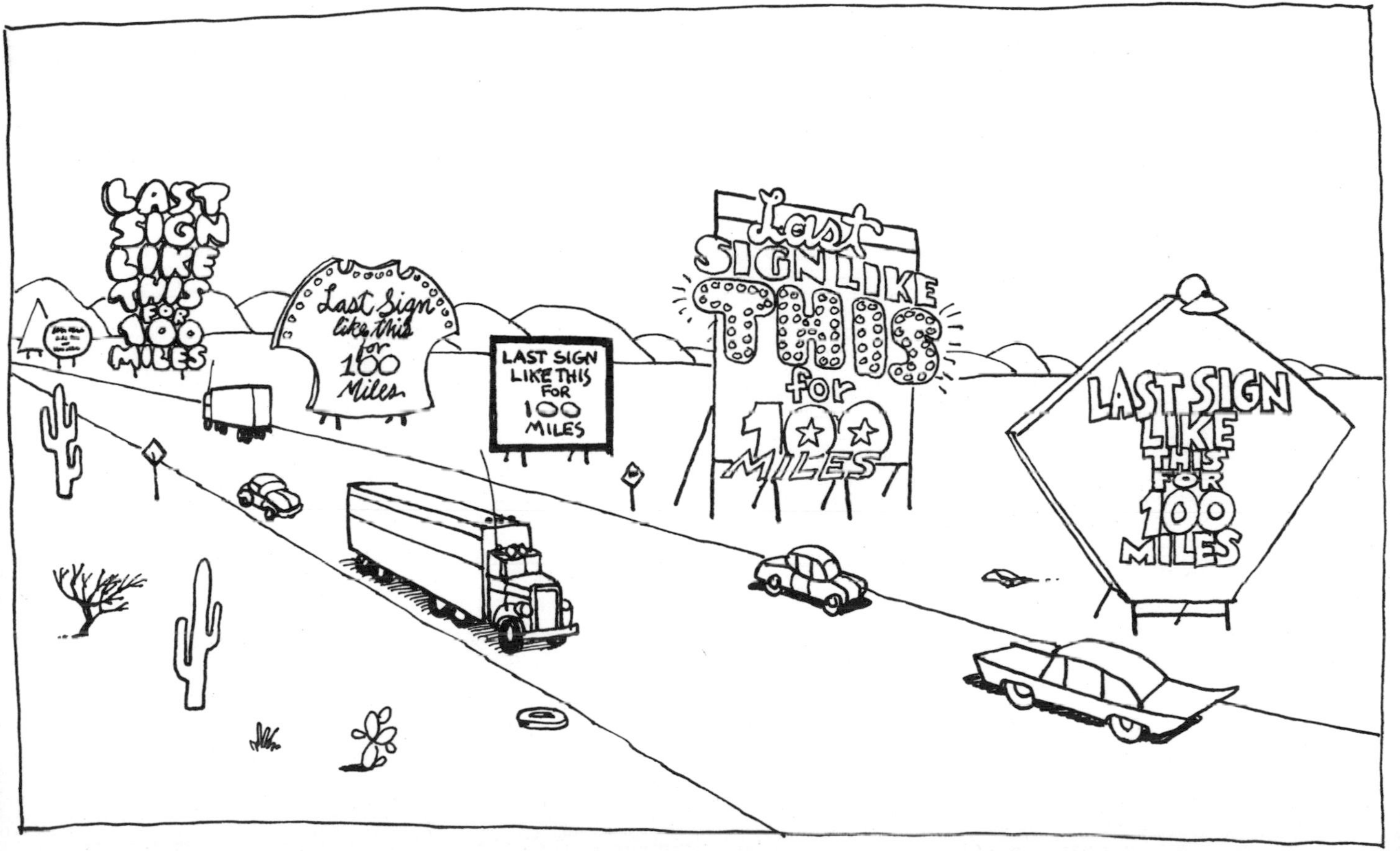

LAST SIGN LIKE THIS FOR 100 MILES
Last Sign like this for 100 Miles
LAST SIGN LIKE THIS FOR 100 MILES
Last SIGN LIKE THIS for 100 MILES
LAST SIGN LIKE THIS FOR 100 MILES

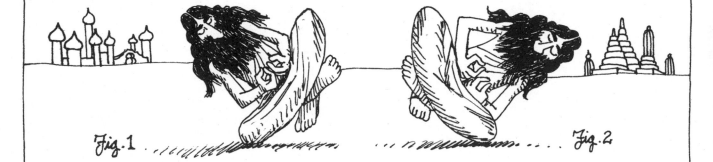

Fig. 1                    Fig. 2

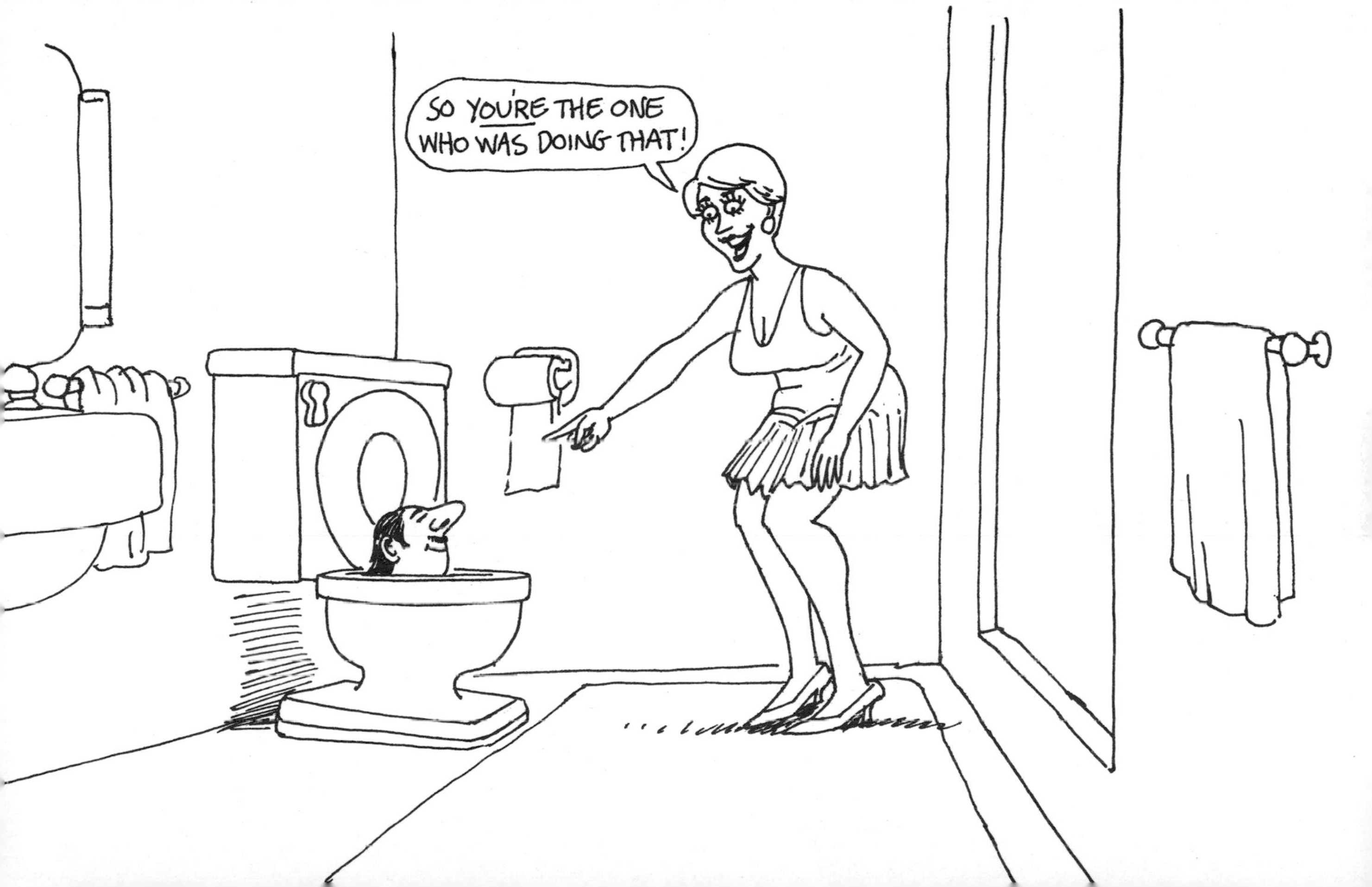
SO YOU'RE THE ONE WHO WAS DOING THAT!

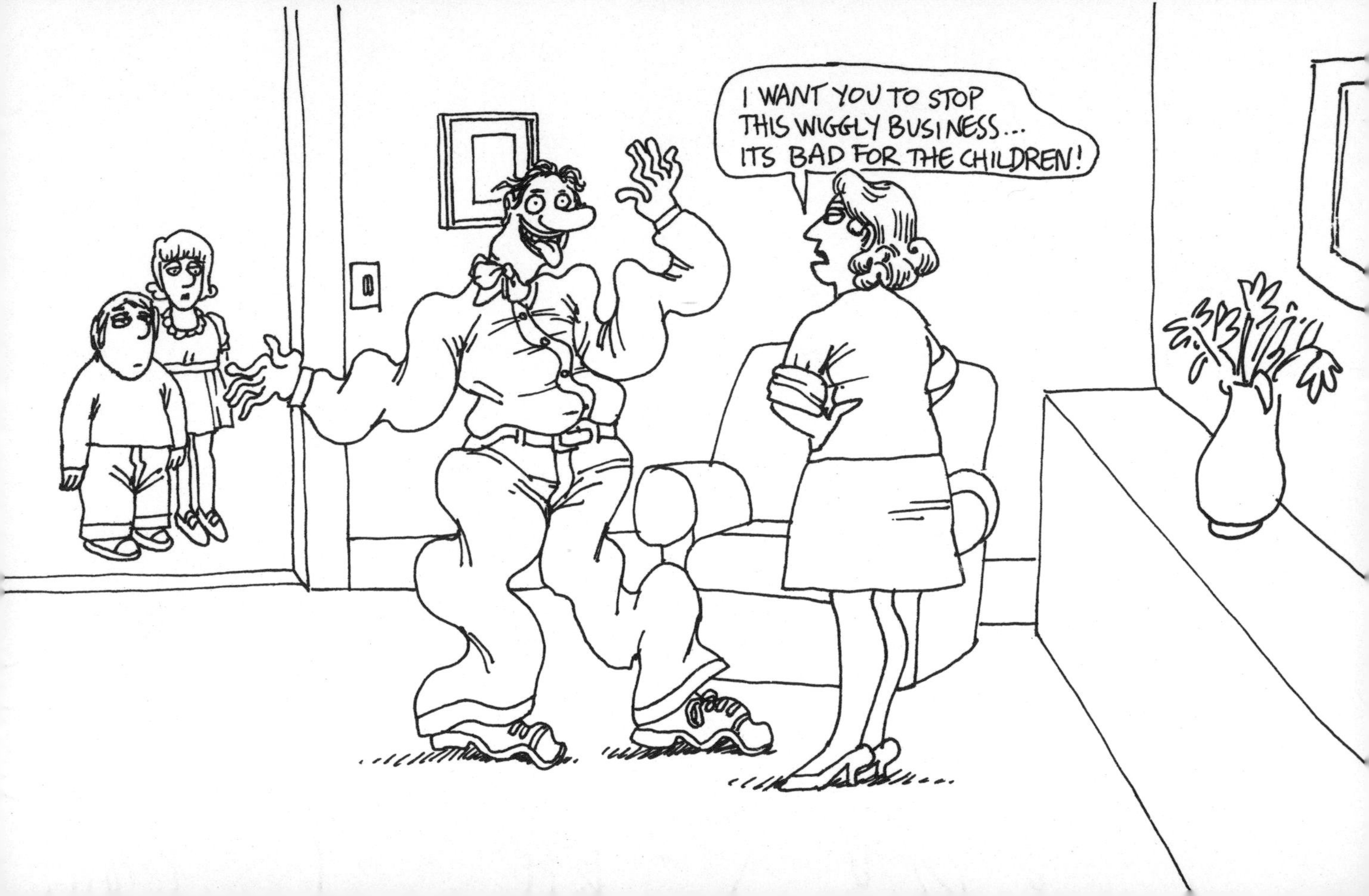
I WANT YOU TO STOP THIS WIGGLY BUSINESS... ITS BAD FOR THE CHILDREN!

MY SQUID'S NAMED NED, OR MAYBE FRED.
HE'S PAINTED RED
TO MATCH HIS BED.
A PEDIGREED SQUID THOROUGHBRED
IS NED, OR FRED, OR IS IT TED?

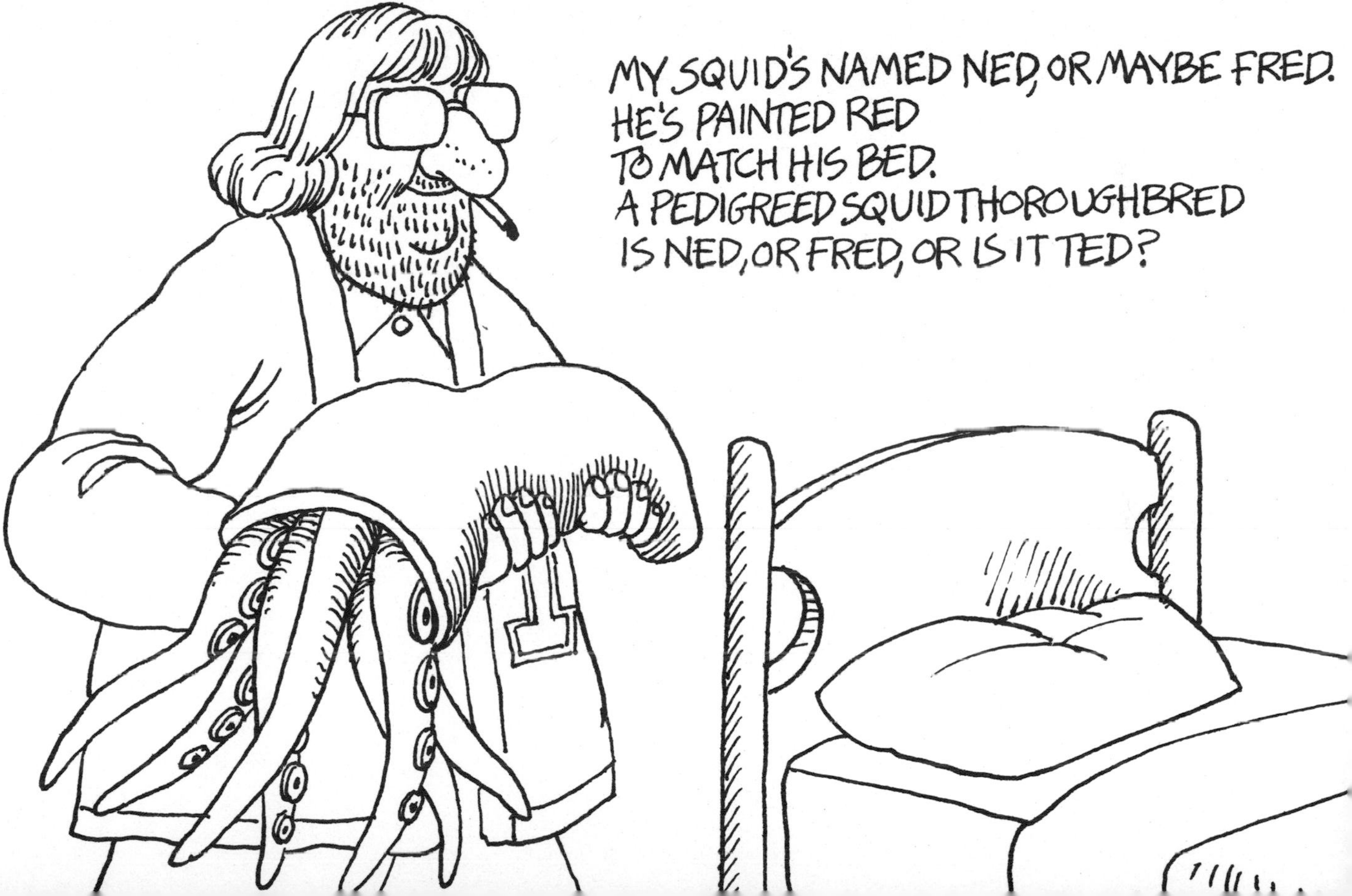

# Best of Show

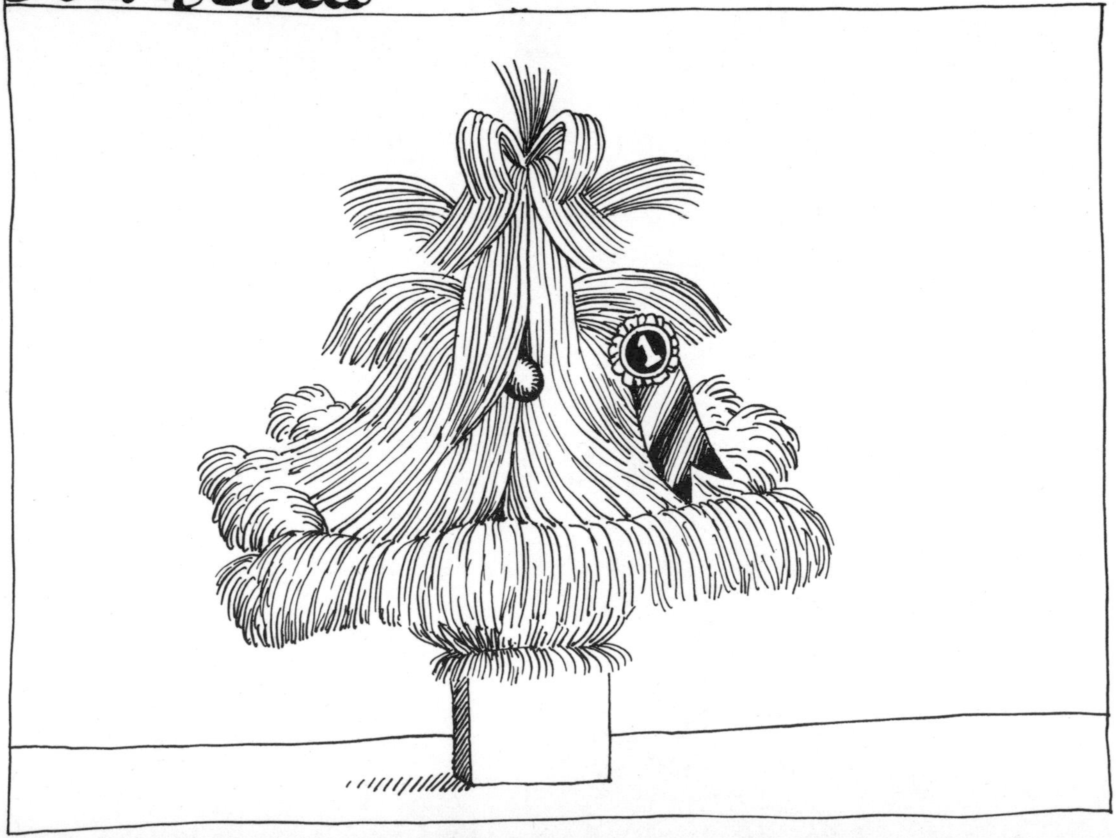
1

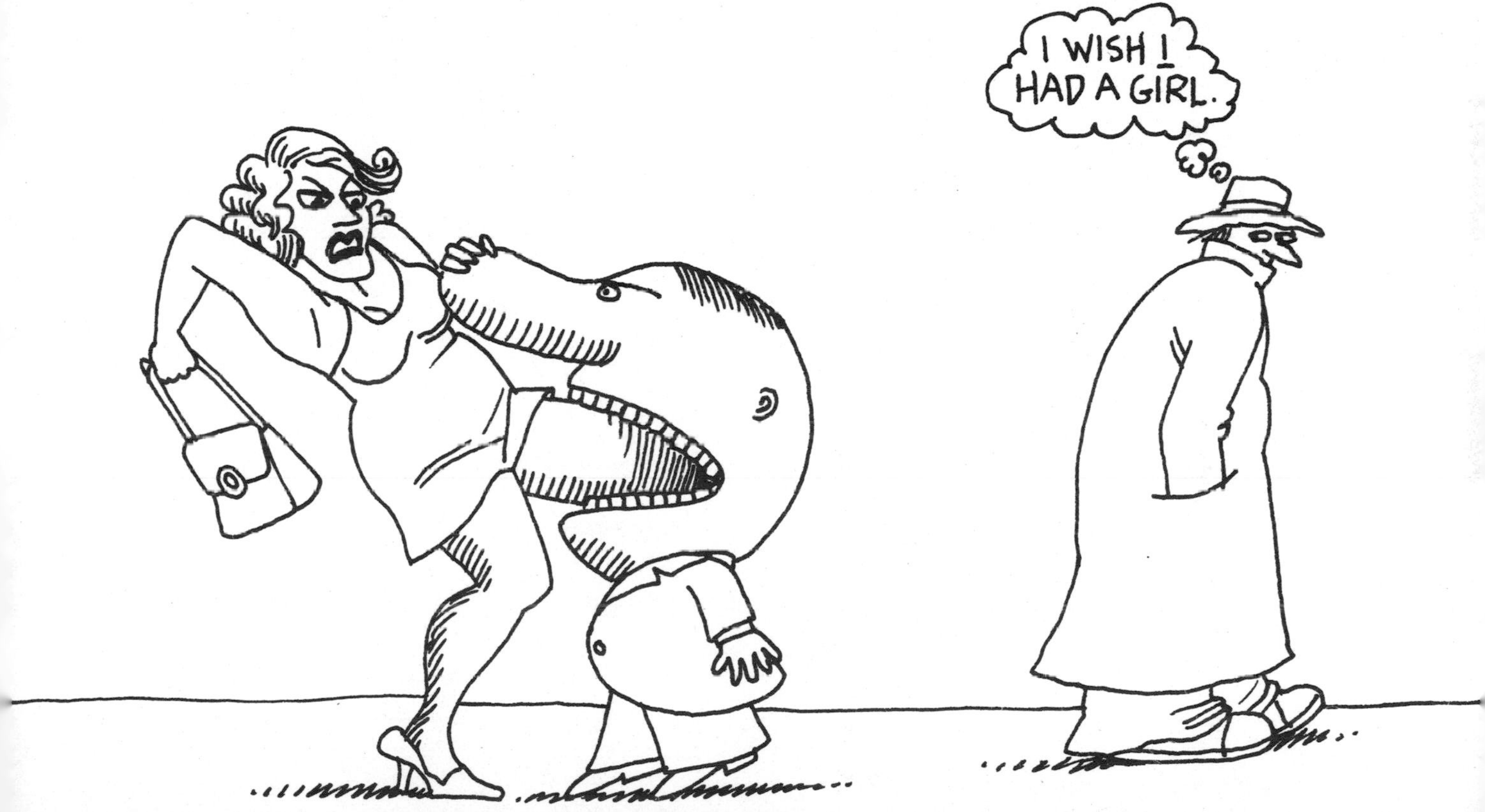
I WISH I HAD A GIRL.

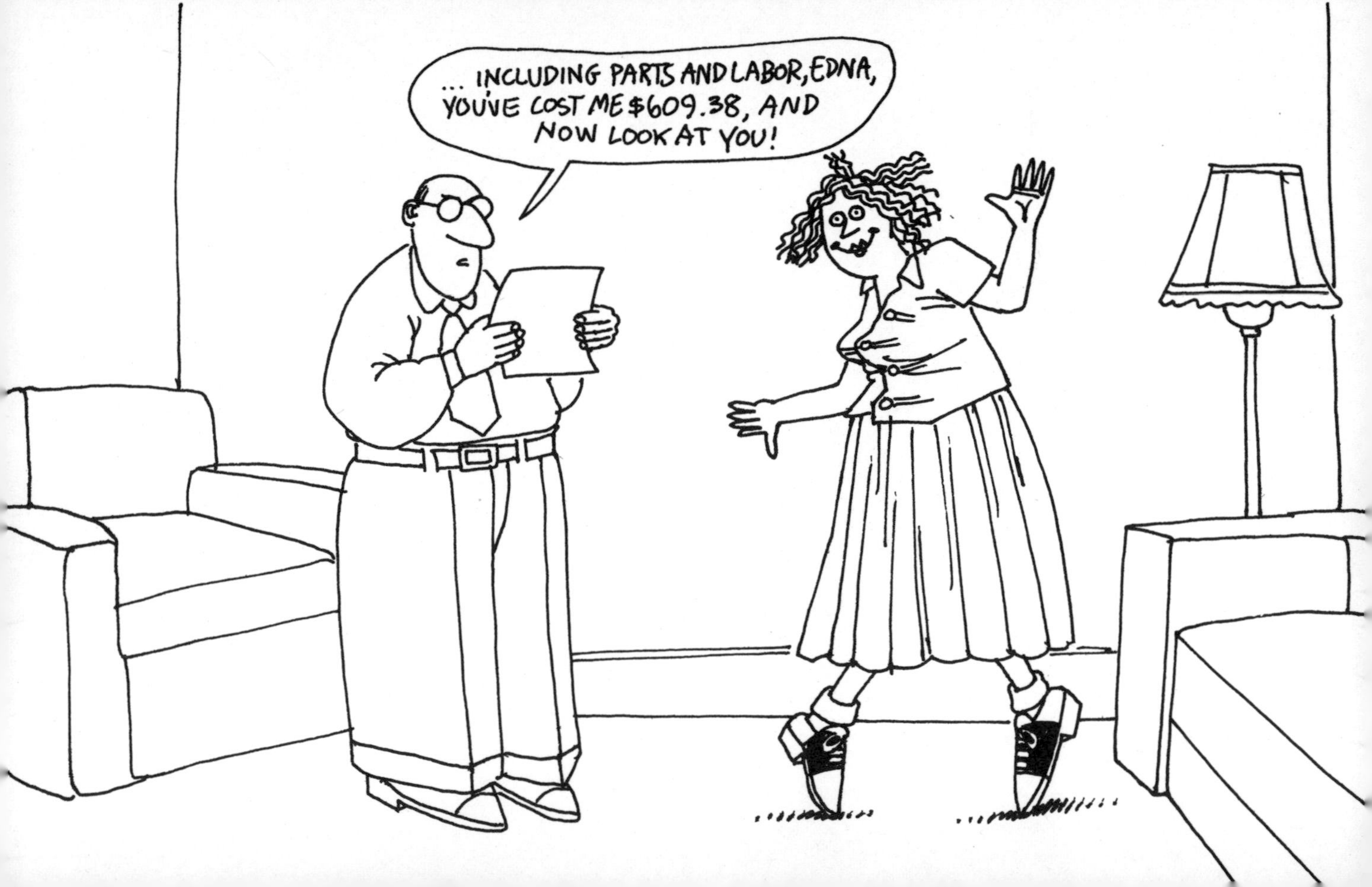
... INCLUDING PARTS AND LABOR, EDNA, YOU'VE COST ME $609.38, AND NOW LOOK AT YOU!

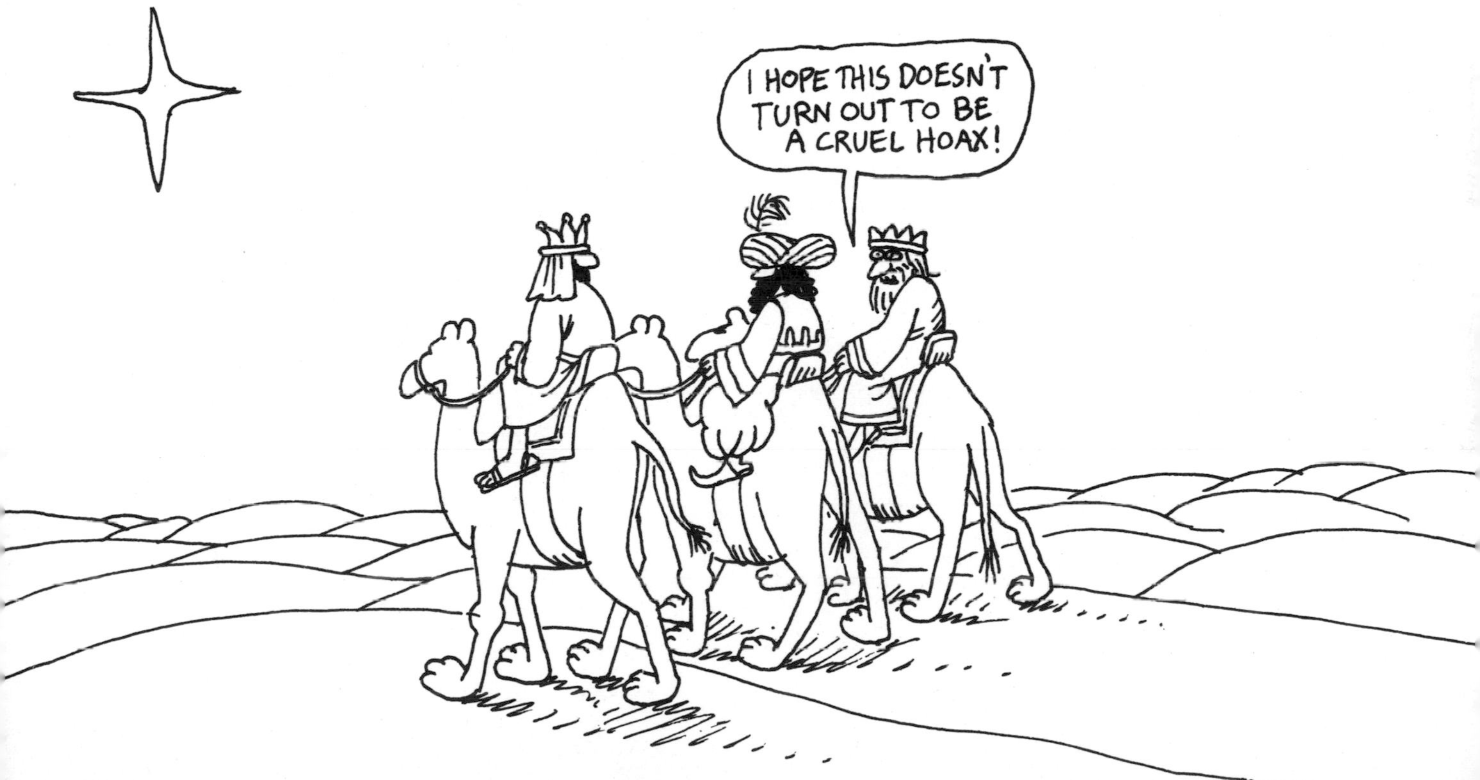
I HOPE THIS DOESN'T TURN OUT TO BE A CRUEL HOAX!

Houdini Escaping from Hong Kong

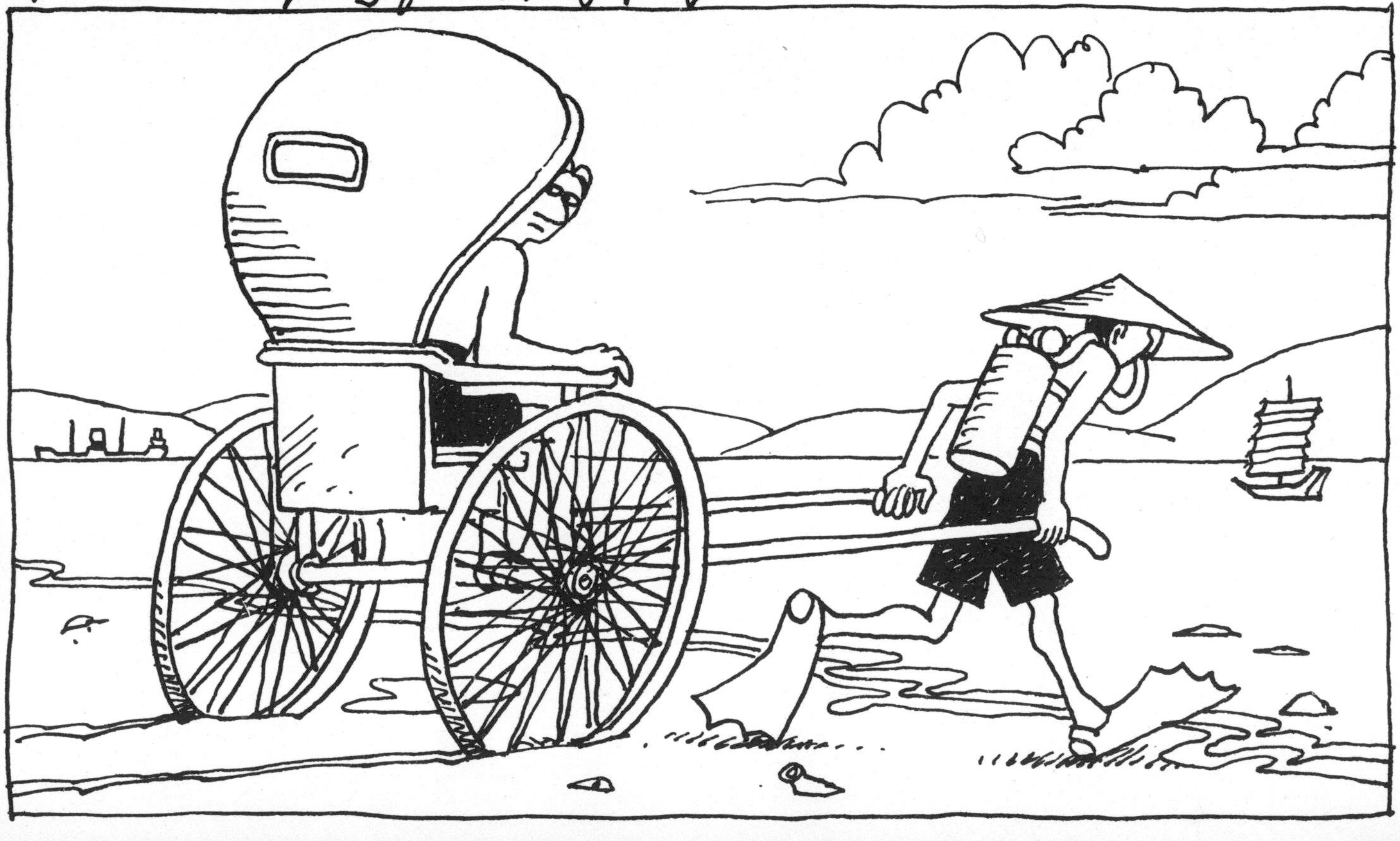

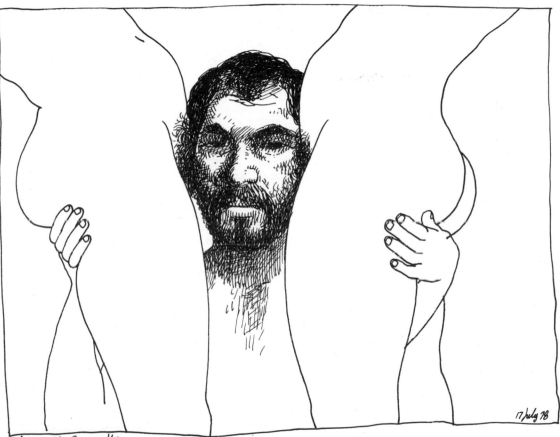

Man with Earmuffs

17 July 78

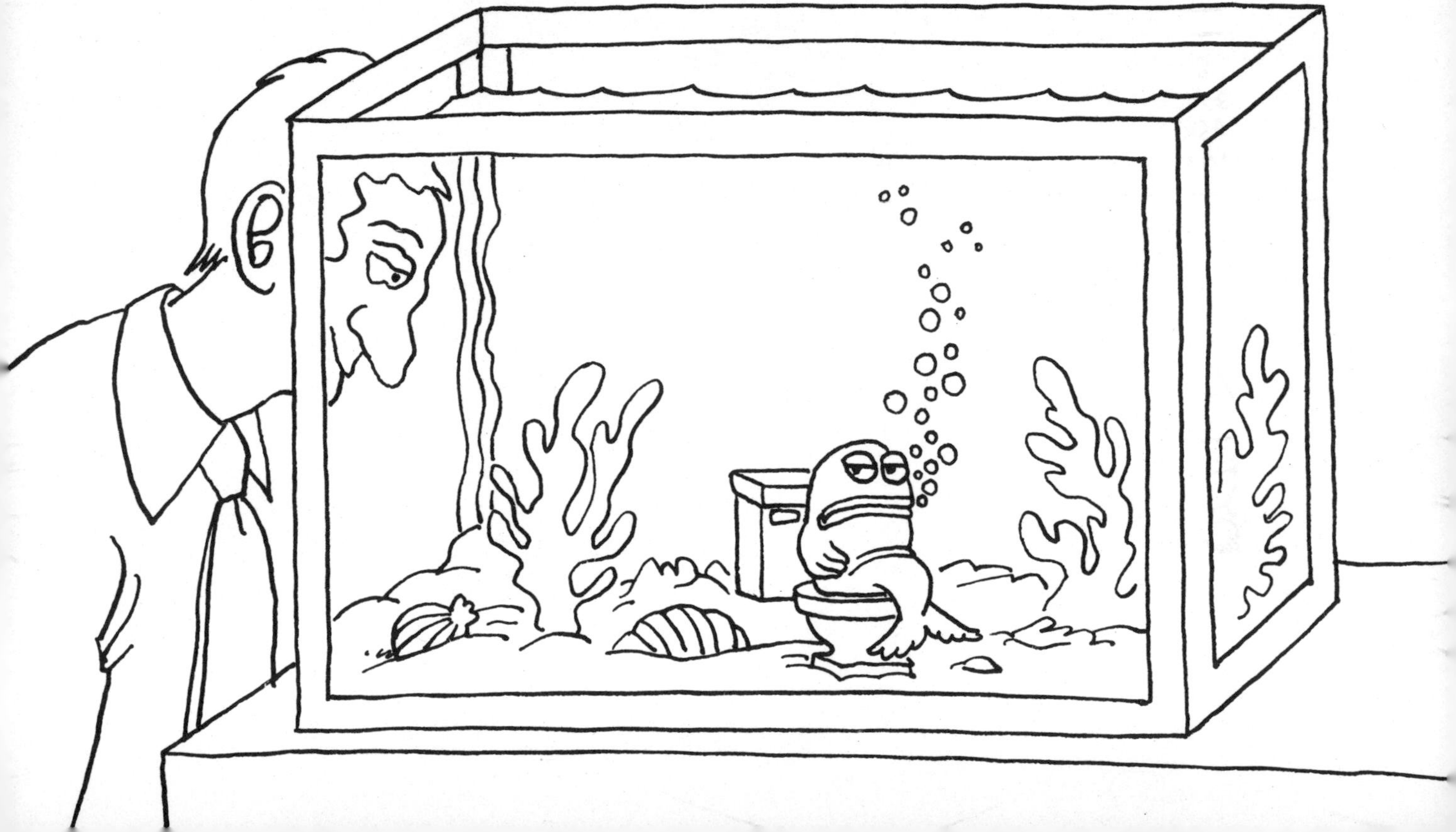

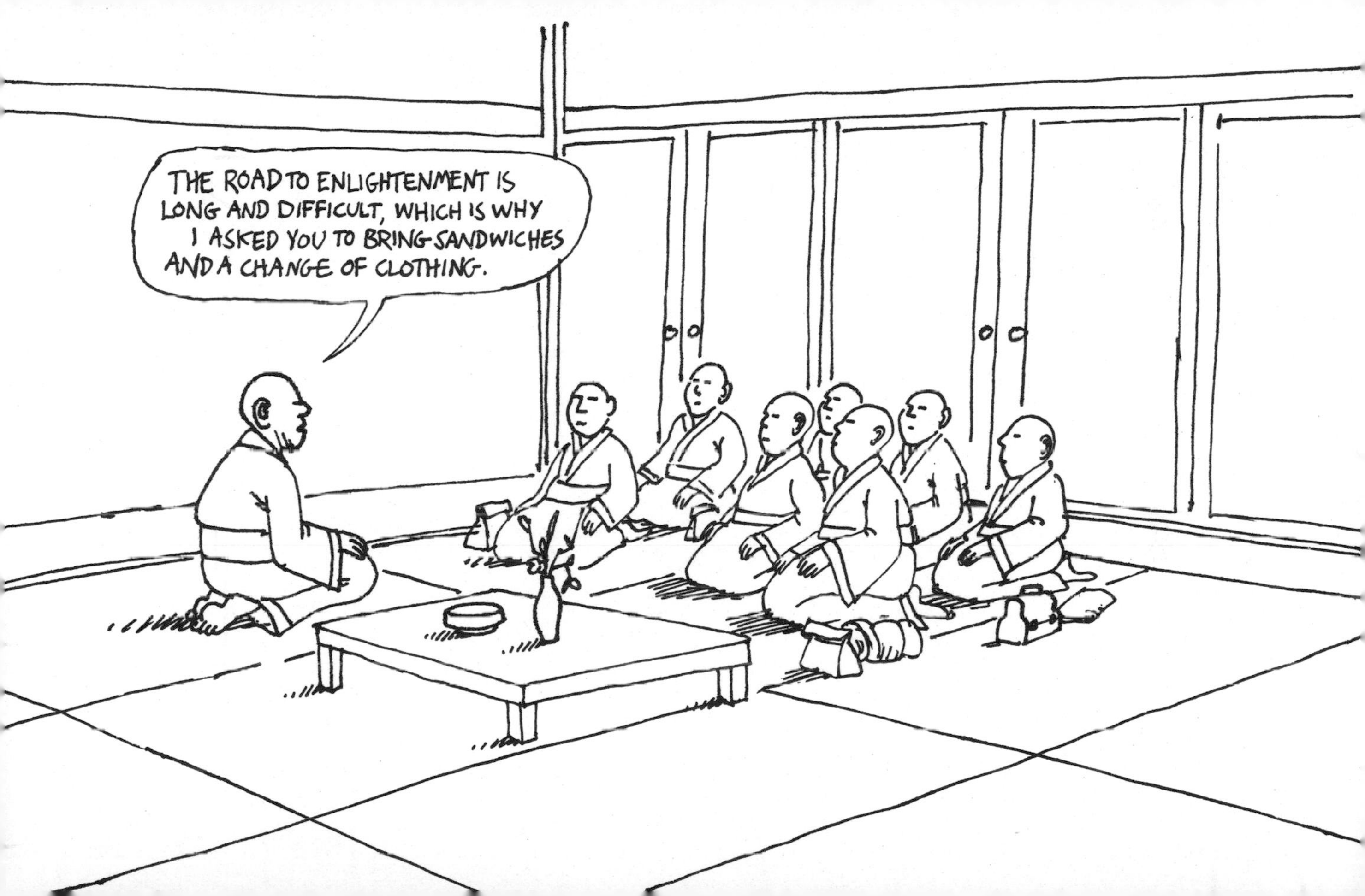
THE ROAD TO ENLIGHTENMENT IS LONG AND DIFFICULT, WHICH IS WHY I ASKED YOU TO BRING SANDWICHES AND A CHANGE OF CLOTHING.

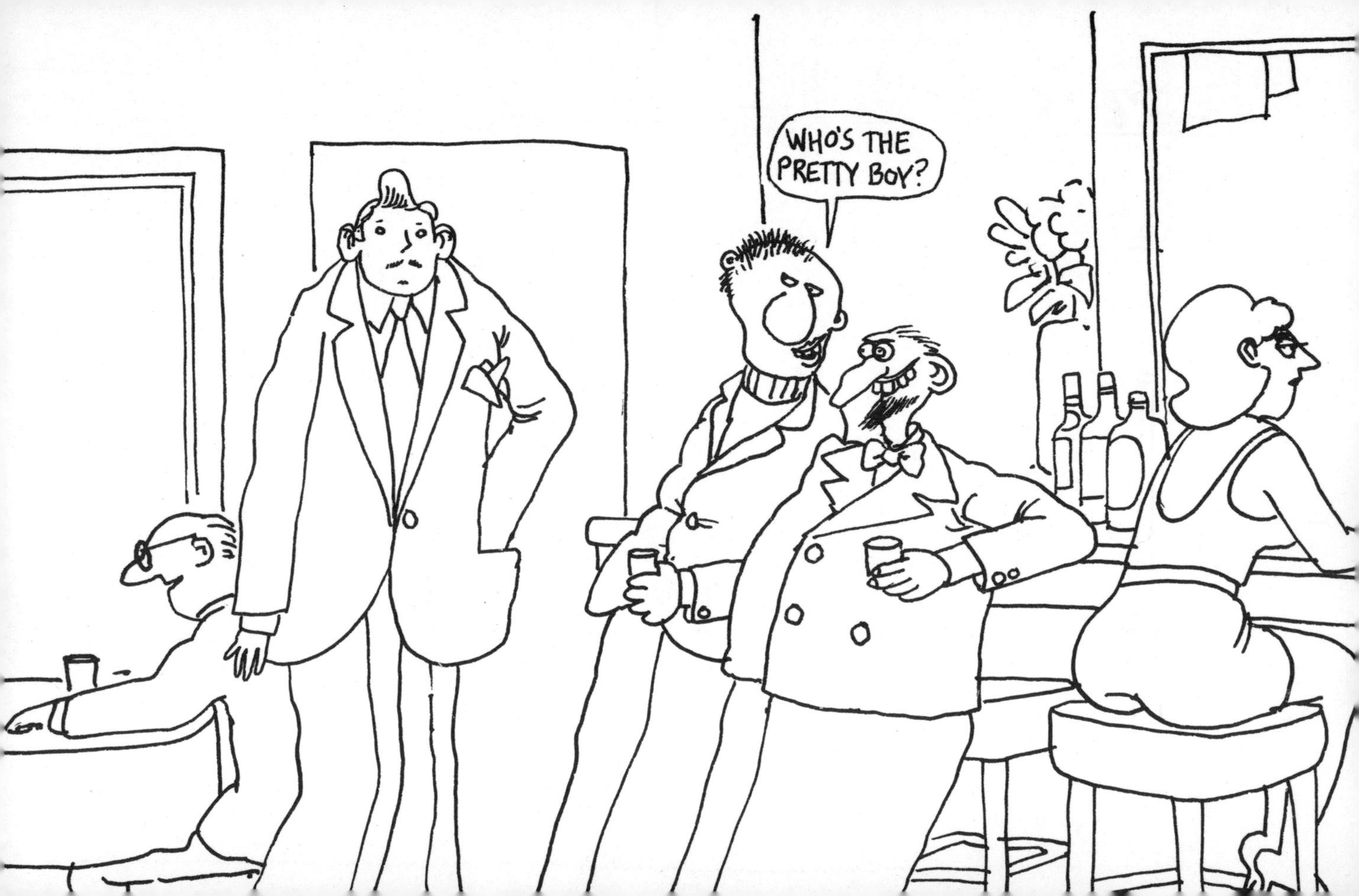
WHO'S THE
PRETTY BOY?

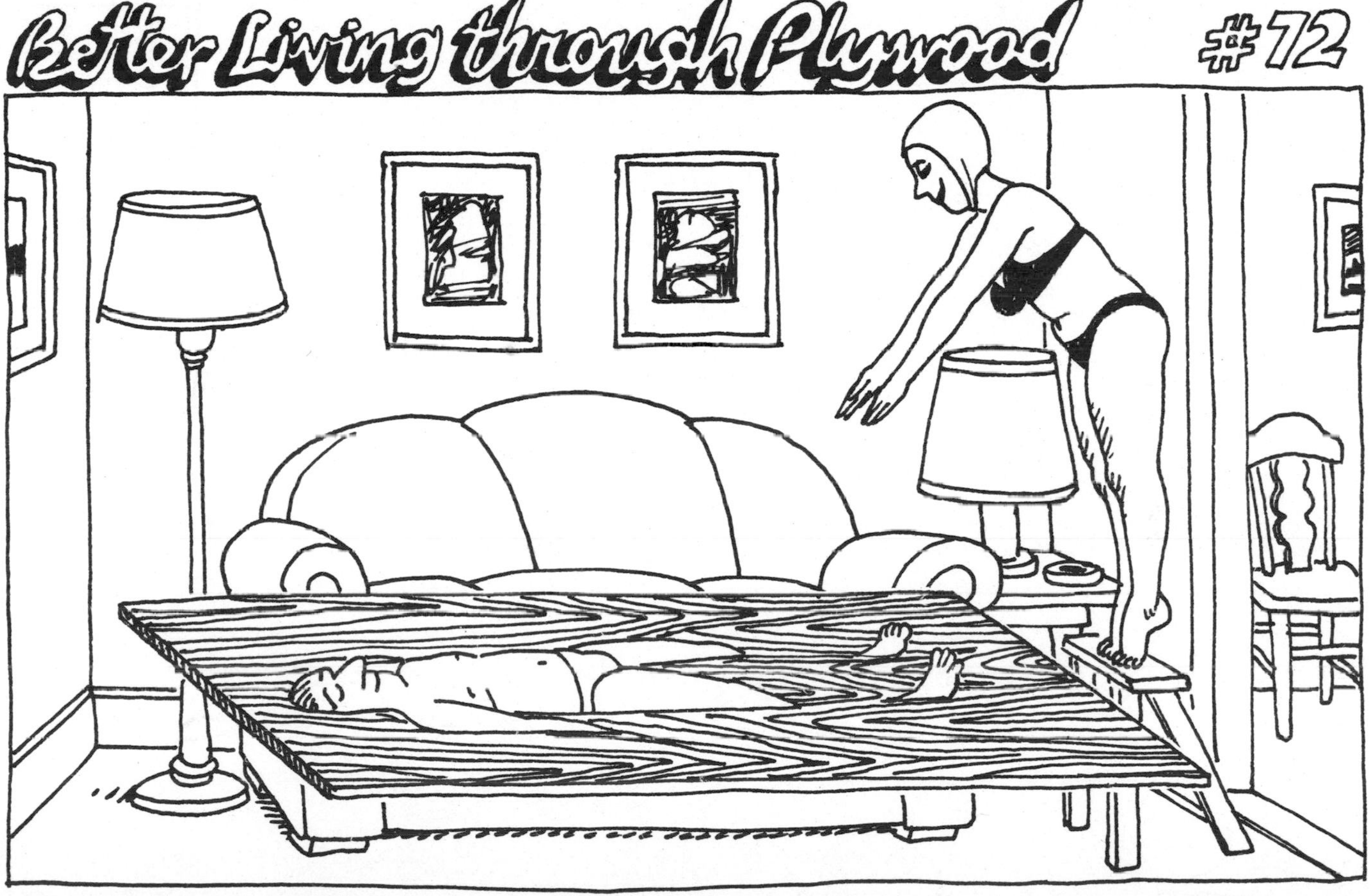
Better Living through Plywood
#72

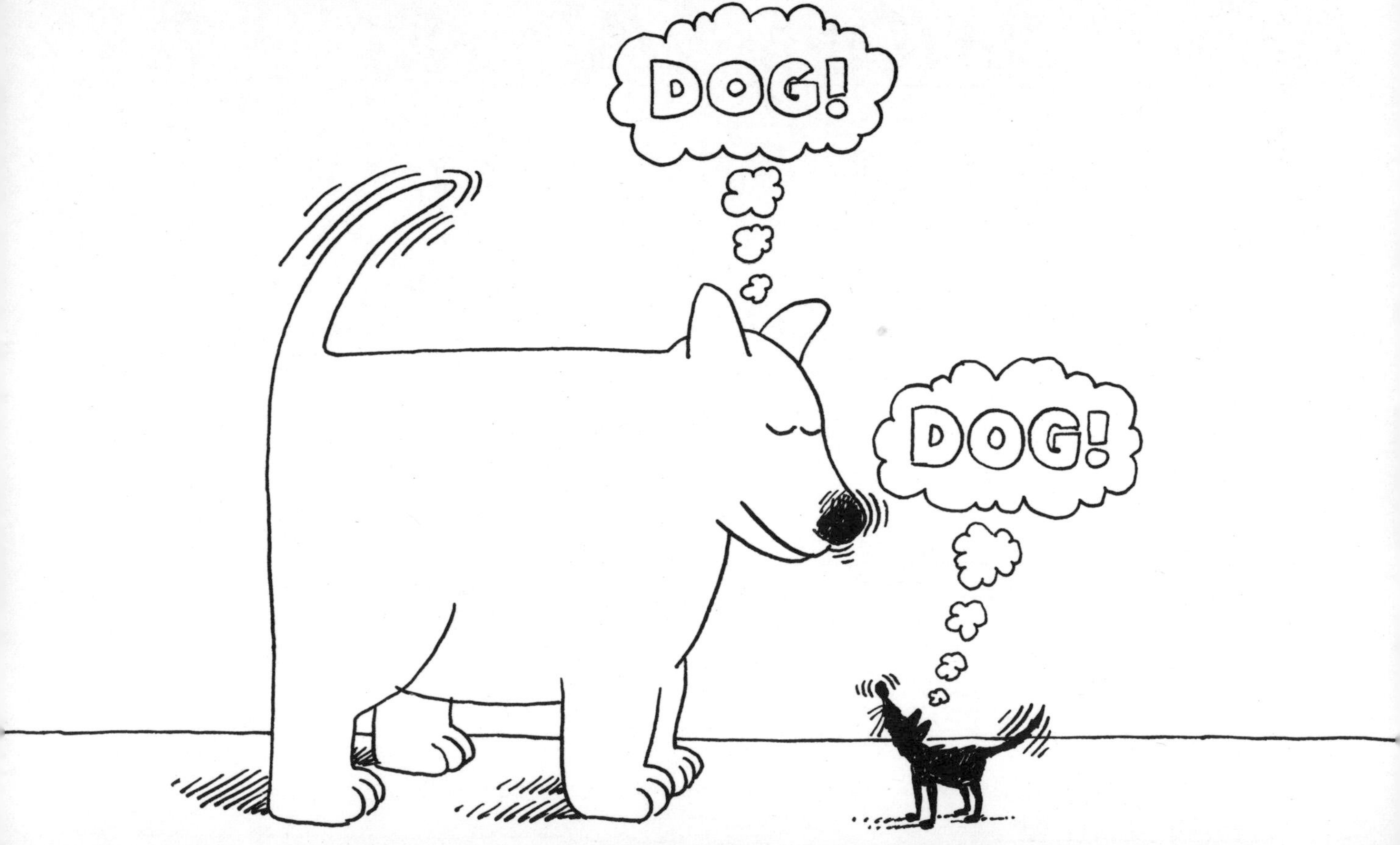
DOG!
DOG!

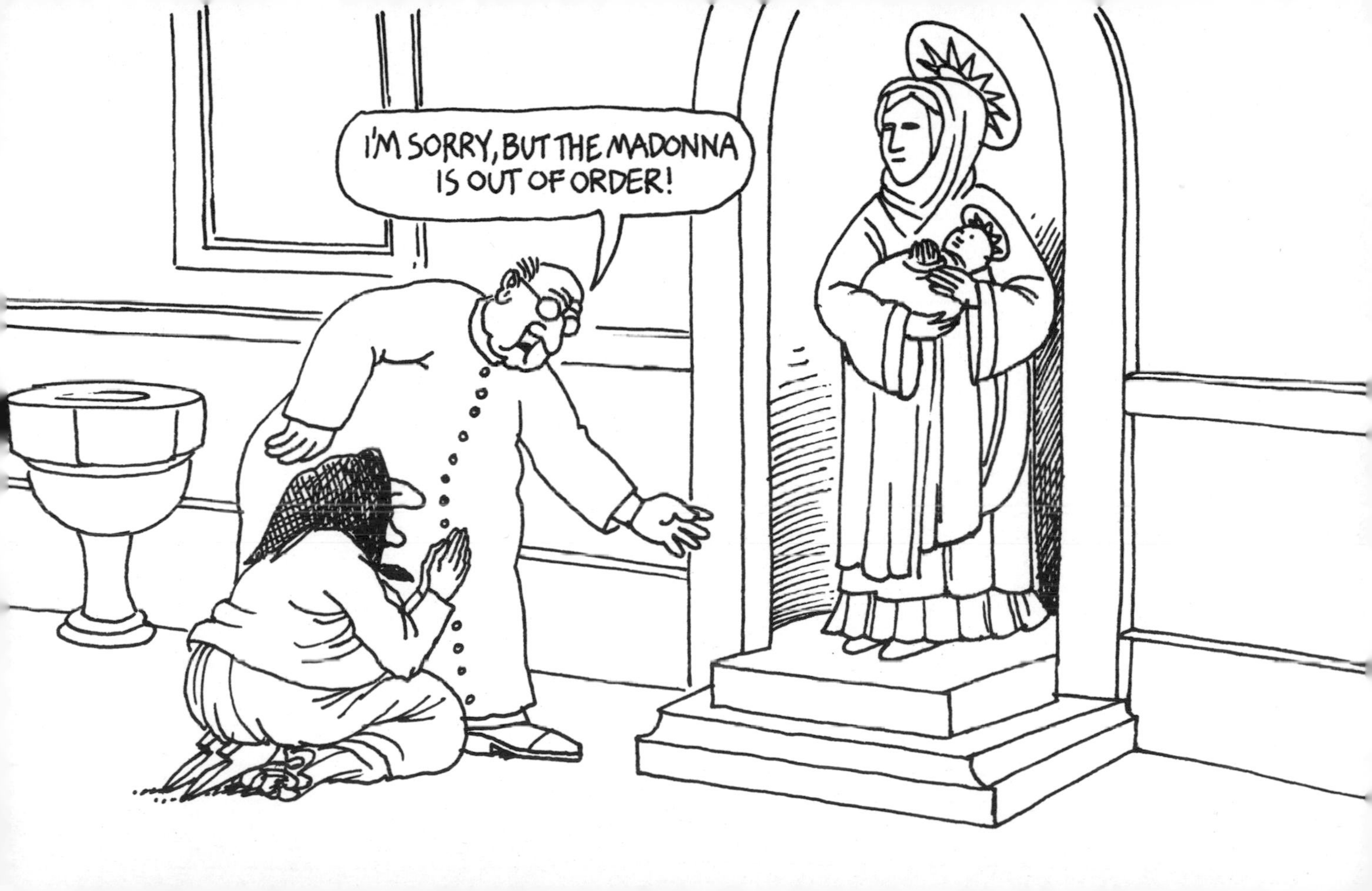
I'M SORRY, BUT THE MADONNA IS OUT OF ORDER!

## Road Food

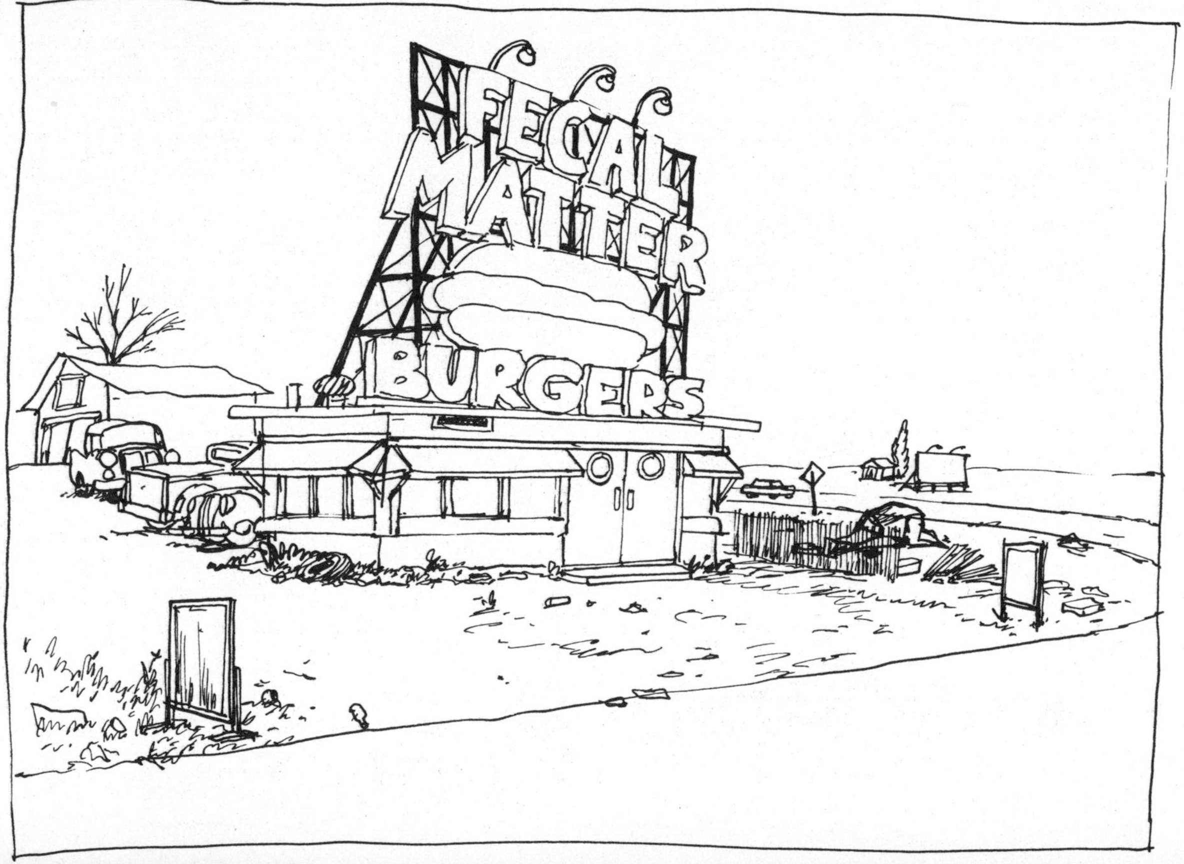
FECAL
MATTER
BURGERS

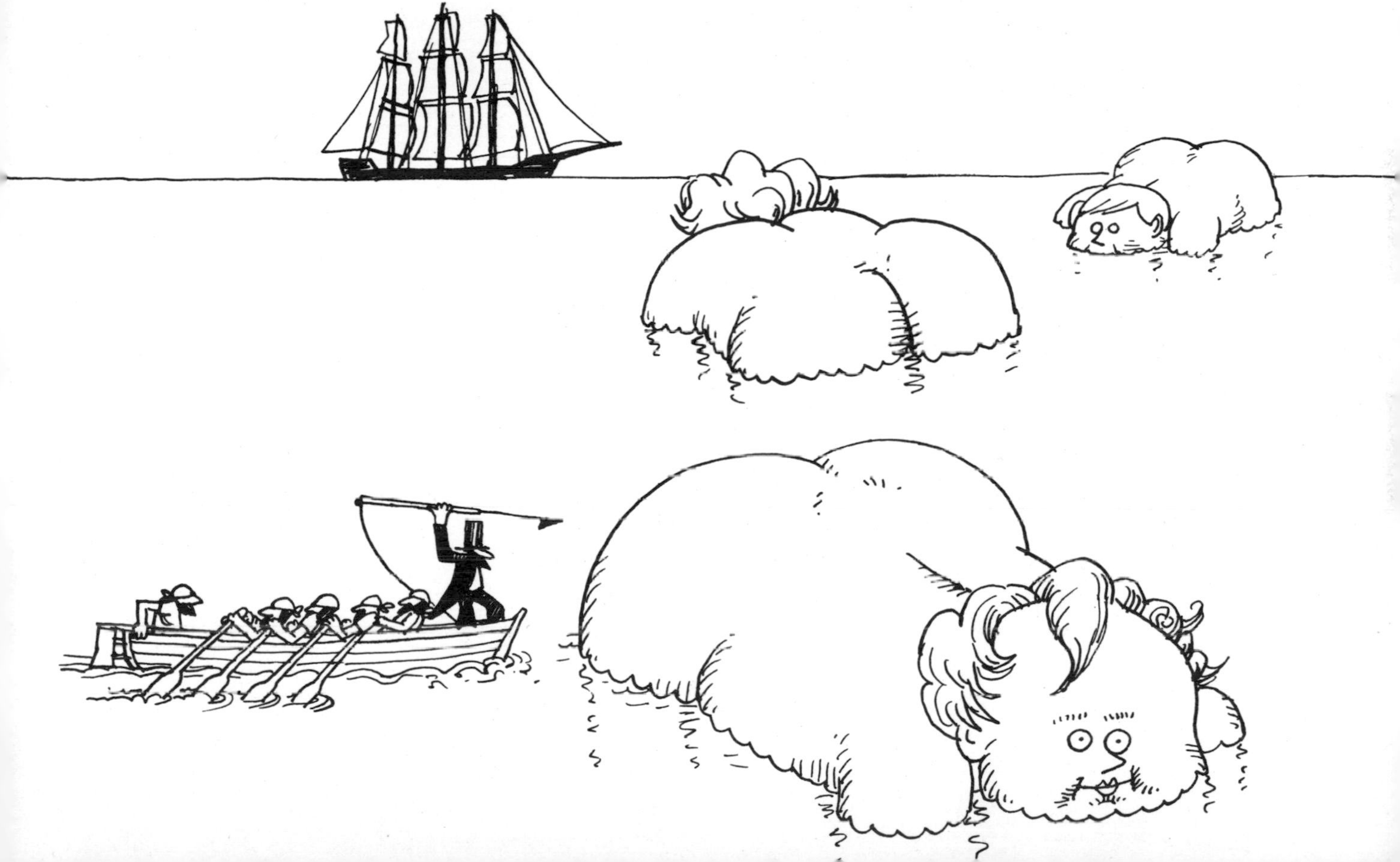

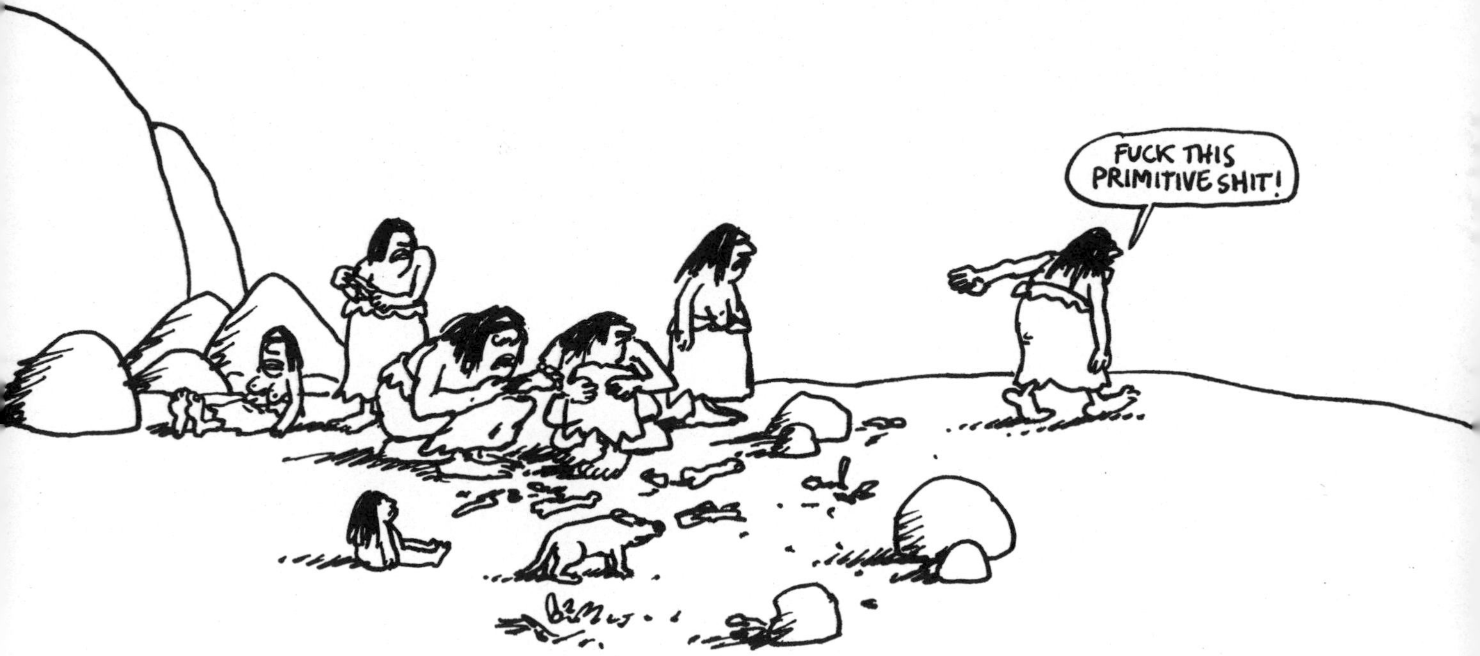
FUCK THIS PRIMITIVE SHIT!

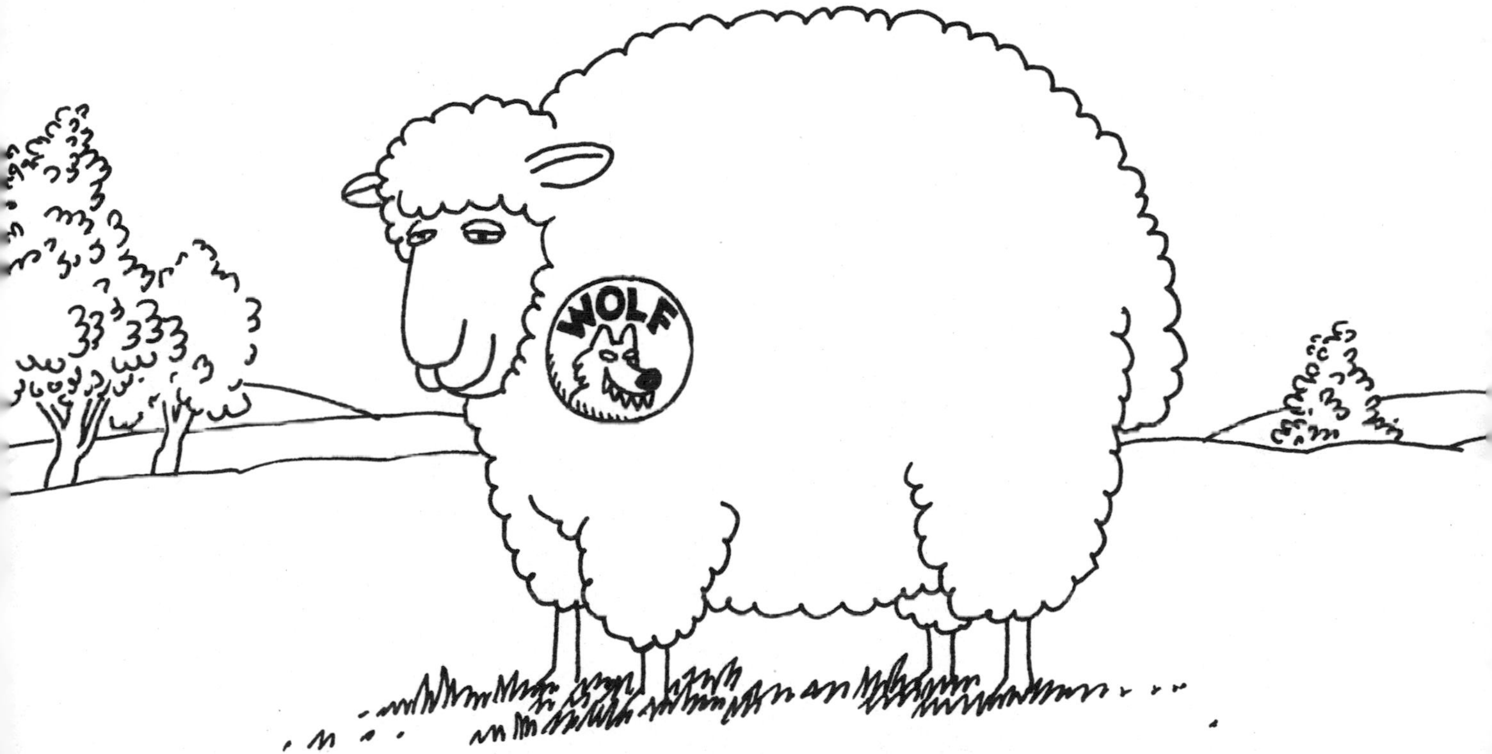
WOLF

Cosmic Pies, Gliding Silently Through Space

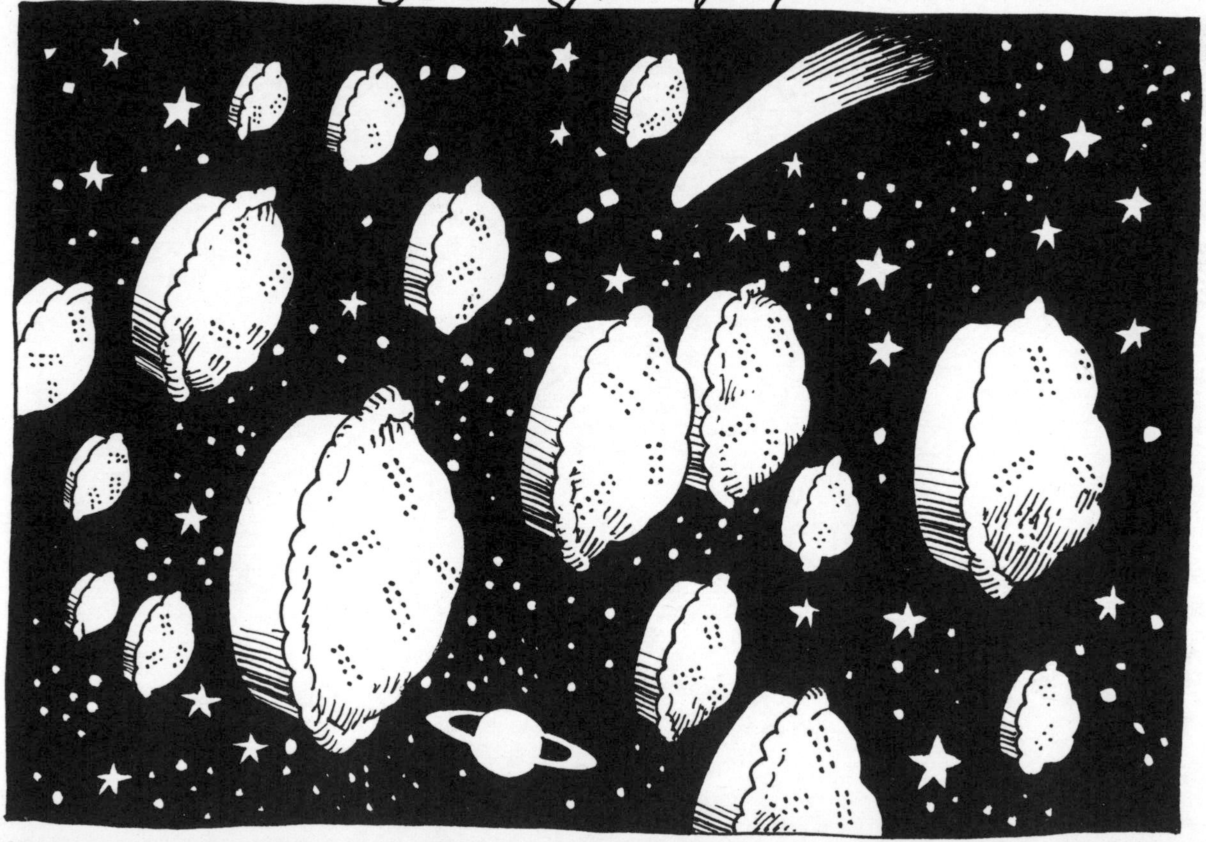

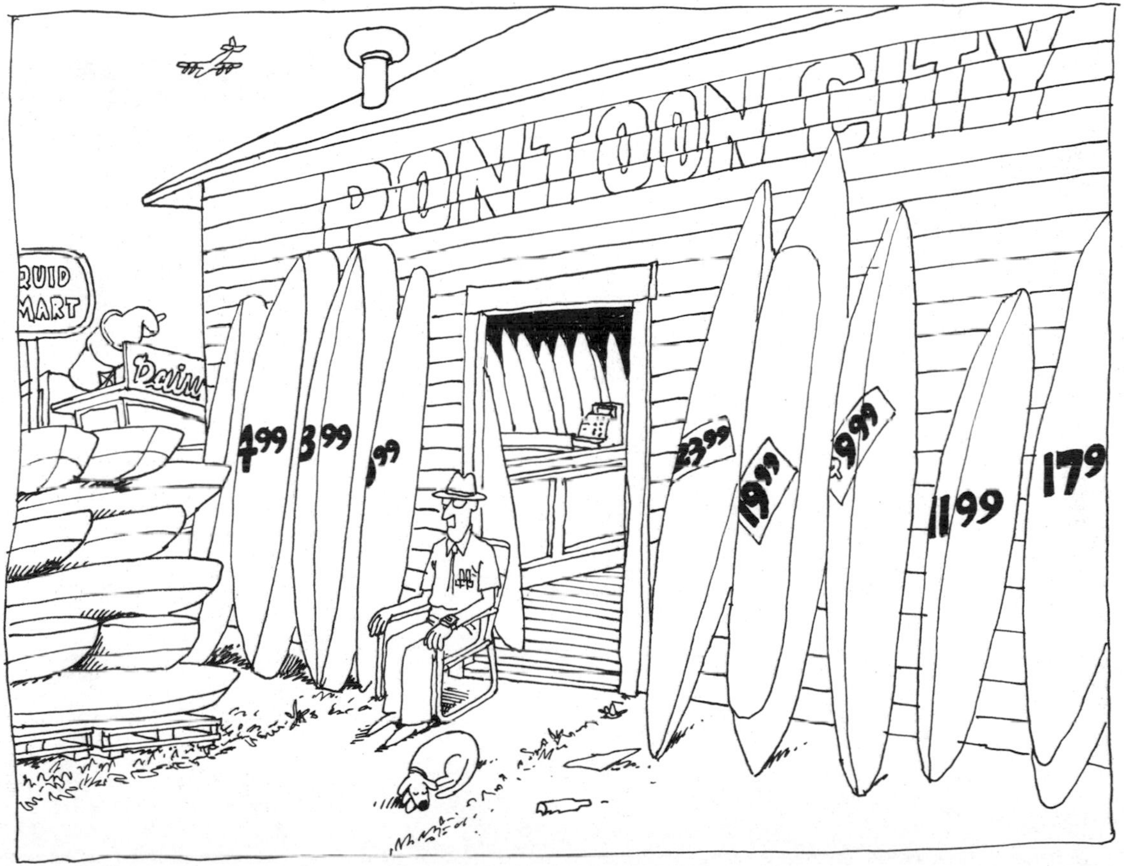
PONTOON CITY
QUID
MART
499
399
2399
1999
1199
179

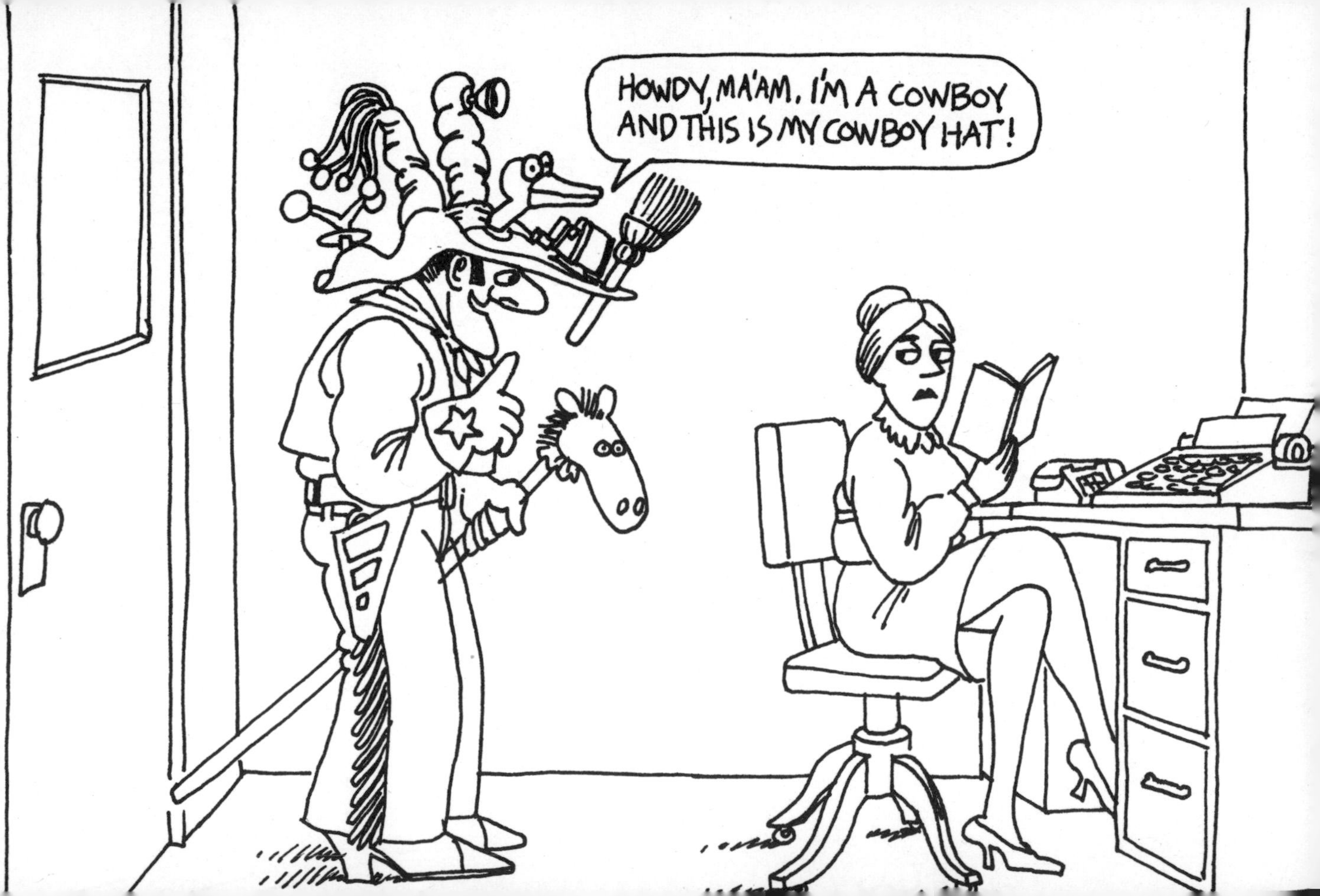
HOWDY, MA'AM. I'M A COWBOY AND THIS IS MY COWBOY HAT!

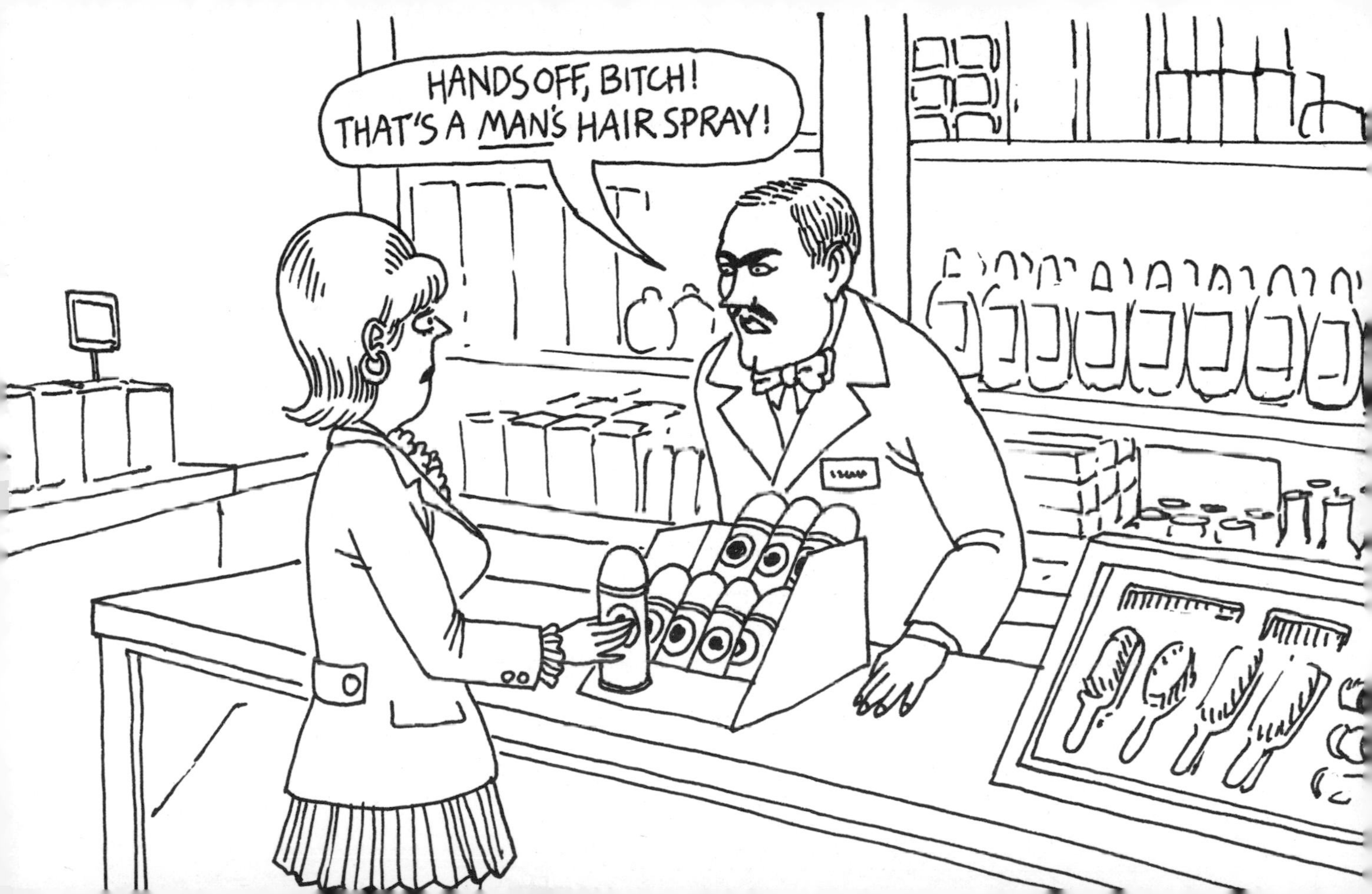
HANDS OFF, BITCH!
THAT'S A MAN'S HAIR SPRAY!

An Illegal Cube Den

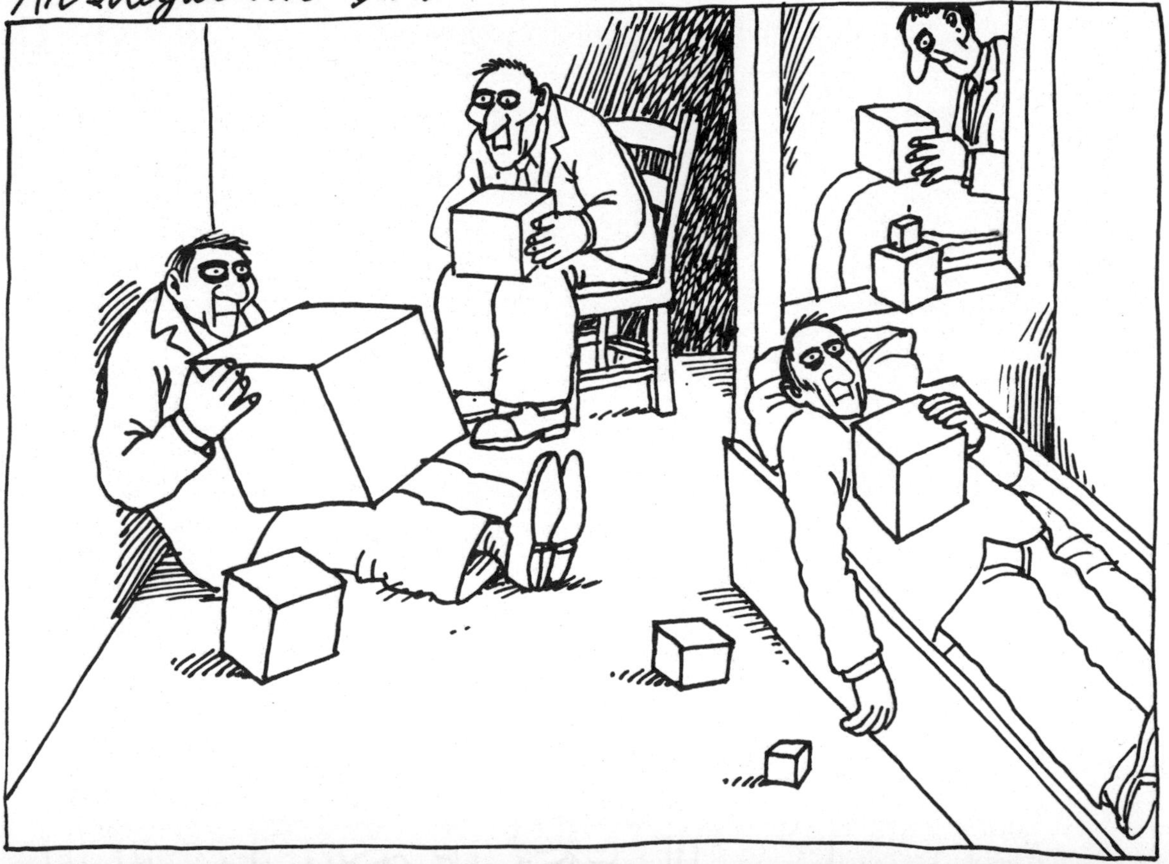

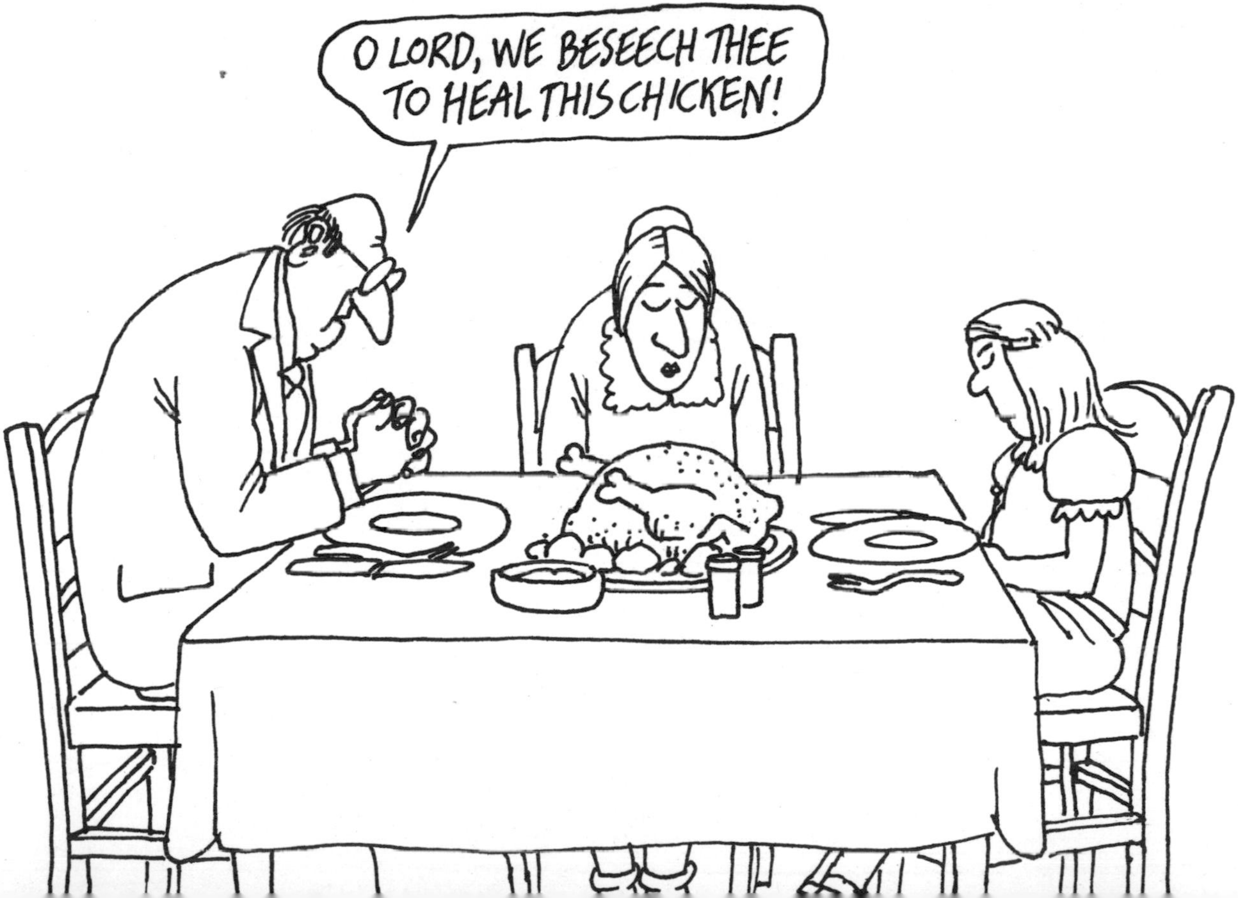
O LORD, WE BESEECH THEE TO HEAL THIS CHICKEN!

# Pork

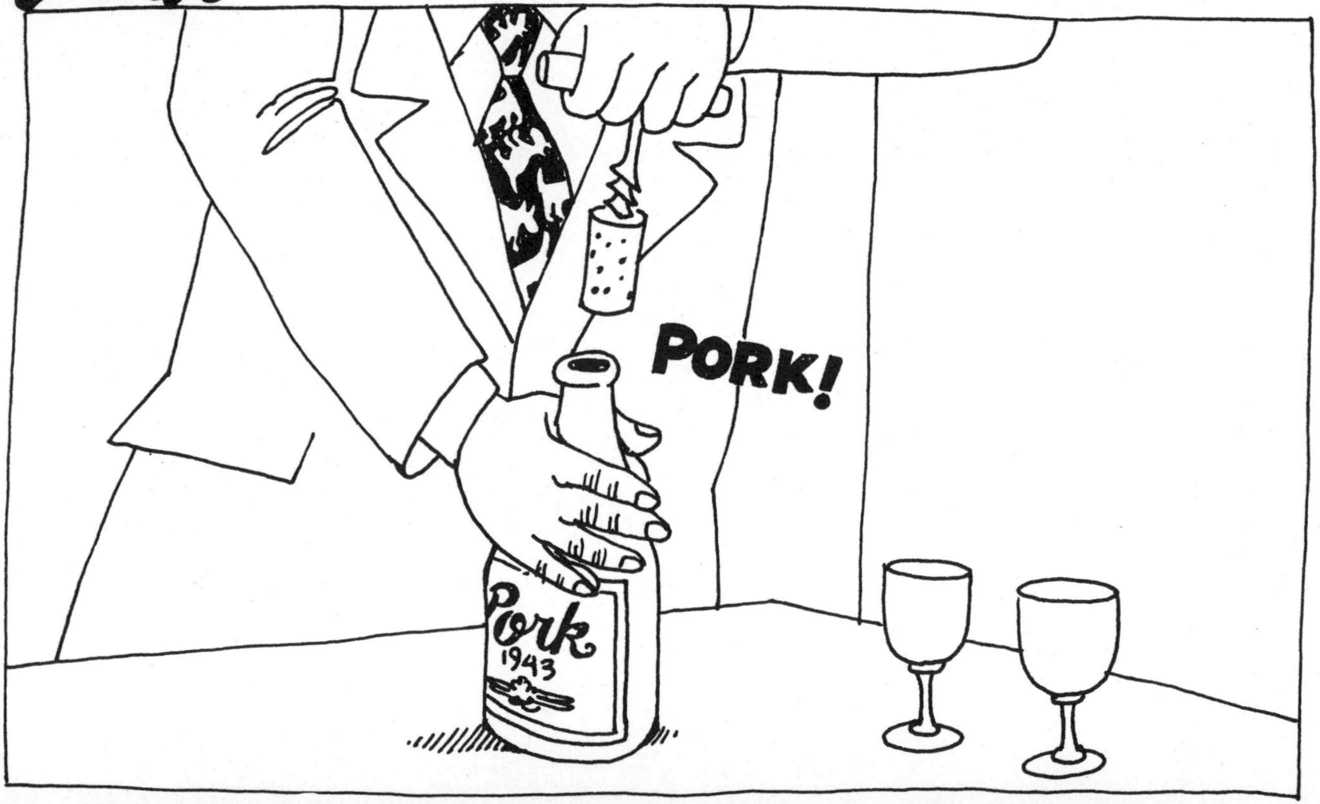

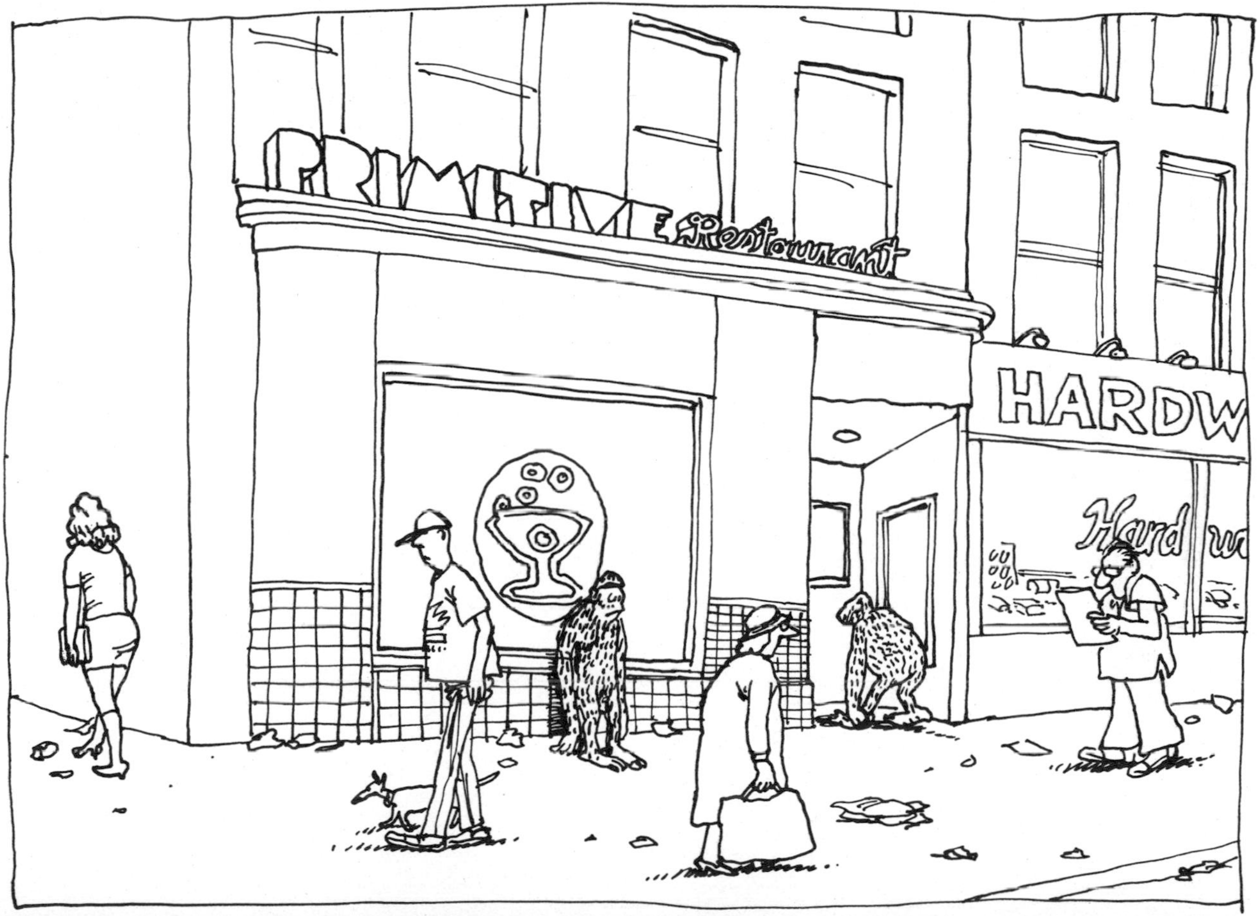
PRIMITIVE Restaurant
HARDW
Hard wa

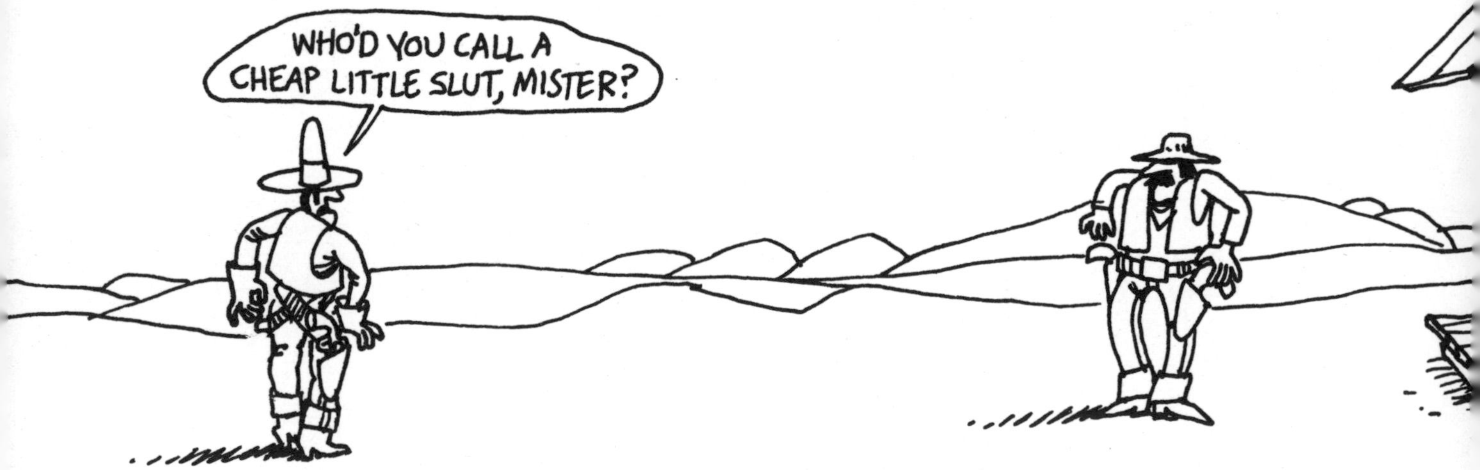
WHO'D YOU CALL A CHEAP LITTLE SLUT, MISTER?

SAINT ROCCO PREACHING TO THE TOILETS

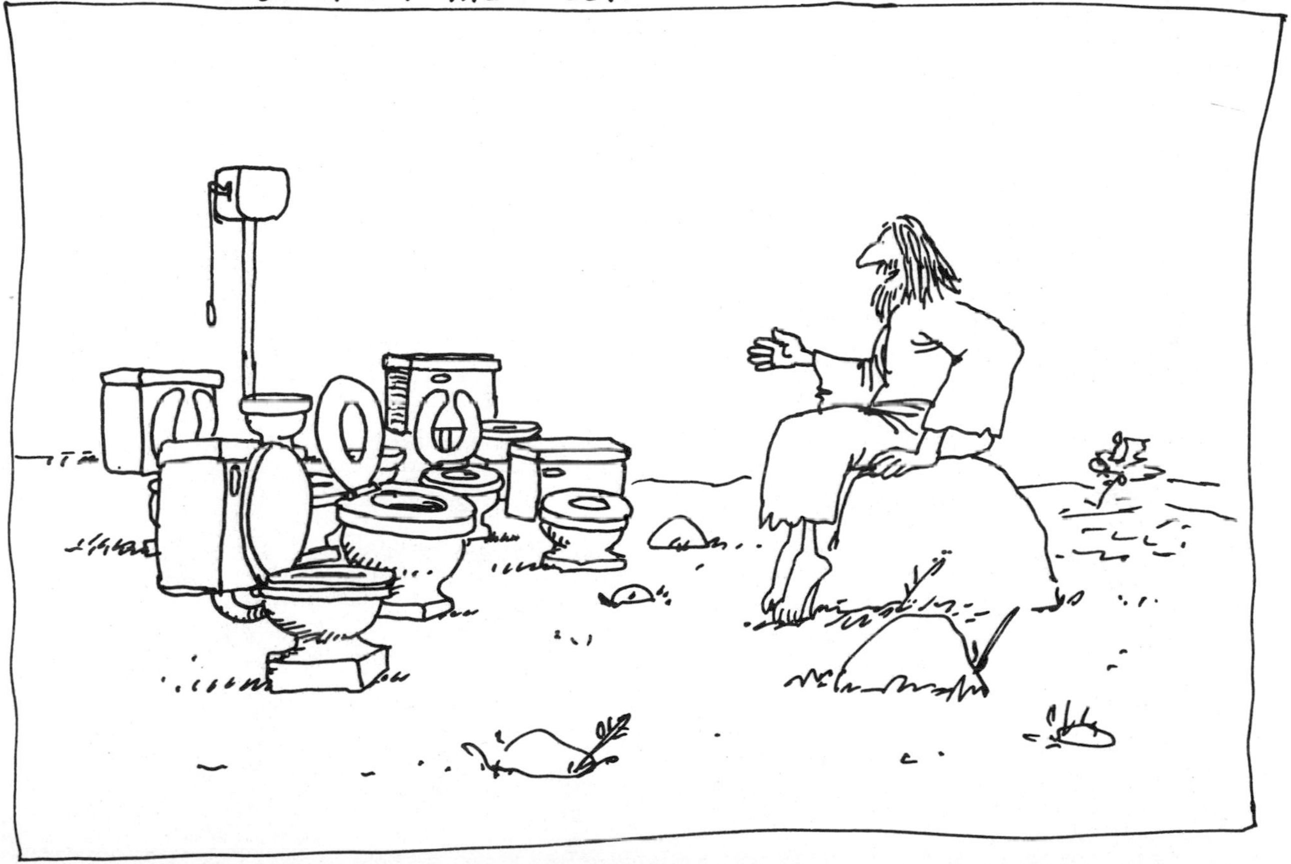

# Basic Sci-Fi

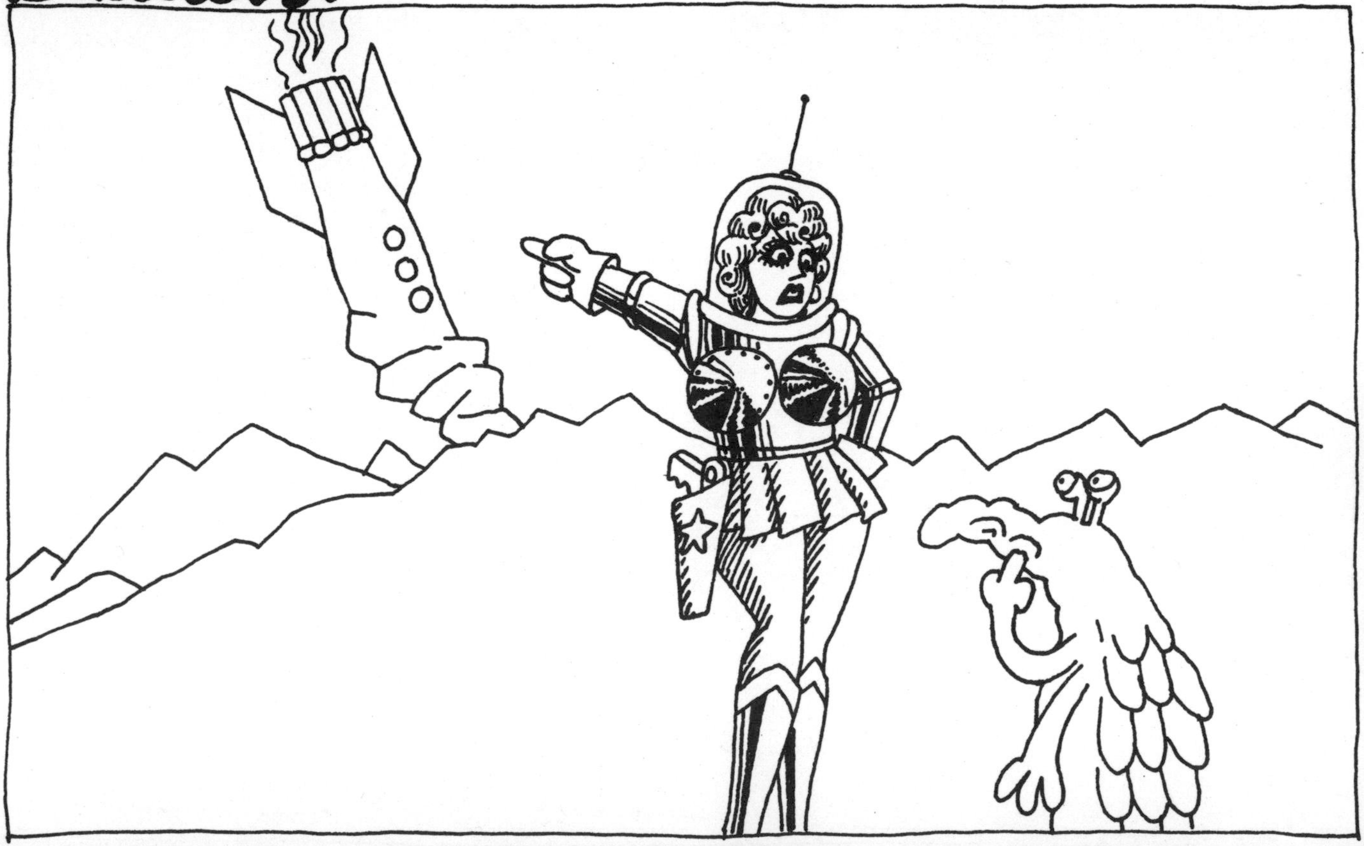

# I Just Flew In From The Coast...

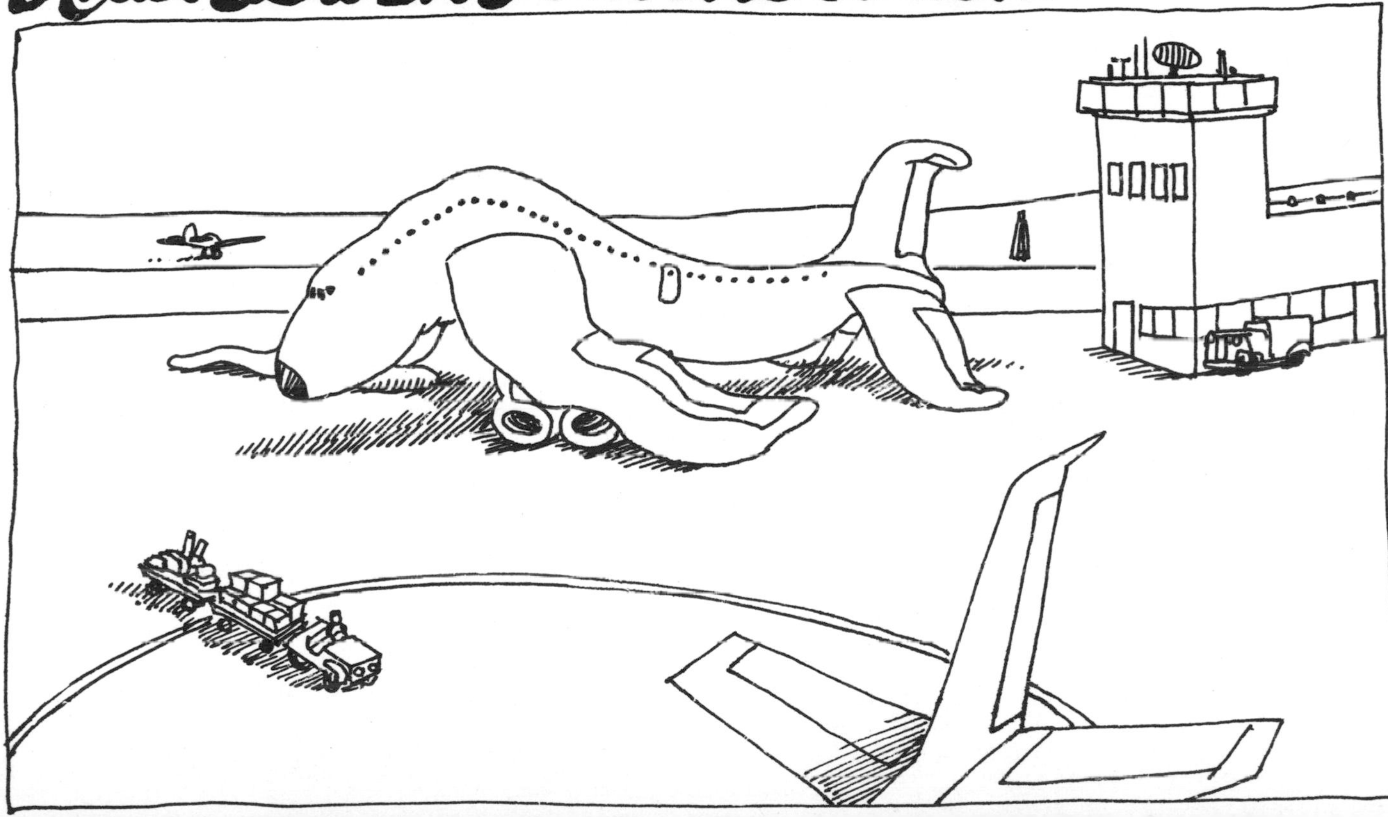

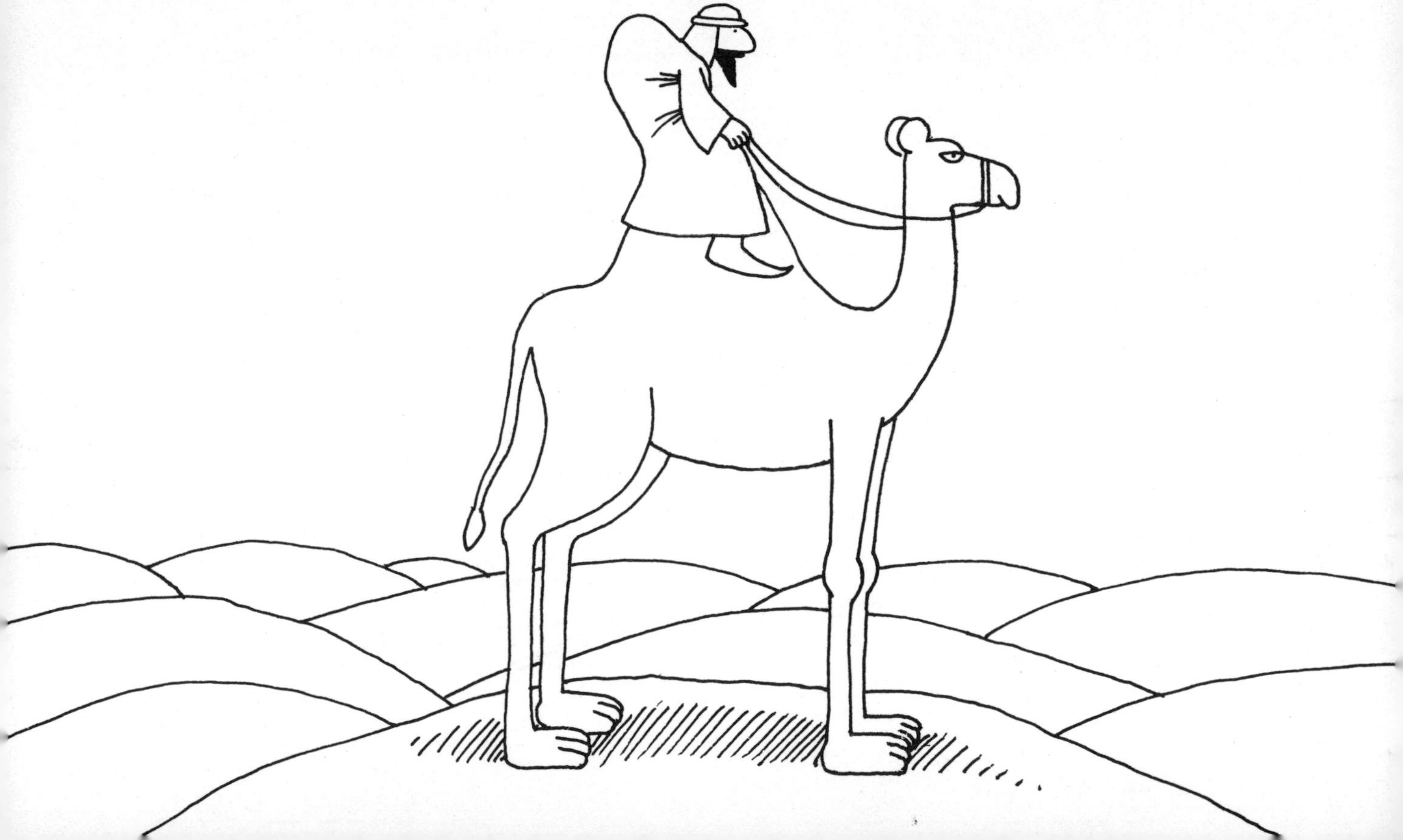

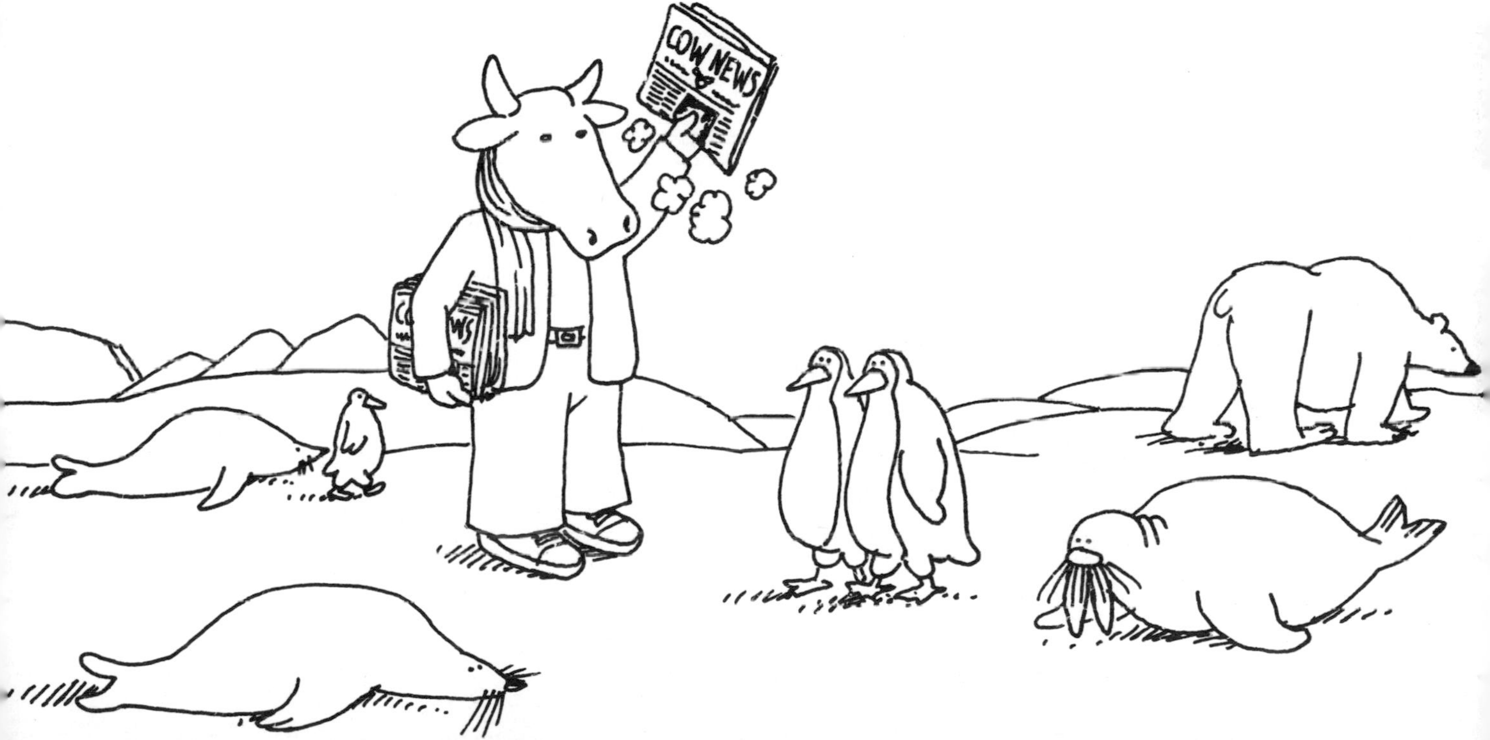
COW NEWS

# Back to Nature

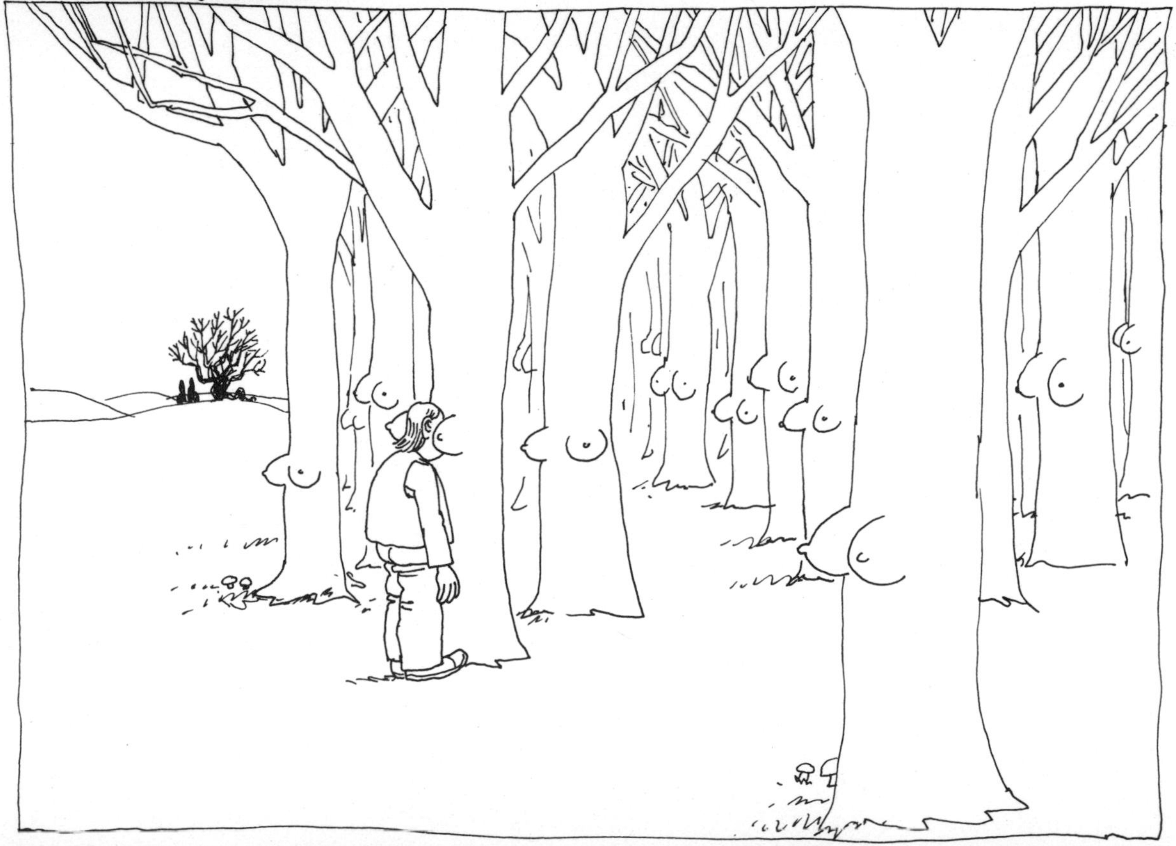

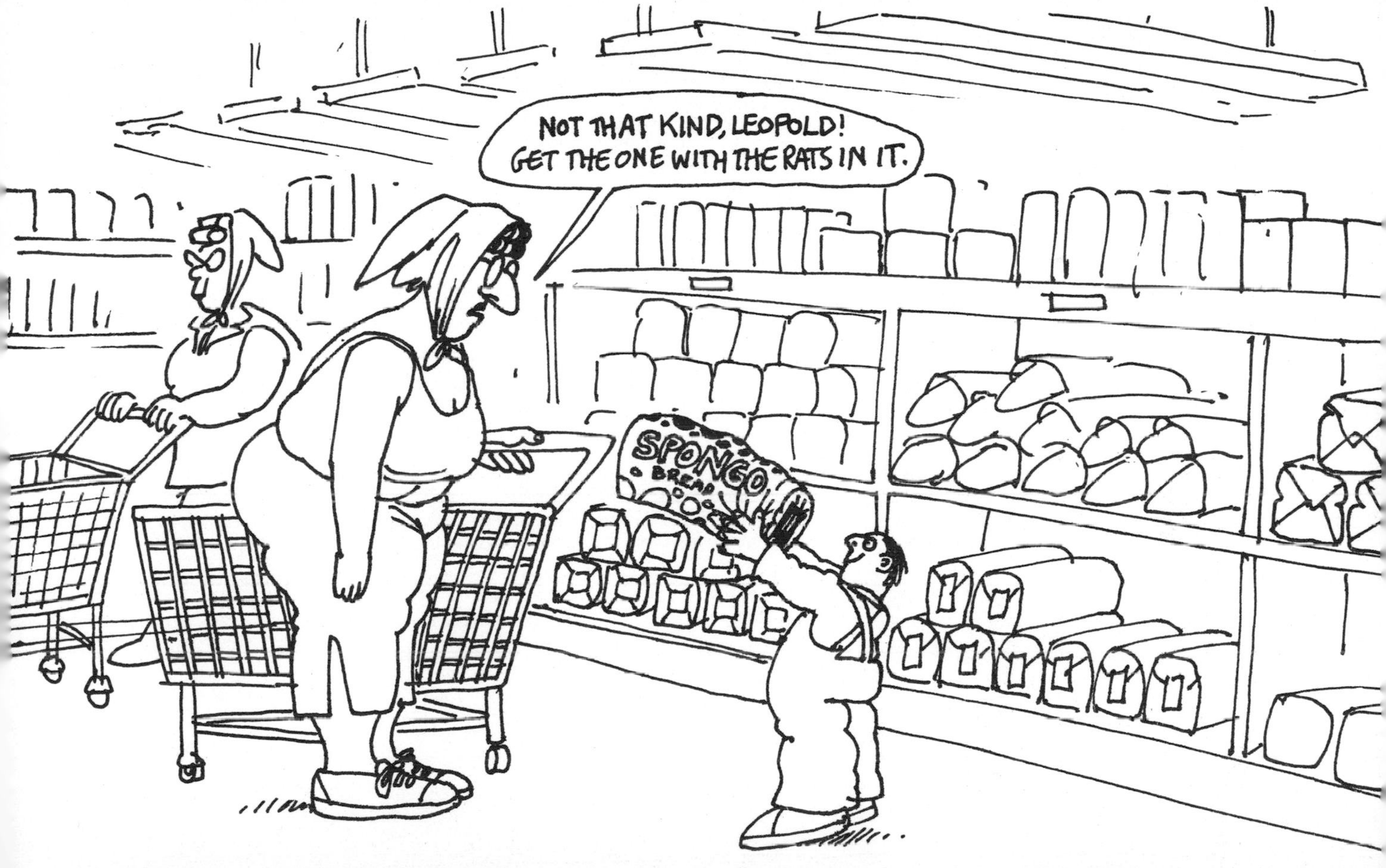
NOT THAT KIND, LEOPOLD!
GET THE ONE WITH THE RATS IN IT.
SPONGO
BREAD

LUCILLE AND HOWARD ENJOYING A BOOK

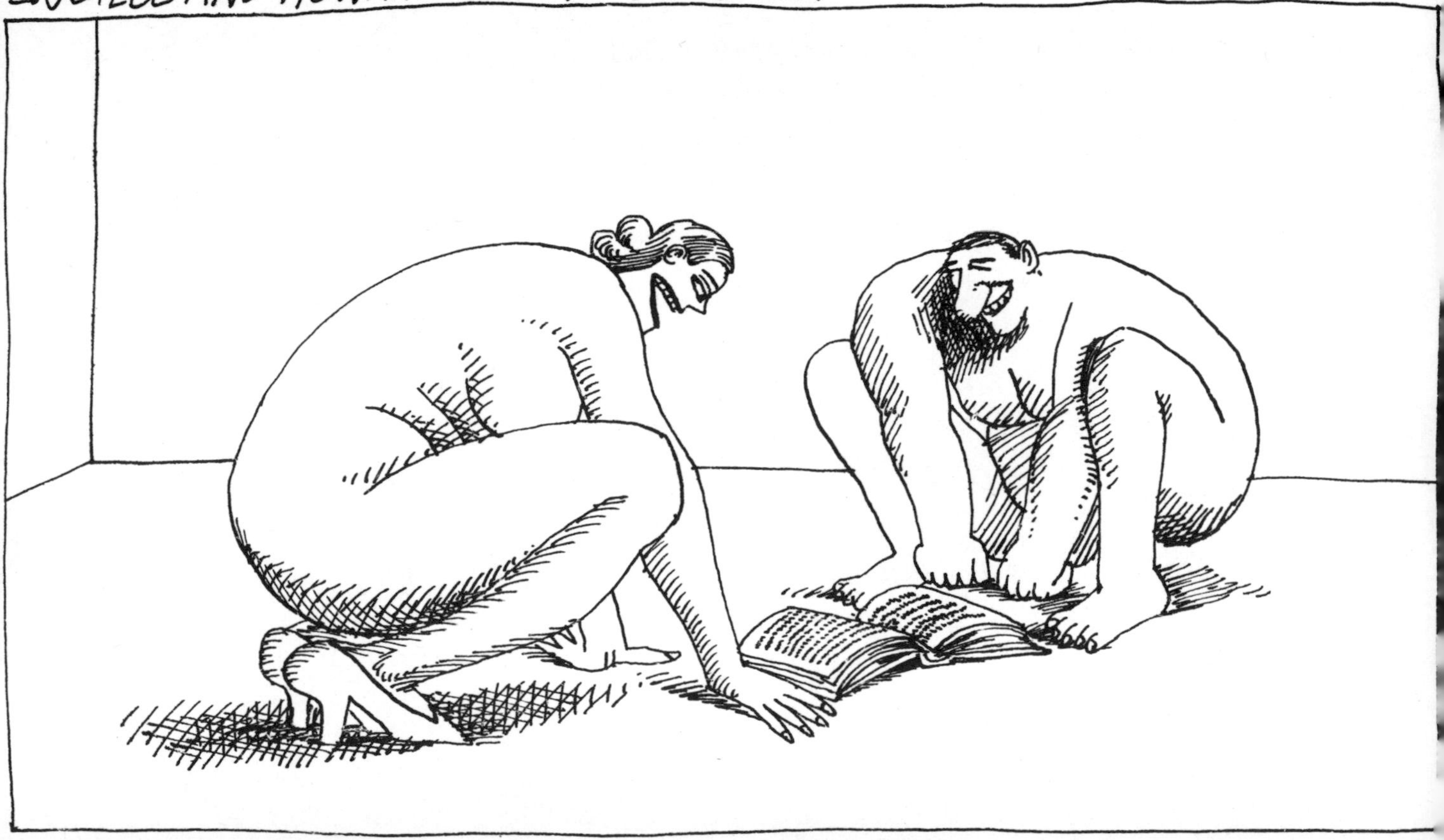

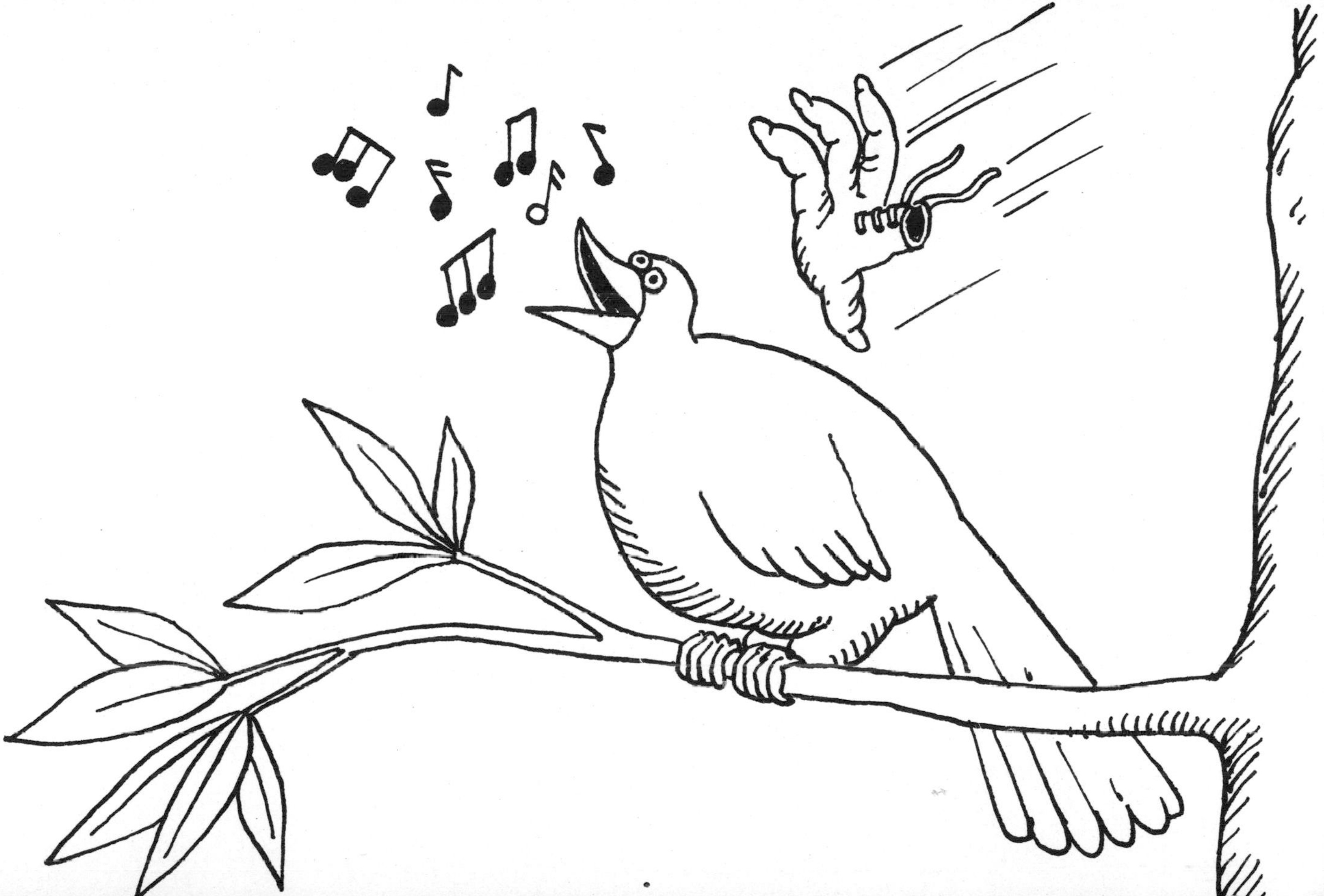

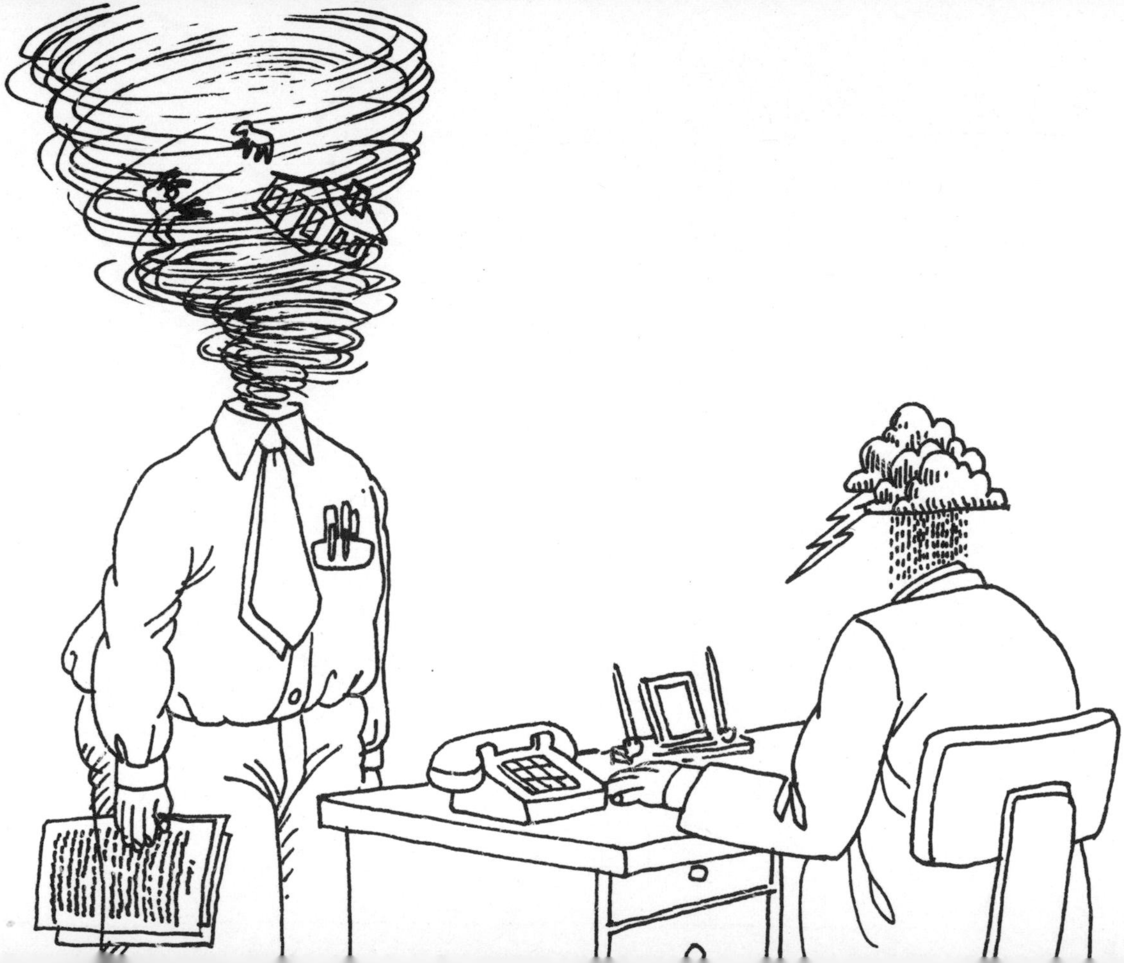

# The Unshaved Heart

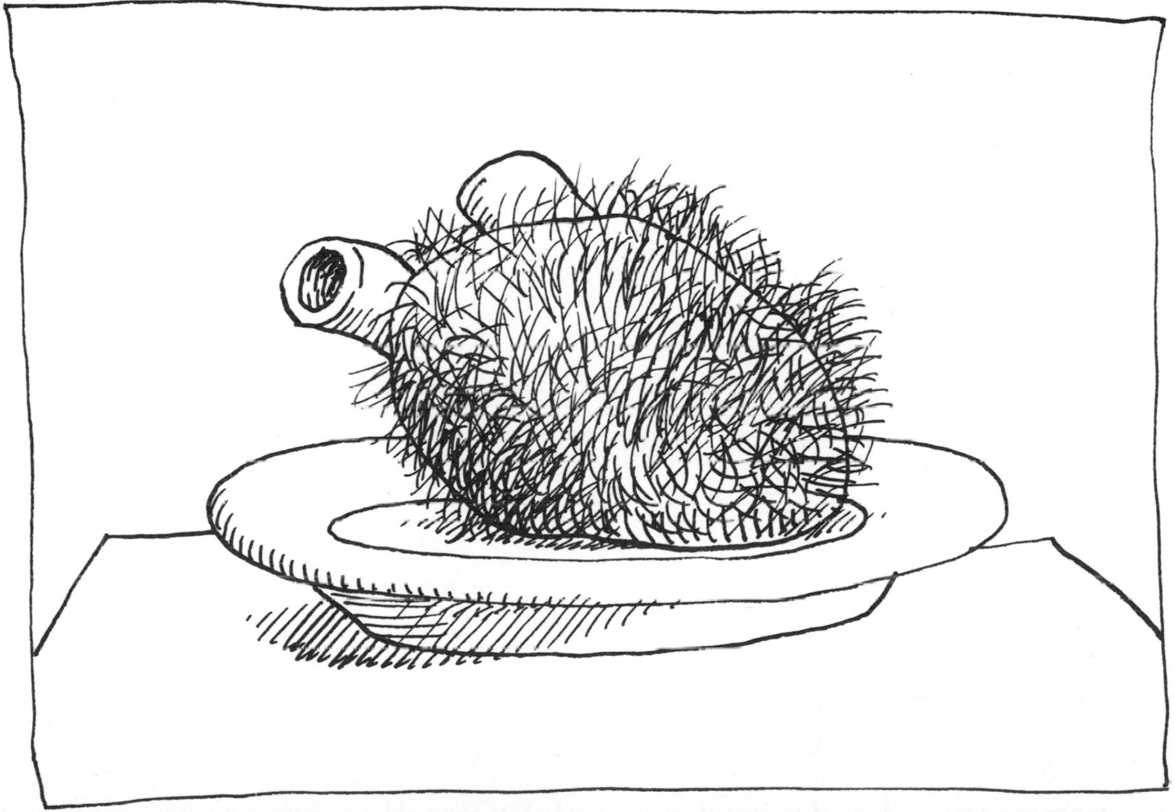

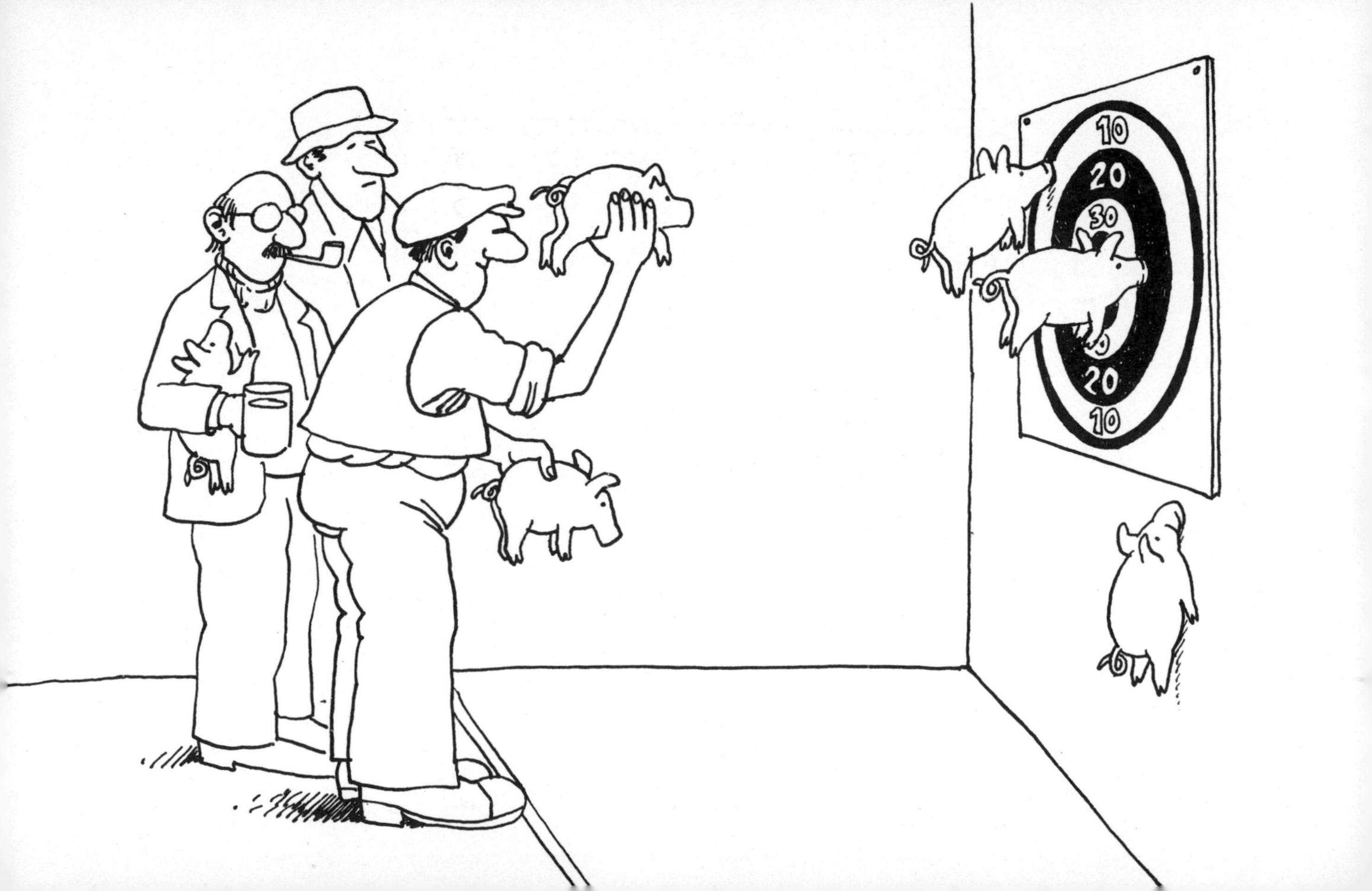
10
20
30
20
10

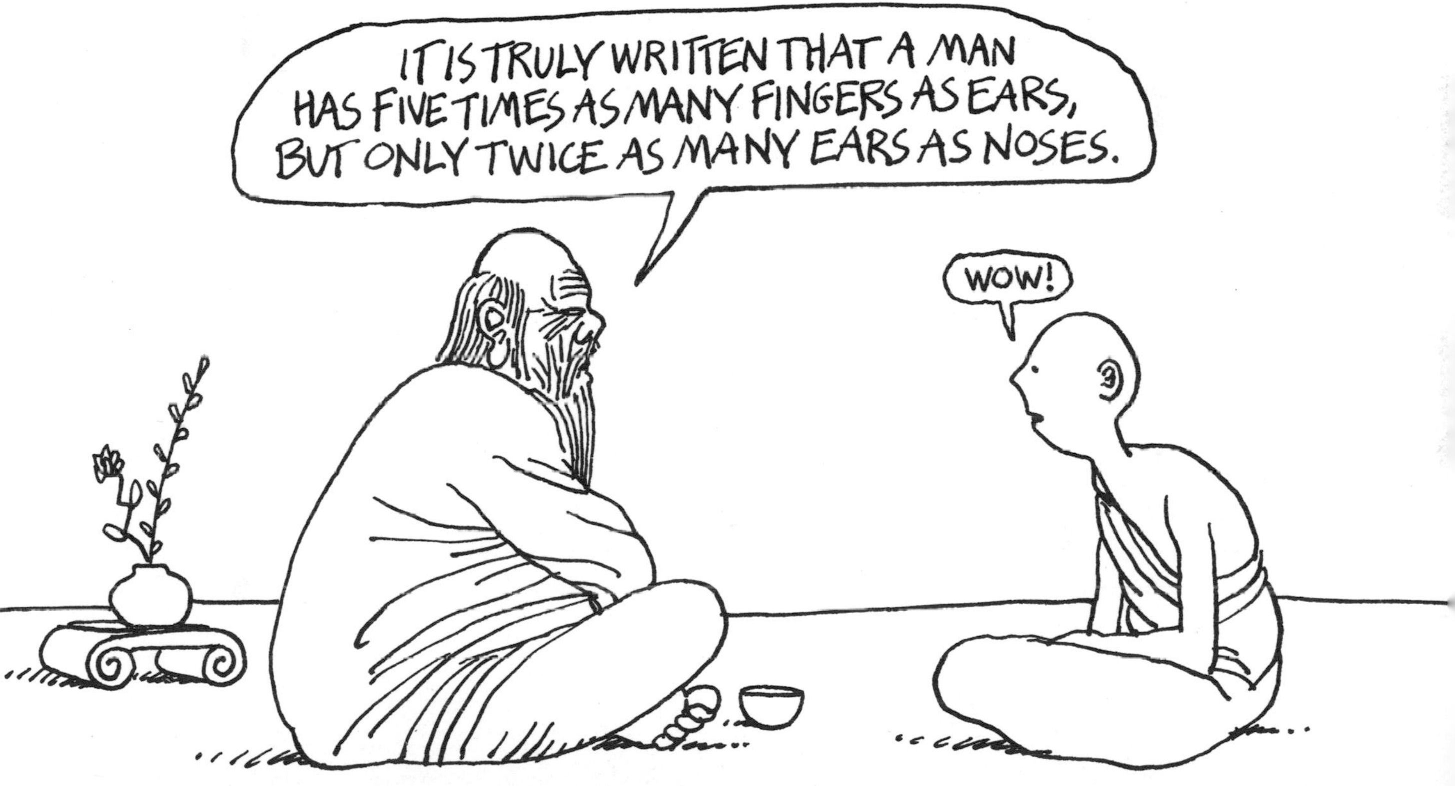
IT IS TRULY WRITTEN THAT A MAN HAS FIVE TIMES AS MANY FINGERS AS EARS, BUT ONLY TWICE AS MANY EARS AS NOSES.
WOW!

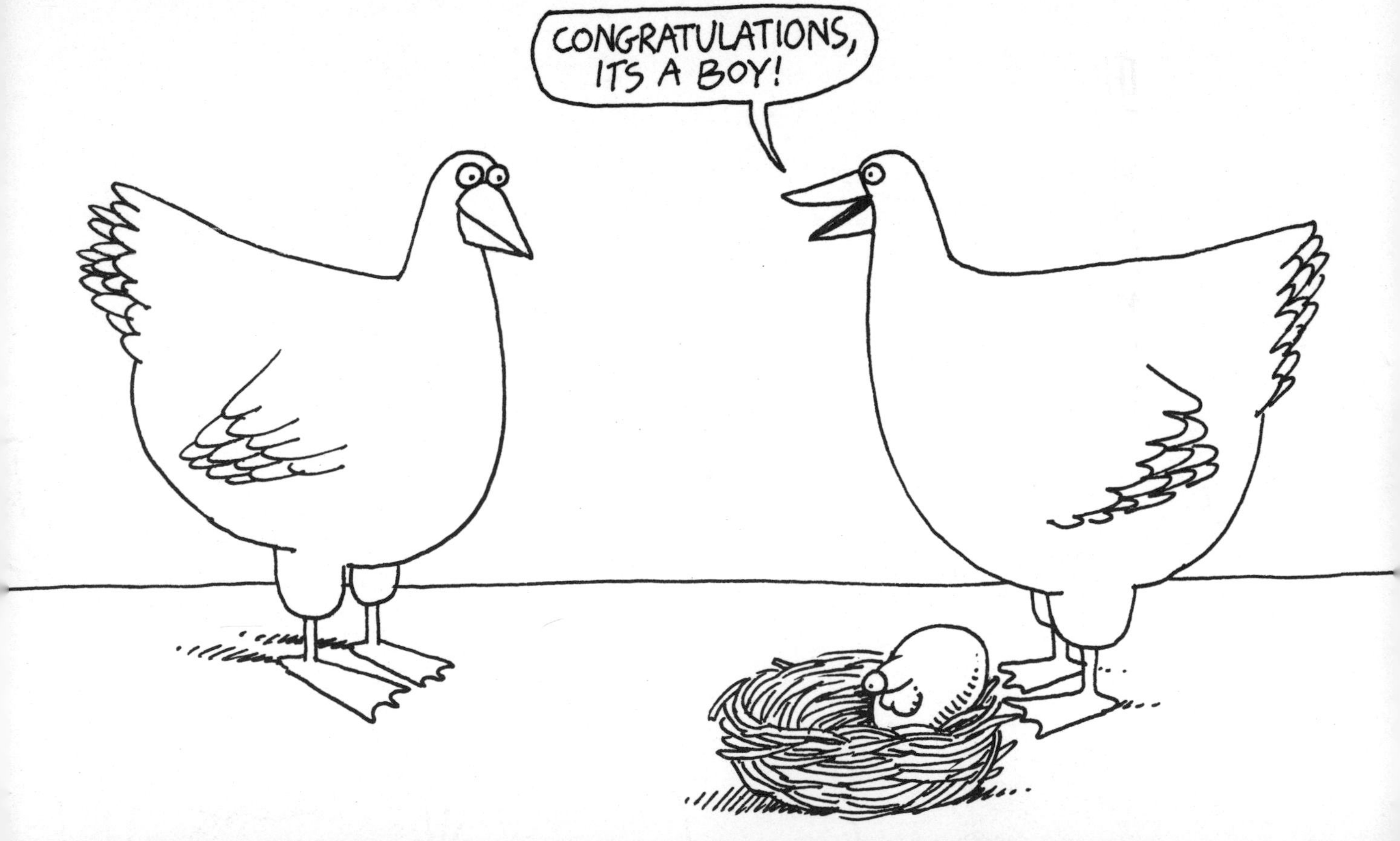
CONGRATULATIONS,
ITS A BOY!

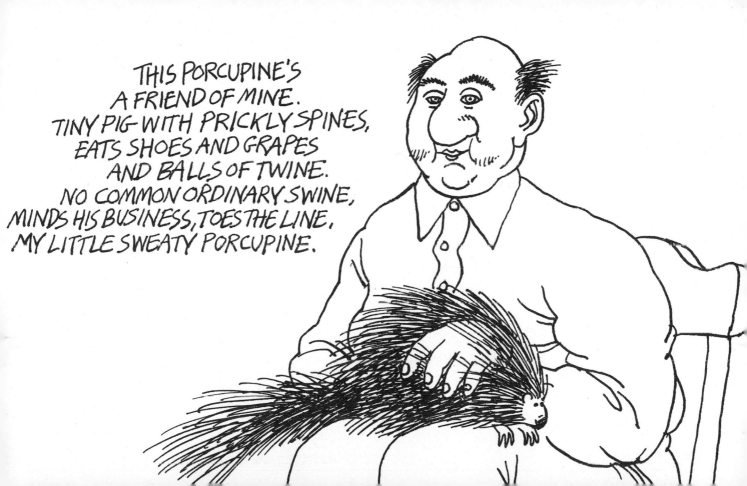

THIS PORCUPINE'S
A FRIEND OF MINE.
TINY PIG WITH PRICKLY SPINES,
EATS SHOES AND GRAPES
AND BALLS OF TWINE.
NO COMMON ORDINARY SWINE,
MINDS HIS BUSINESS, TOES THE LINE,
MY LITTLE SWEATY PORCUPINE.

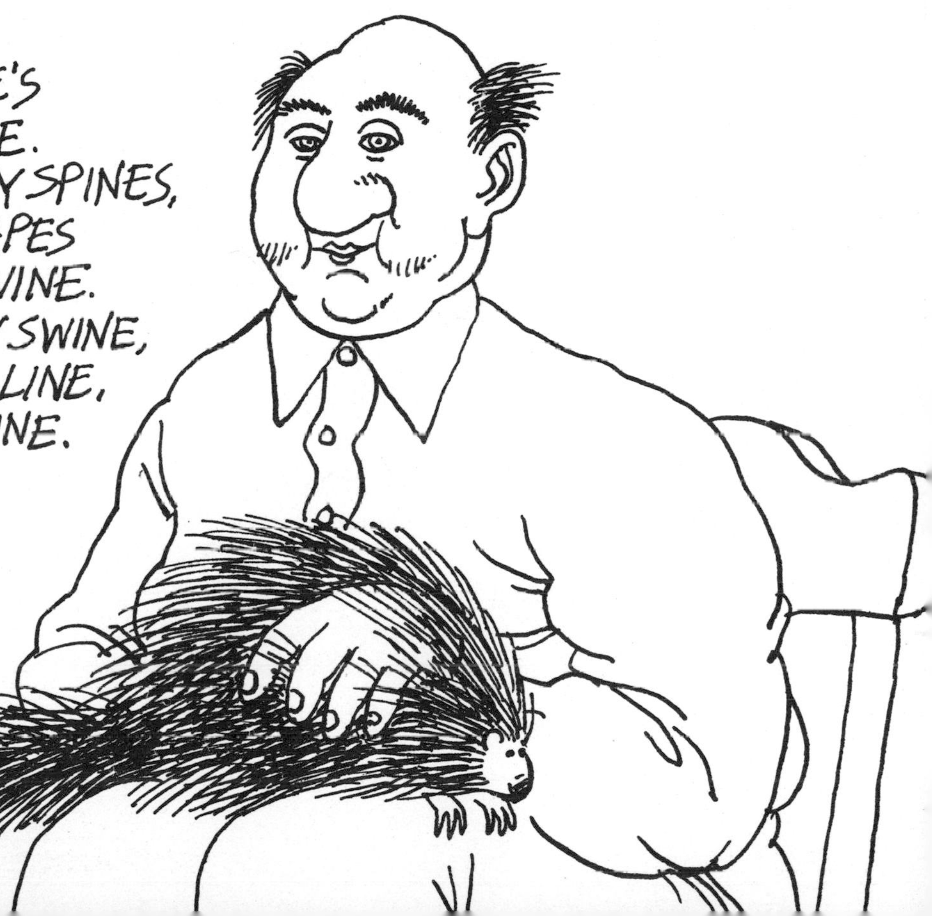

The Critic

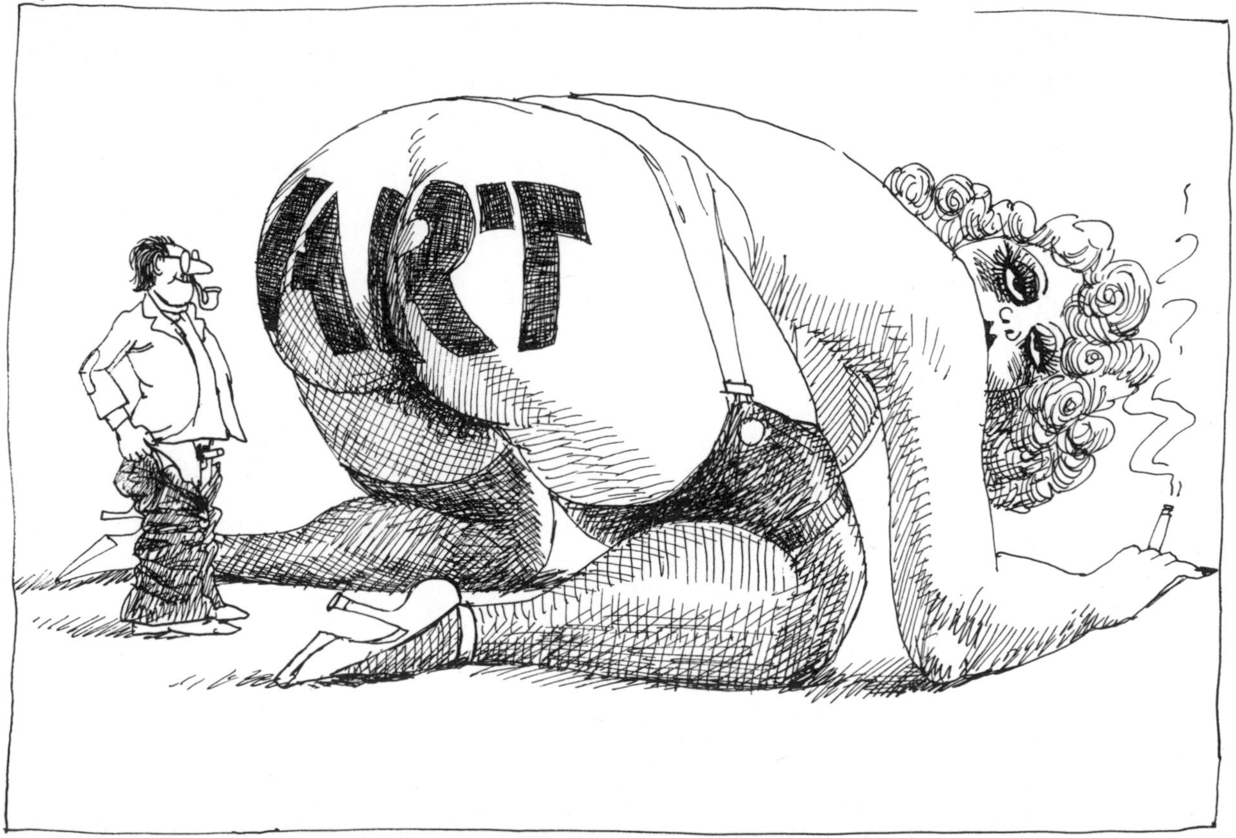
ART

**BARF BOLD** *A Decorative Typeface*

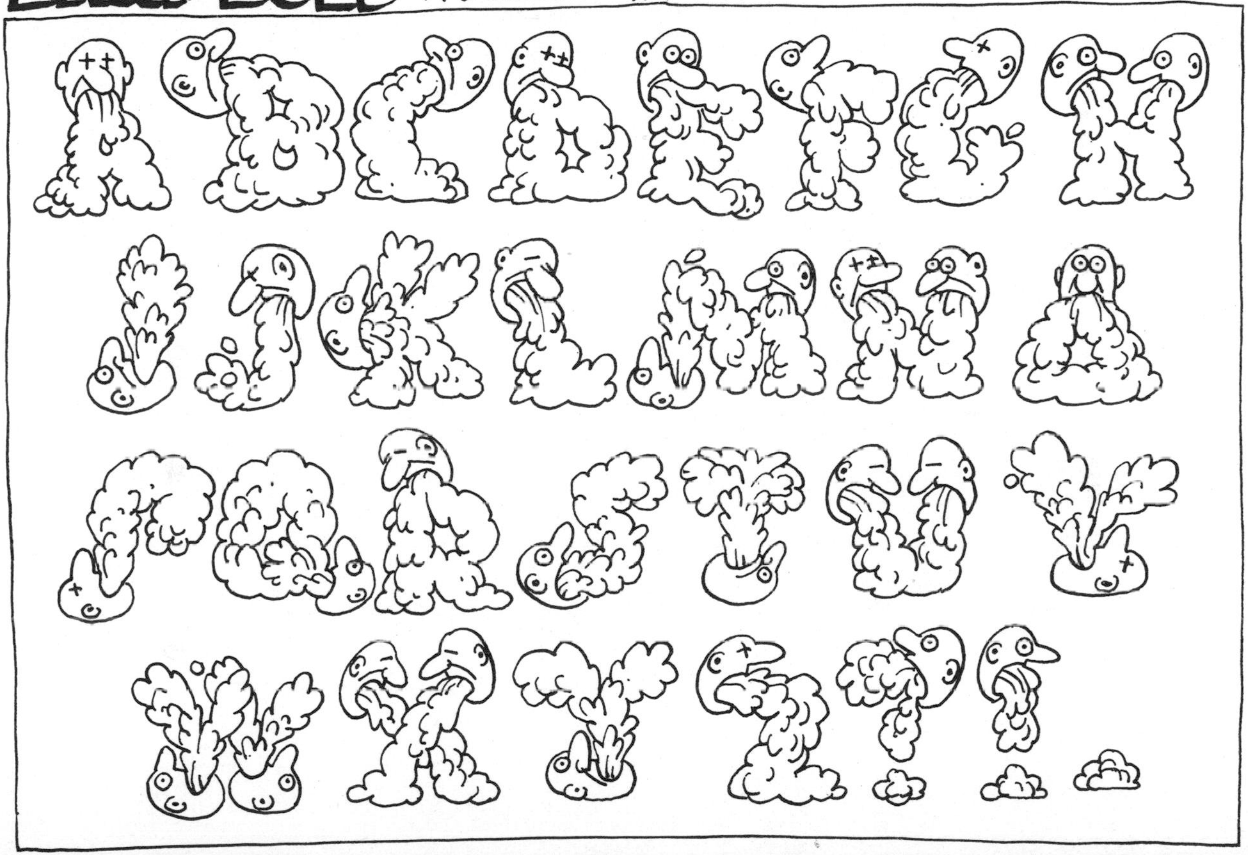

# Better Living through Plywood #66

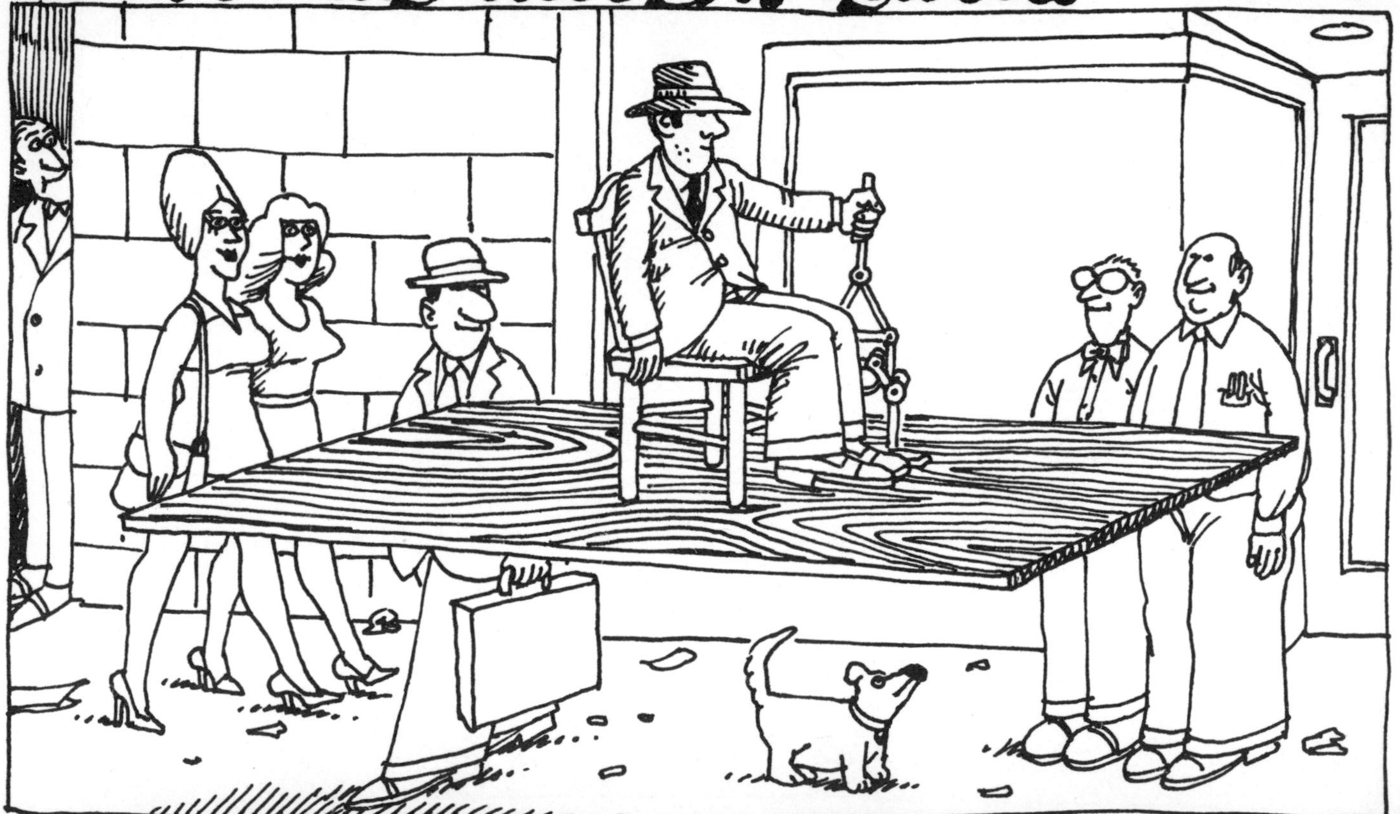

John the Baptist with a Side of Fries

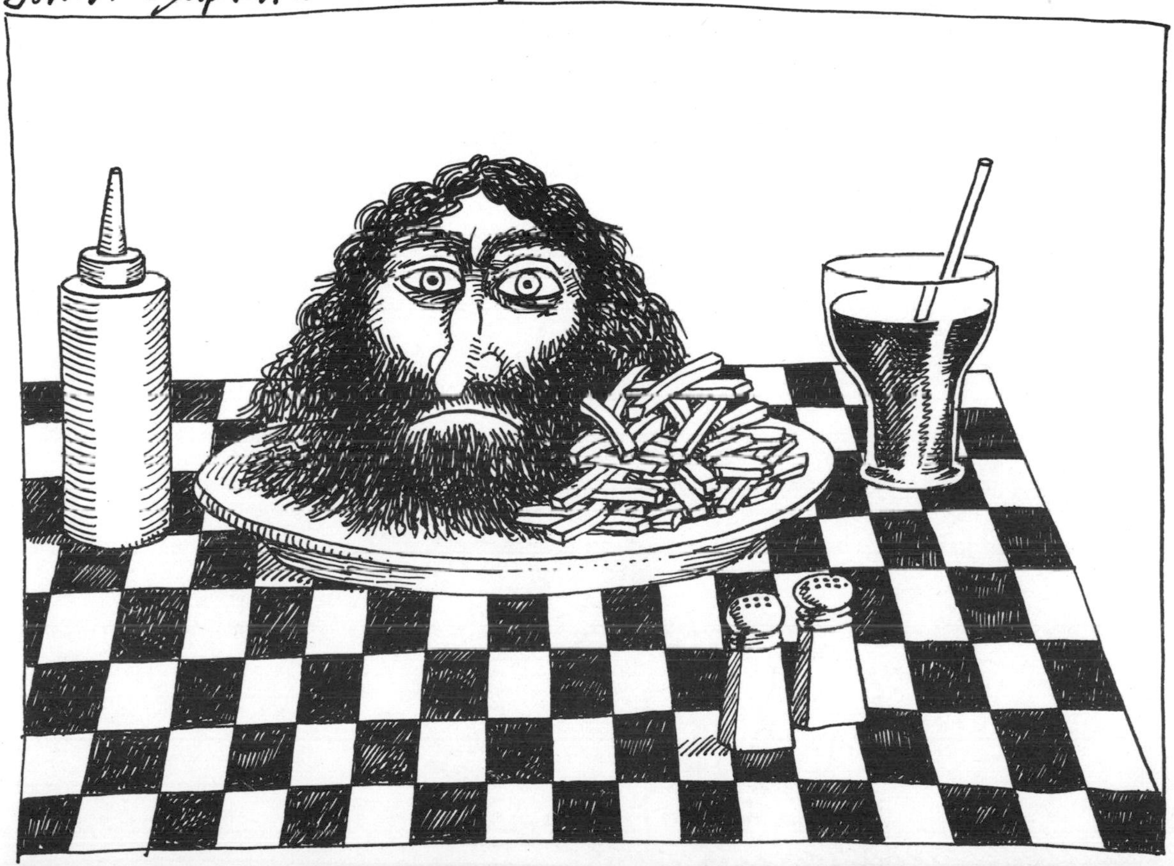

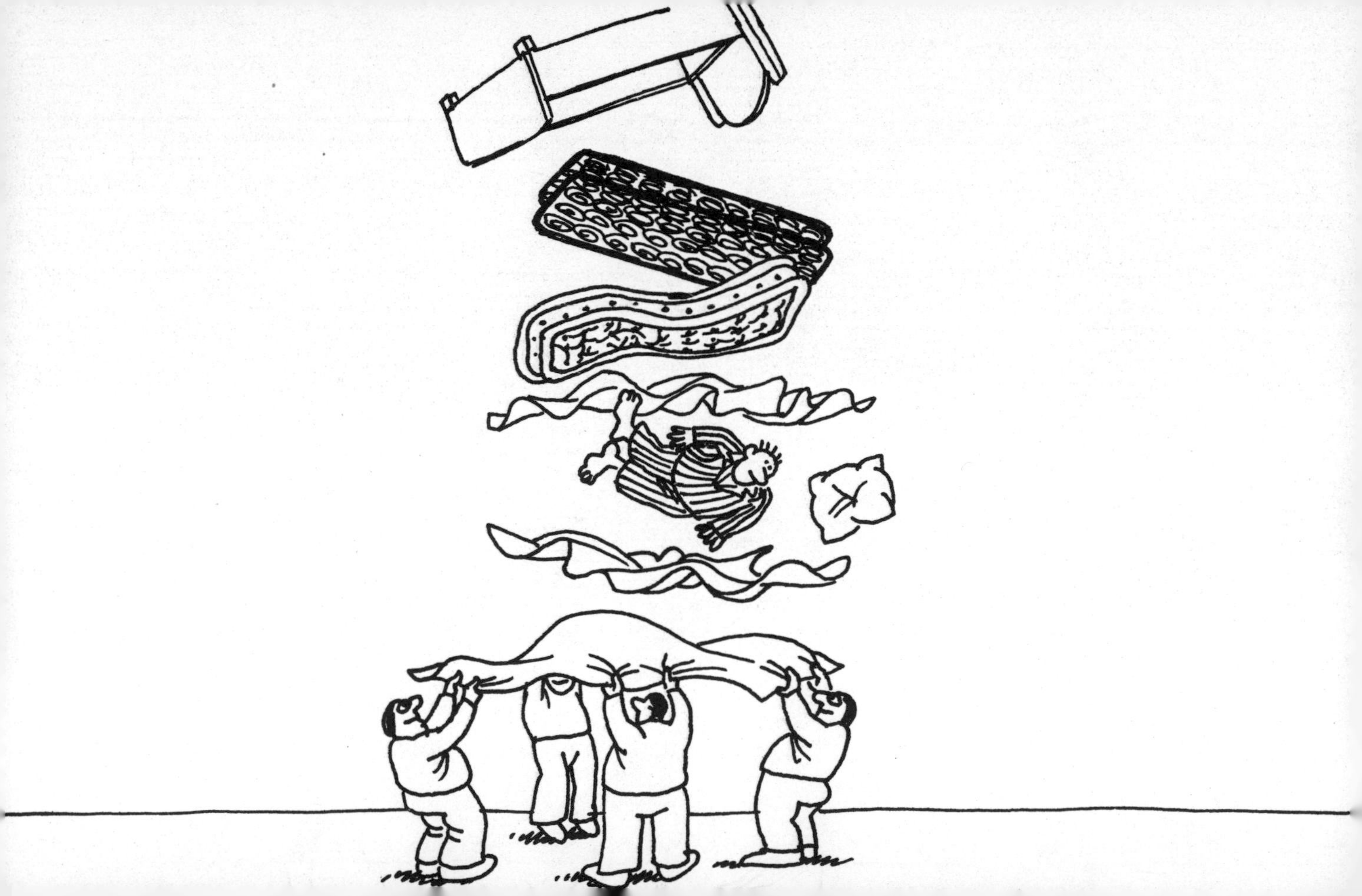

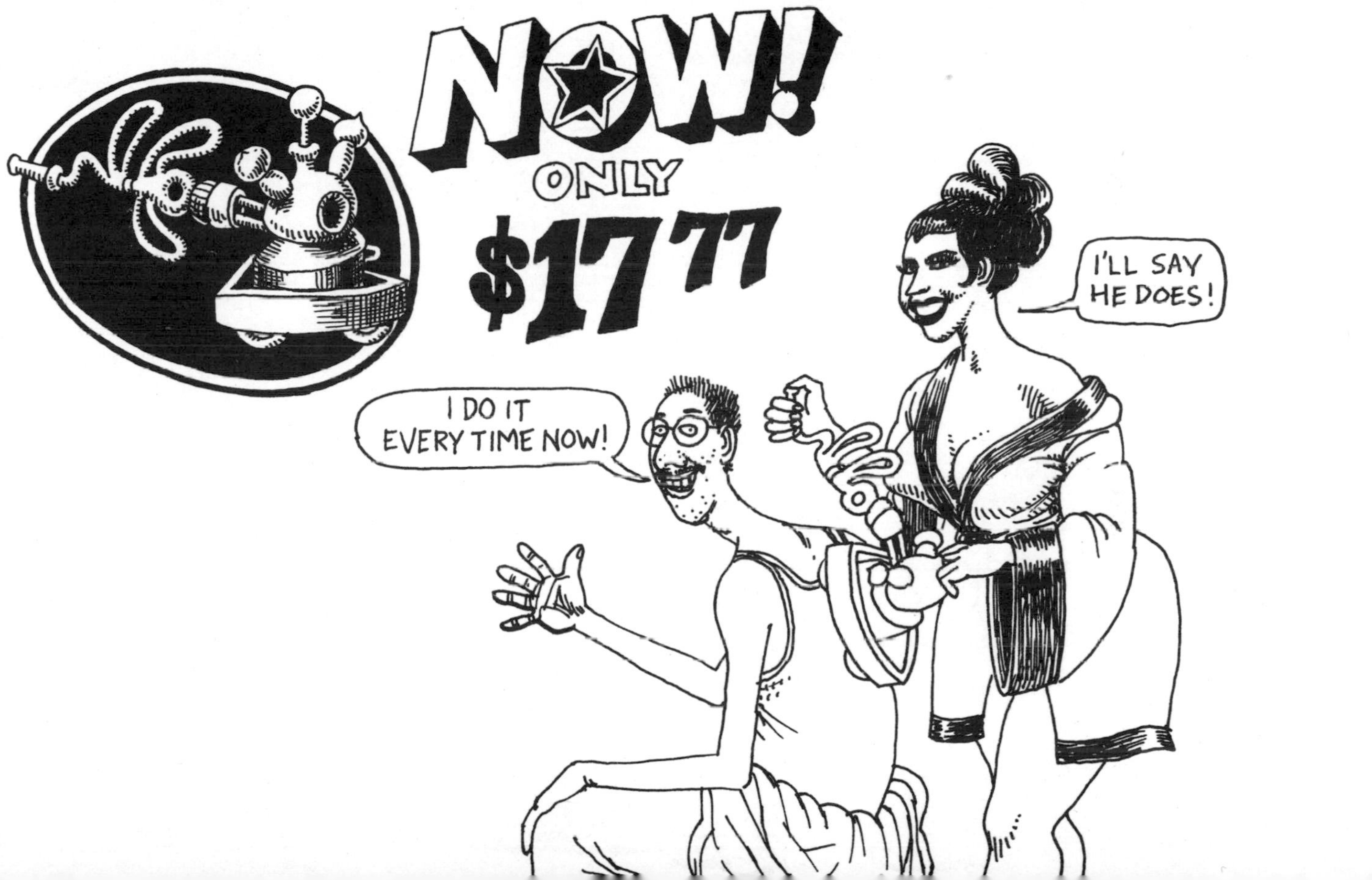
NOW!
ONLY
$17.77
I'LL SAY HE DOES!
I DO IT EVERY TIME NOW!

# Cornish Game Clams

A FALSE START IN SIX PARTS

I

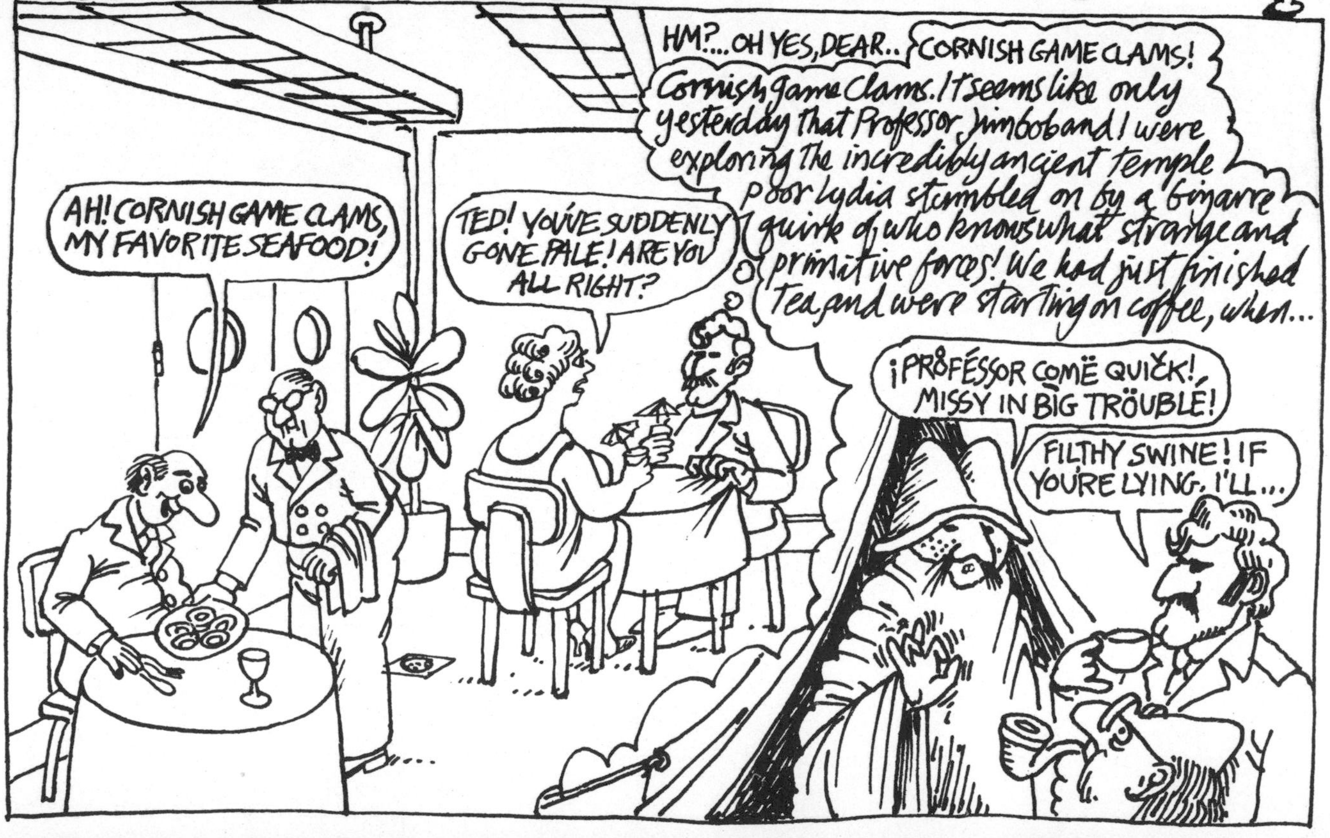

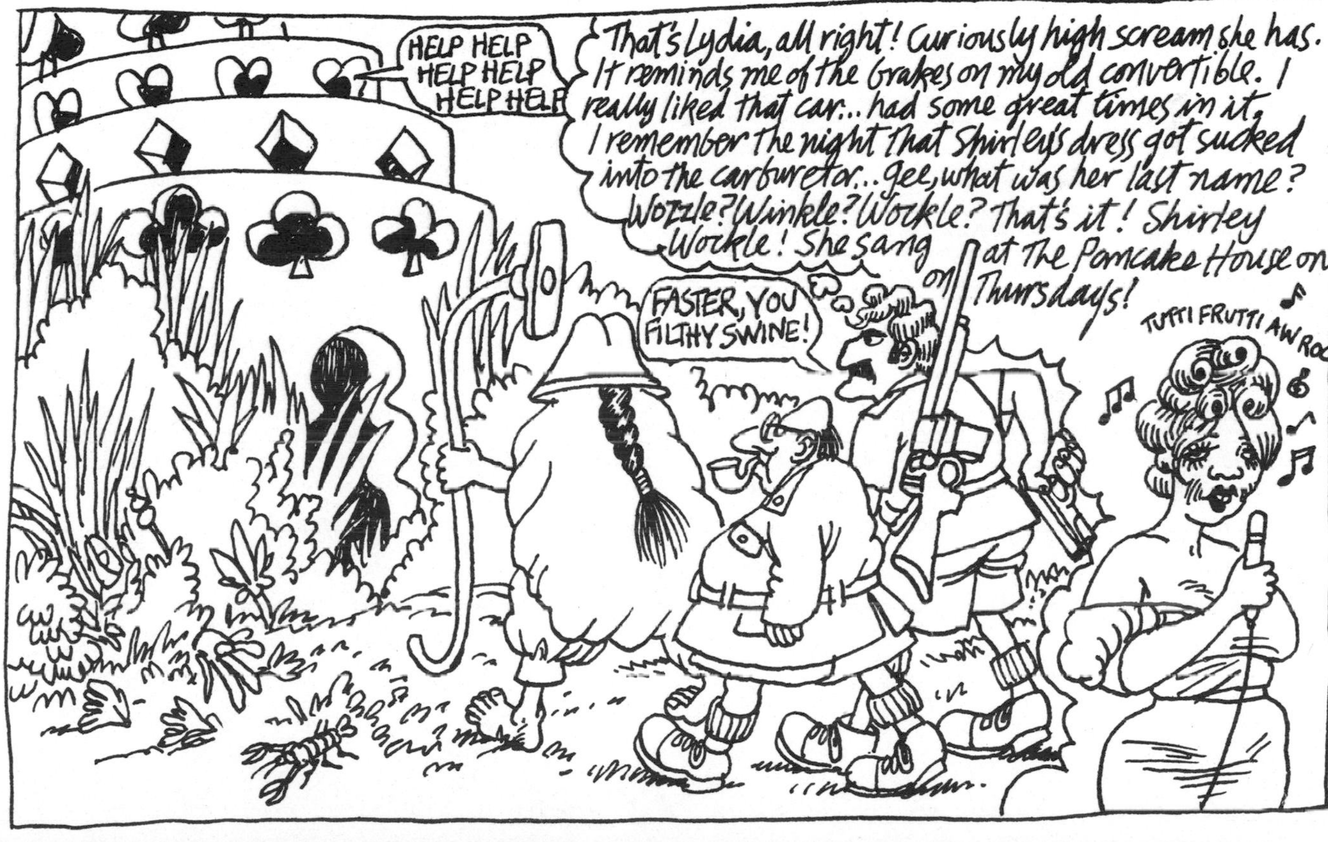
HELP HELP
HELP HELP
HELP HELP
That's Lydia, all right! Curiously high scream she has. It reminds me of the brakes on my old convertible. I really liked that car... had some great times in it. I remember the night that Shirley's dress got sucked into the carburetor... gee, what was her last name? Wozzle? Winkle? Wockle? That's it! Shirley Wockle! She sang on at The Pancake House on Thursdays!
FASTER, YOU FILTHY SWINE!
TUTTI FRUTTI AW ROO

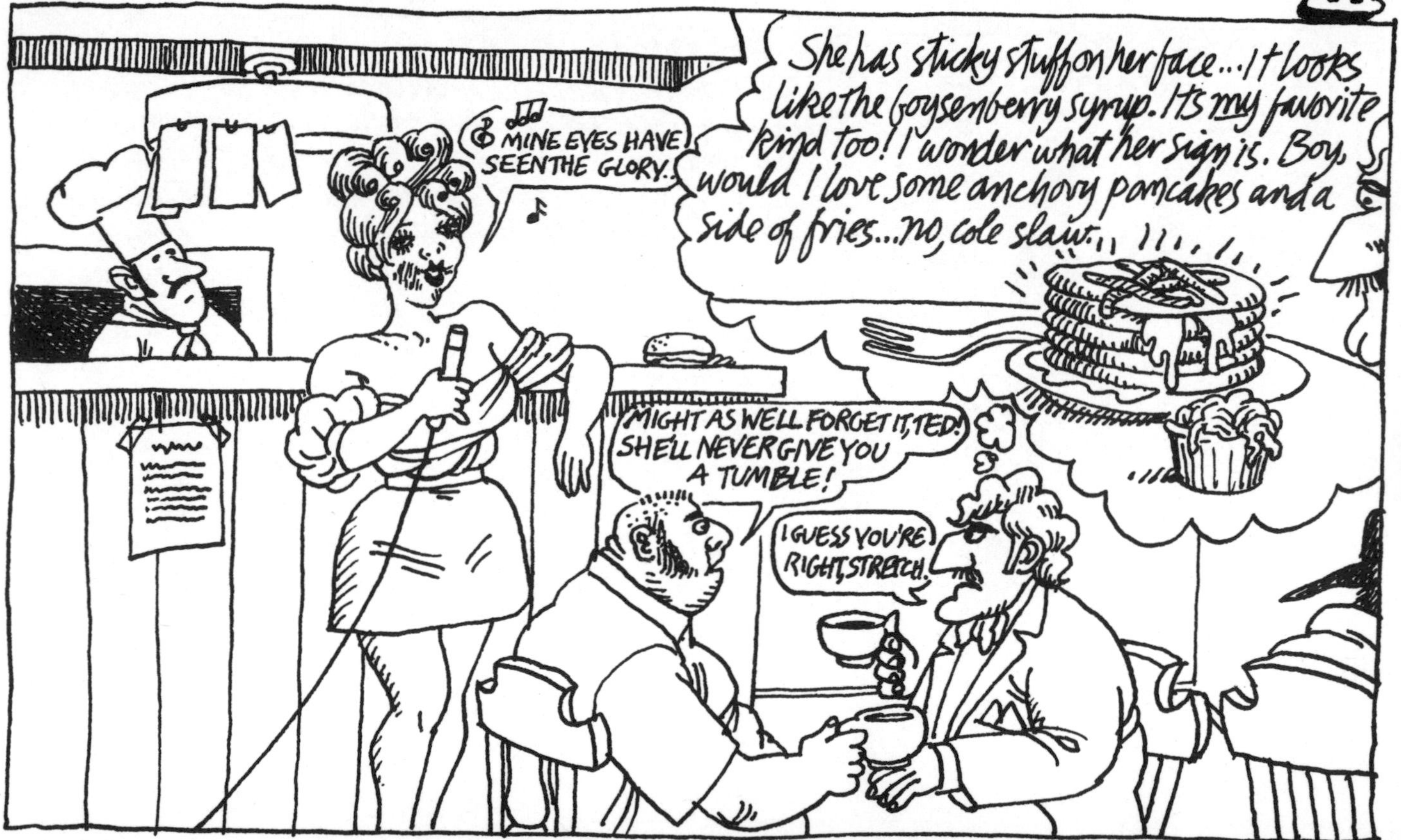
MINE EYES HAVE SEEN THE GLORY..
She has sticky stuff on her face... It looks like the boysenberry syrup. It's my favorite kind too! I wonder what her sign is. Boy, would I love some anchovy pancakes and a side of fries...no, cole slaw.
MIGHT AS WELL FORGET IT, TED! SHE'LL NEVER GIVE YOU A TUMBLE!
I GUESS YOU'RE RIGHT, STRETCH.

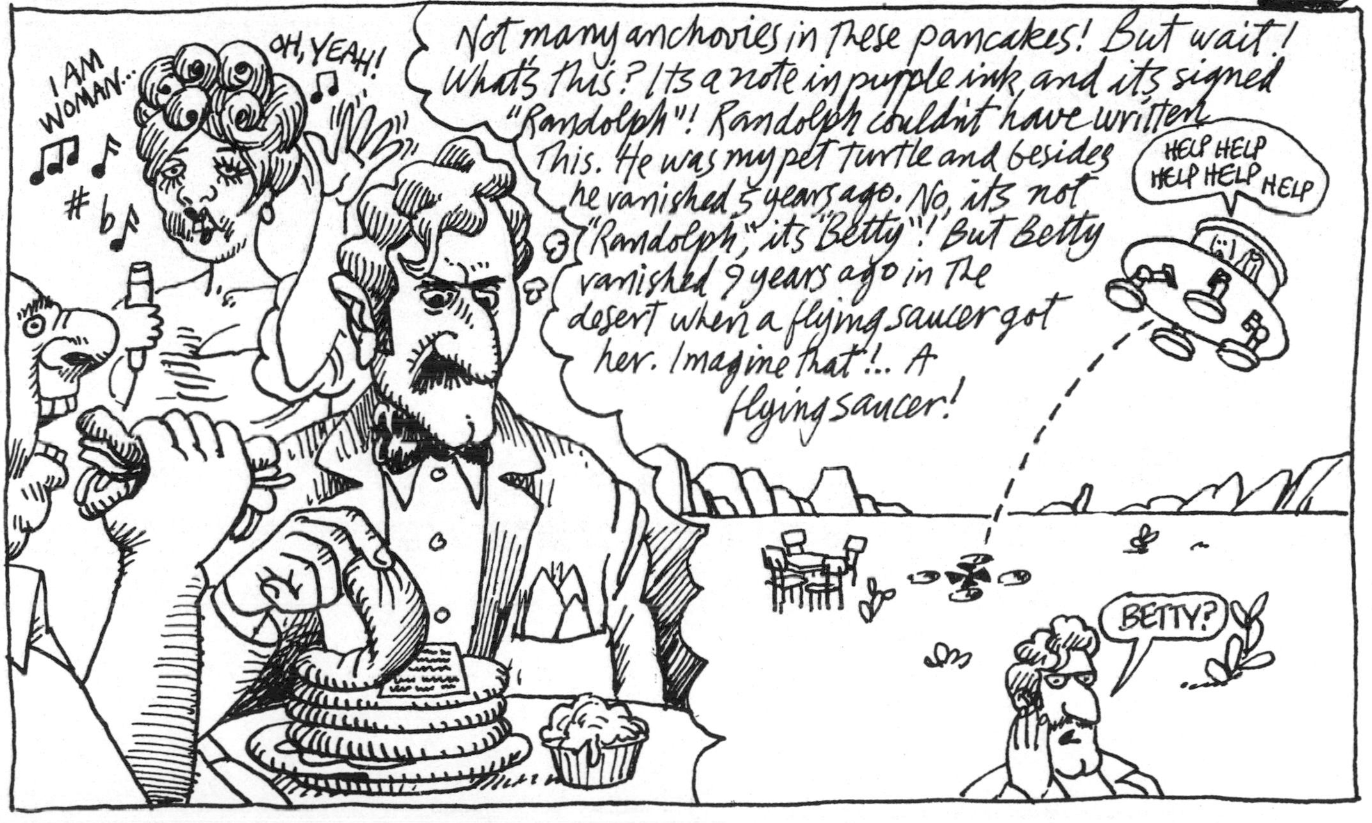

I AM WOMAN...
OH, YEAH!
Not many anchovies in these pancakes! But wait! What's this? It's a note in purple ink, and it's signed "Randolph"! Randolph couldn't have written this. He was my pet turtle and besides he vanished 5 years ago. No, it's not "Randolph," it's "Betty"! But Betty vanished 9 years ago in the desert when a flying saucer got her. Imagine that!.. A flying saucer!
HELP HELP HELP HELP HELP
BETTY?

V

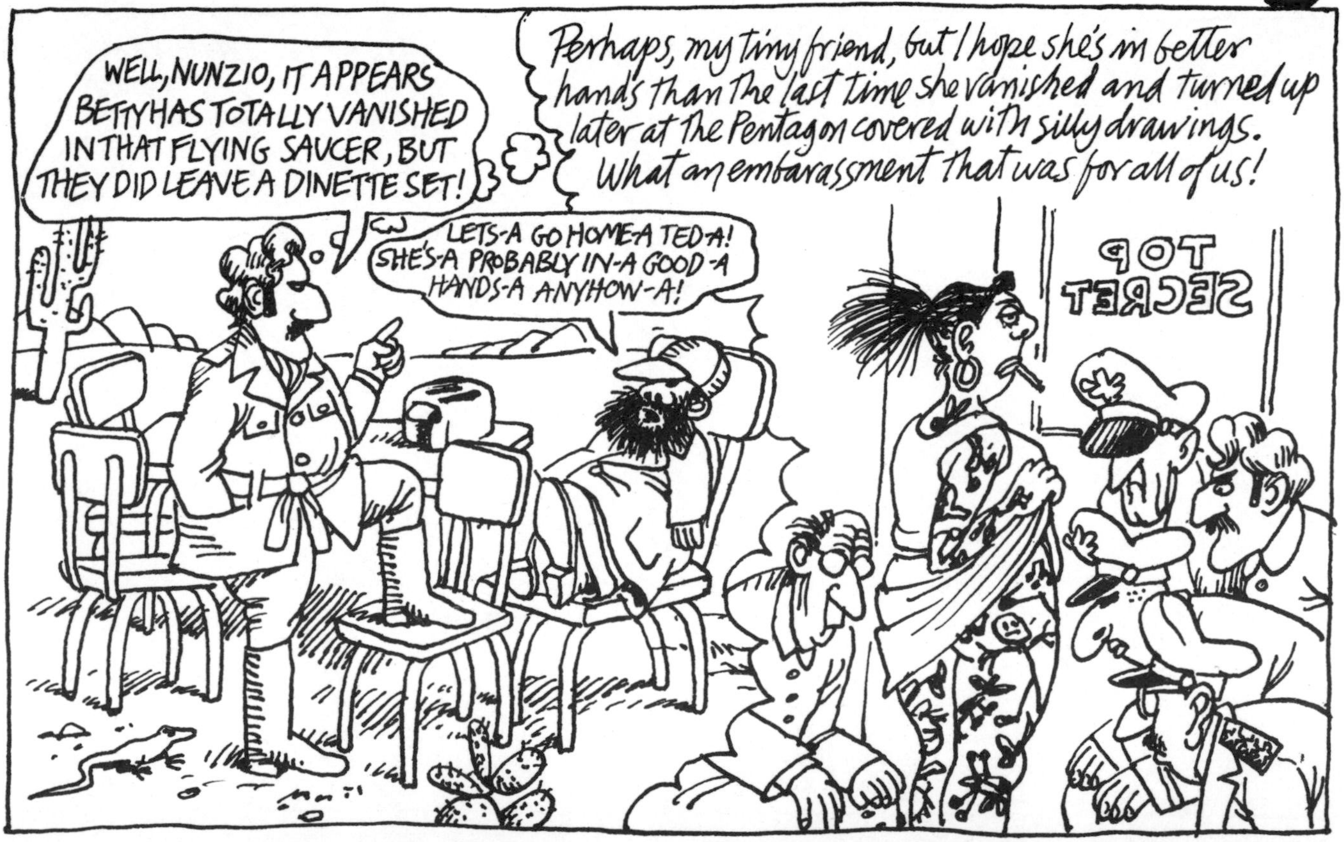
WELL, NUNZIO, IT APPEARS BETTY HAS TOTALLY VANISHED IN THAT FLYING SAUCER, BUT THEY DID LEAVE A DINETTE SET!
LETS-A GO HOME-A TED-A! SHE'S-A PROBABLY IN-A GOOD-A HANDS-A ANYHOW-A!
Perhaps, my tiny friend, but I hope she's in better hands than the last time she vanished and turned up later at the Pentagon covered with silly drawings. What an embarassment that was for all of us!
TOP SECRET

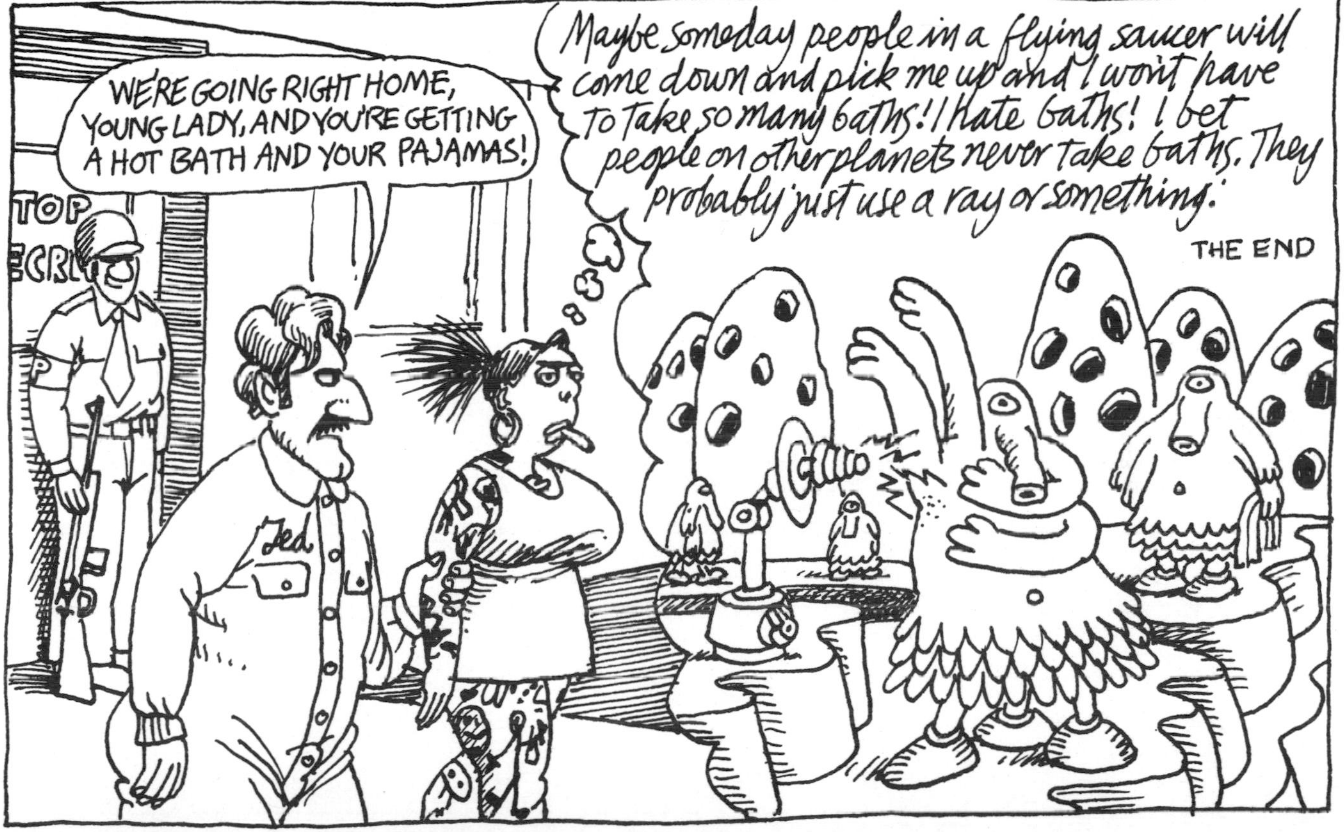
WE'RE GOING RIGHT HOME, YOUNG LADY, AND YOU'RE GETTING A HOT BATH AND YOUR PAJAMAS!
Maybe someday people in a flying saucer will come down and pick me up and I won't have to take so many baths! I hate baths! I bet people on other planets never take baths. They probably just use a ray or something.
THE END
TOP SECRET
Ted

# Inside a Modern Balloon

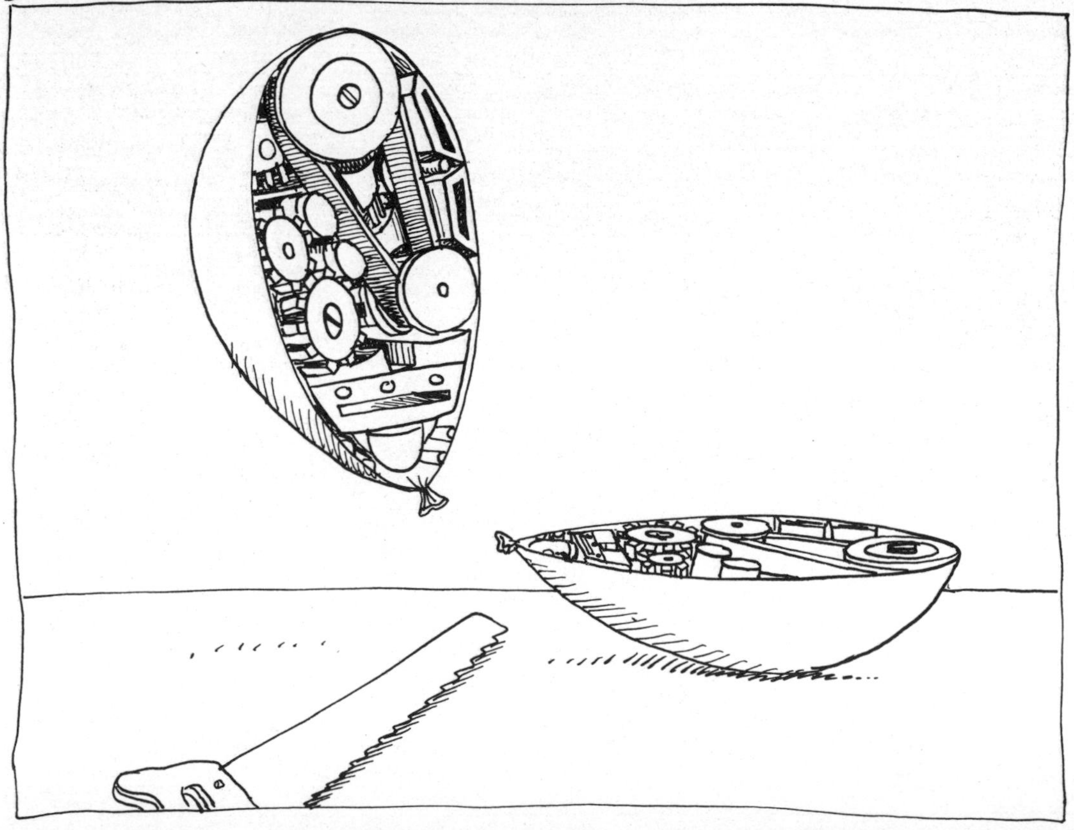

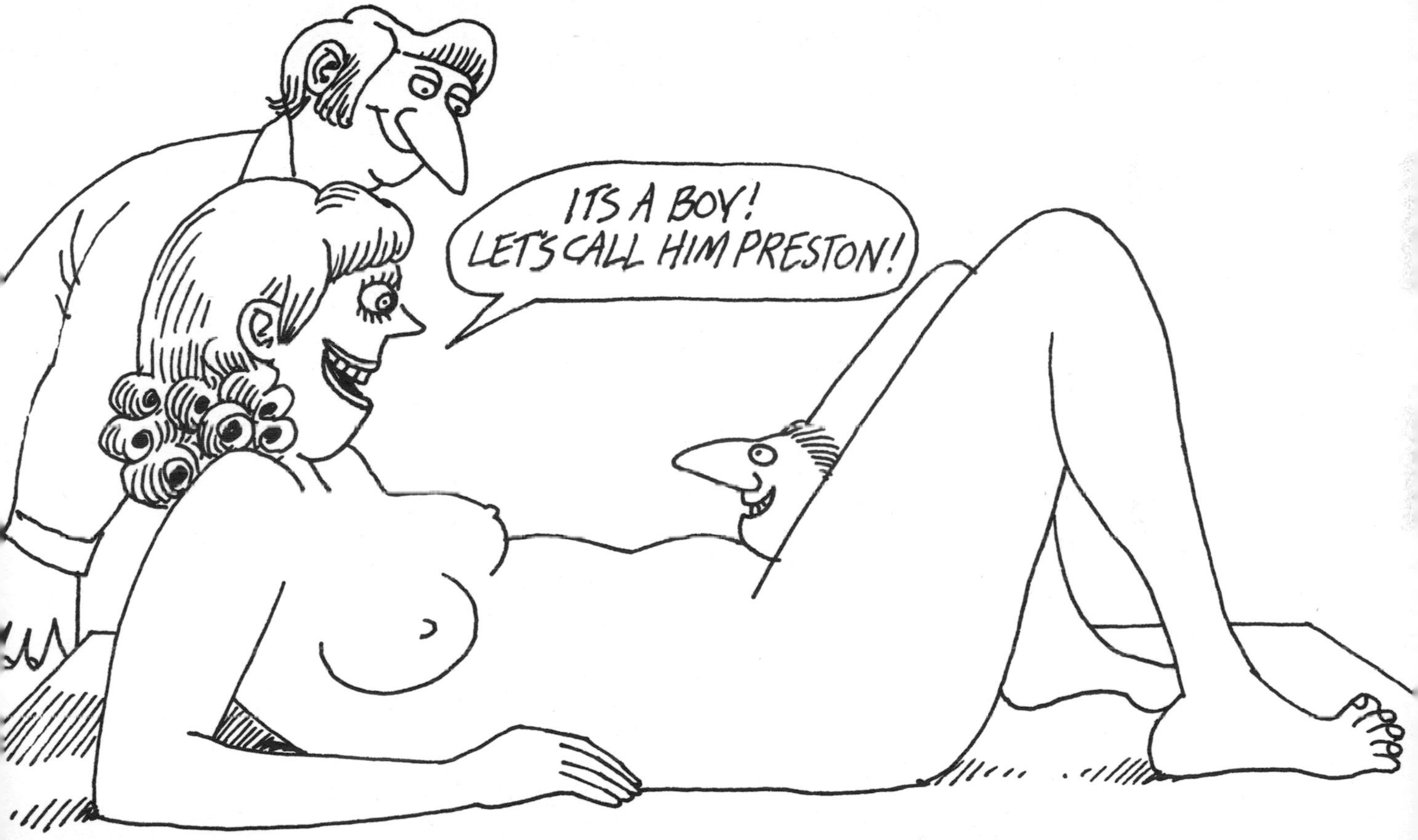
ITS A BOY!
LET'S CALL HIM PRESTON!

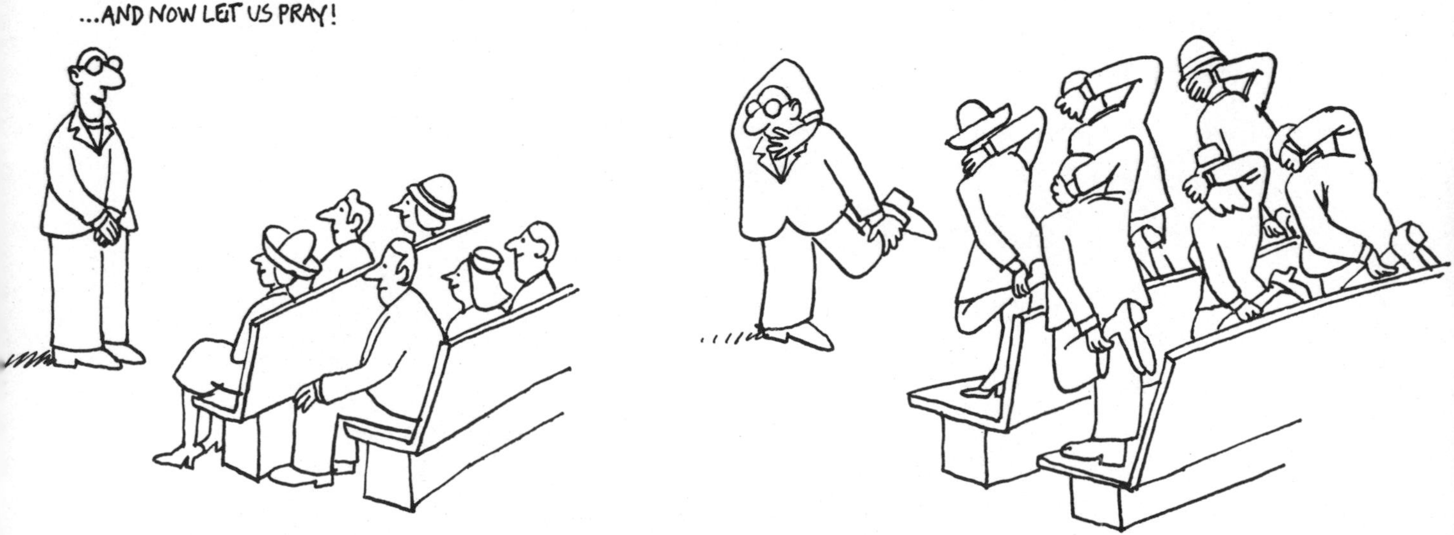
...AND NOW LET US PRAY!

Fucked Again

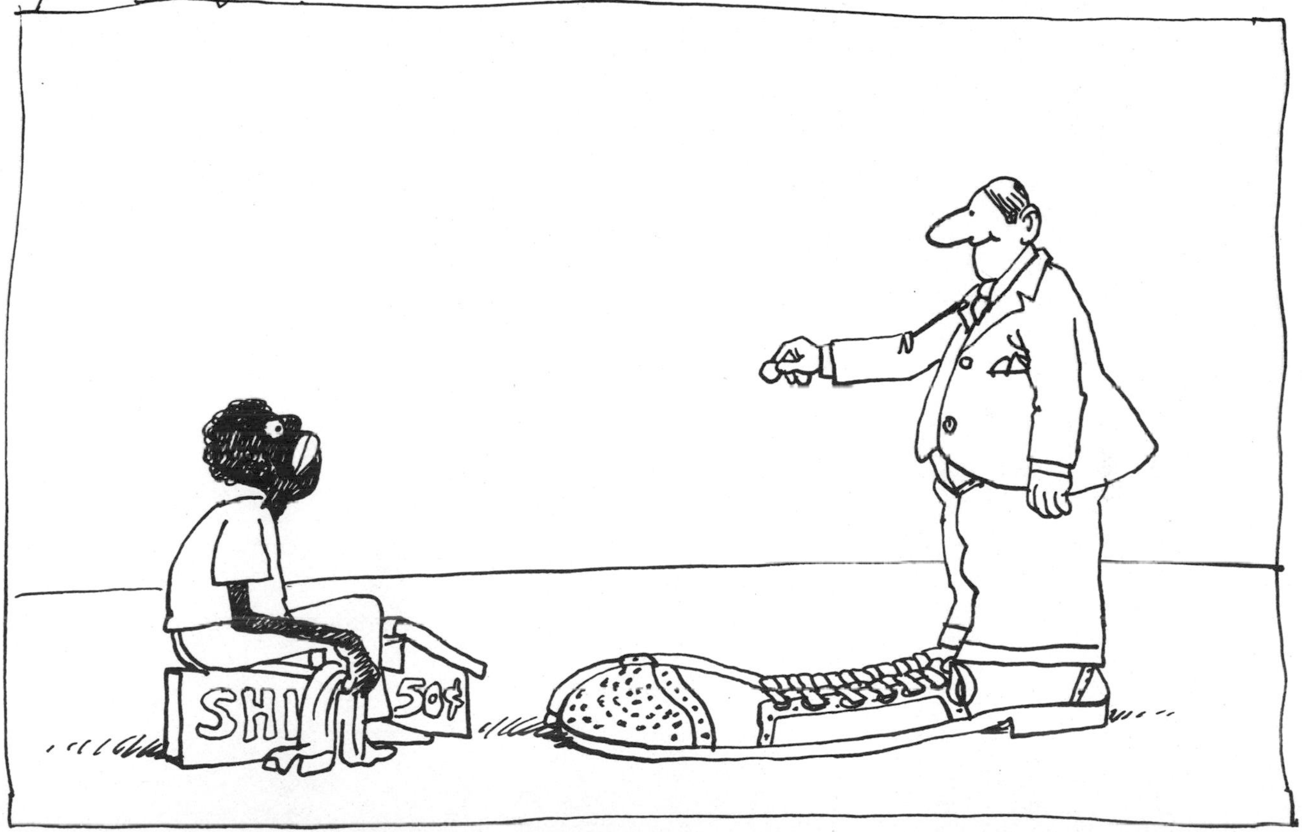
SHI
50¢

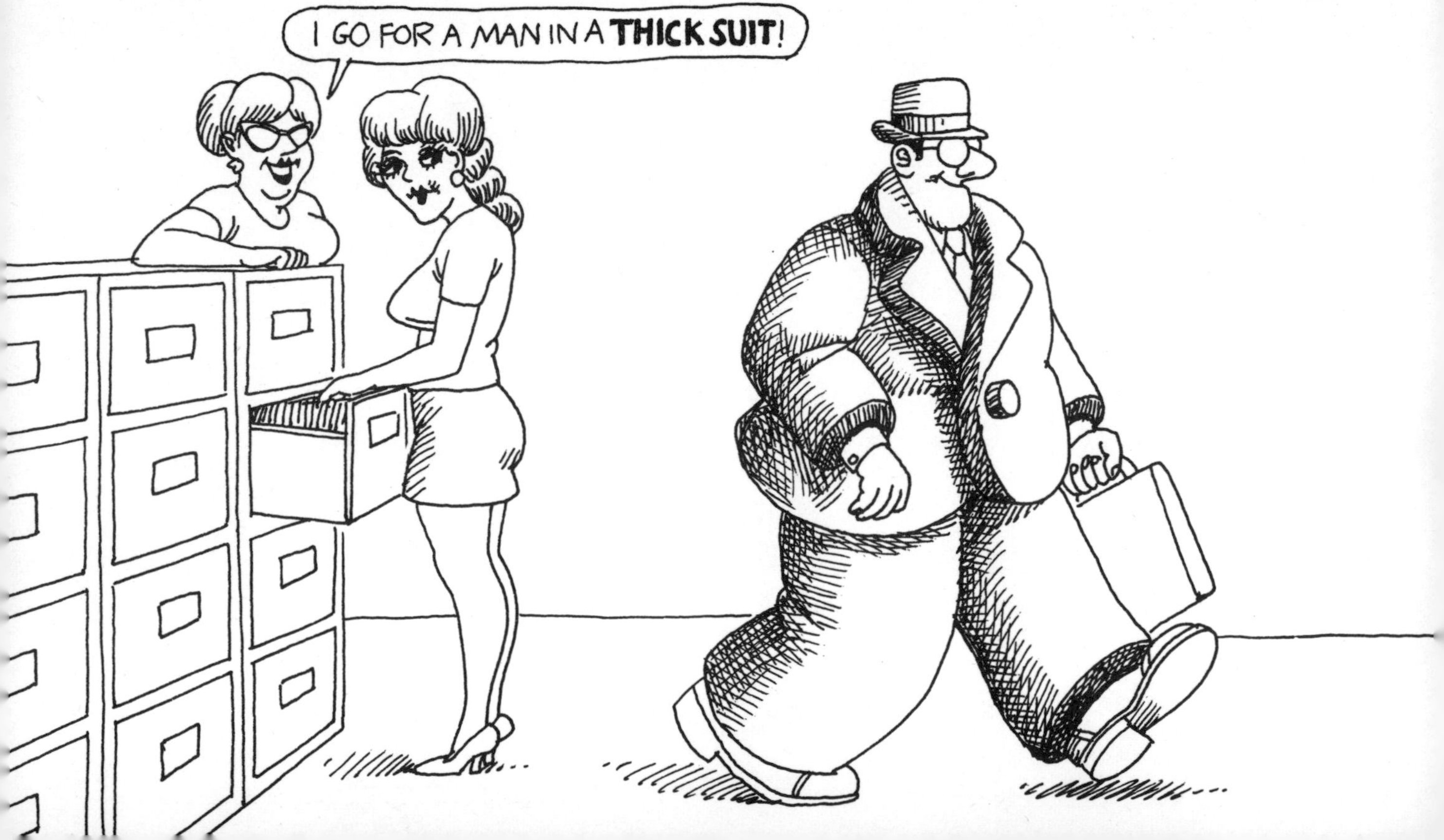
I GO FOR A MAN IN A **THICK SUIT**!

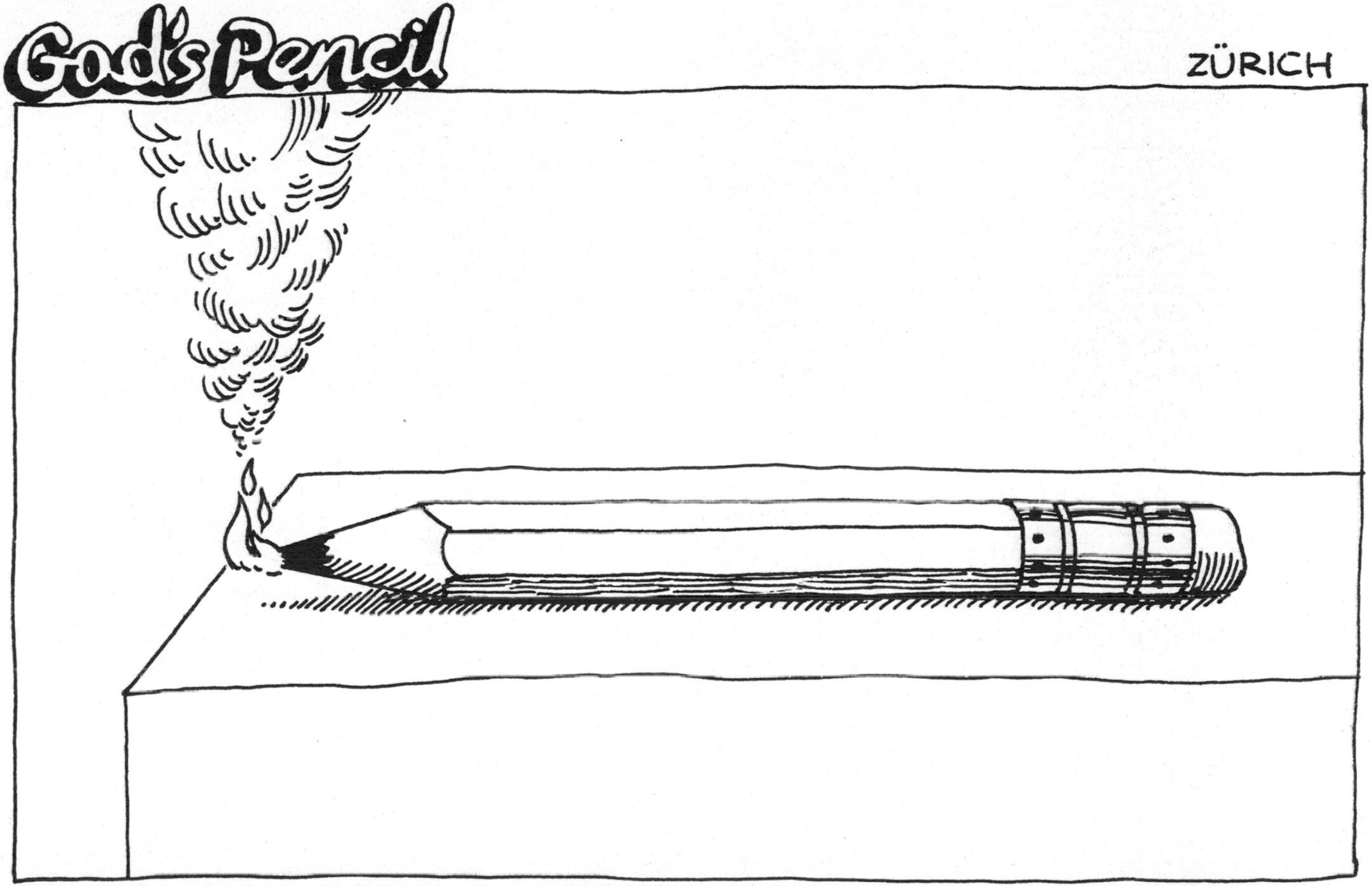
God's Pencil
ZÜRICH

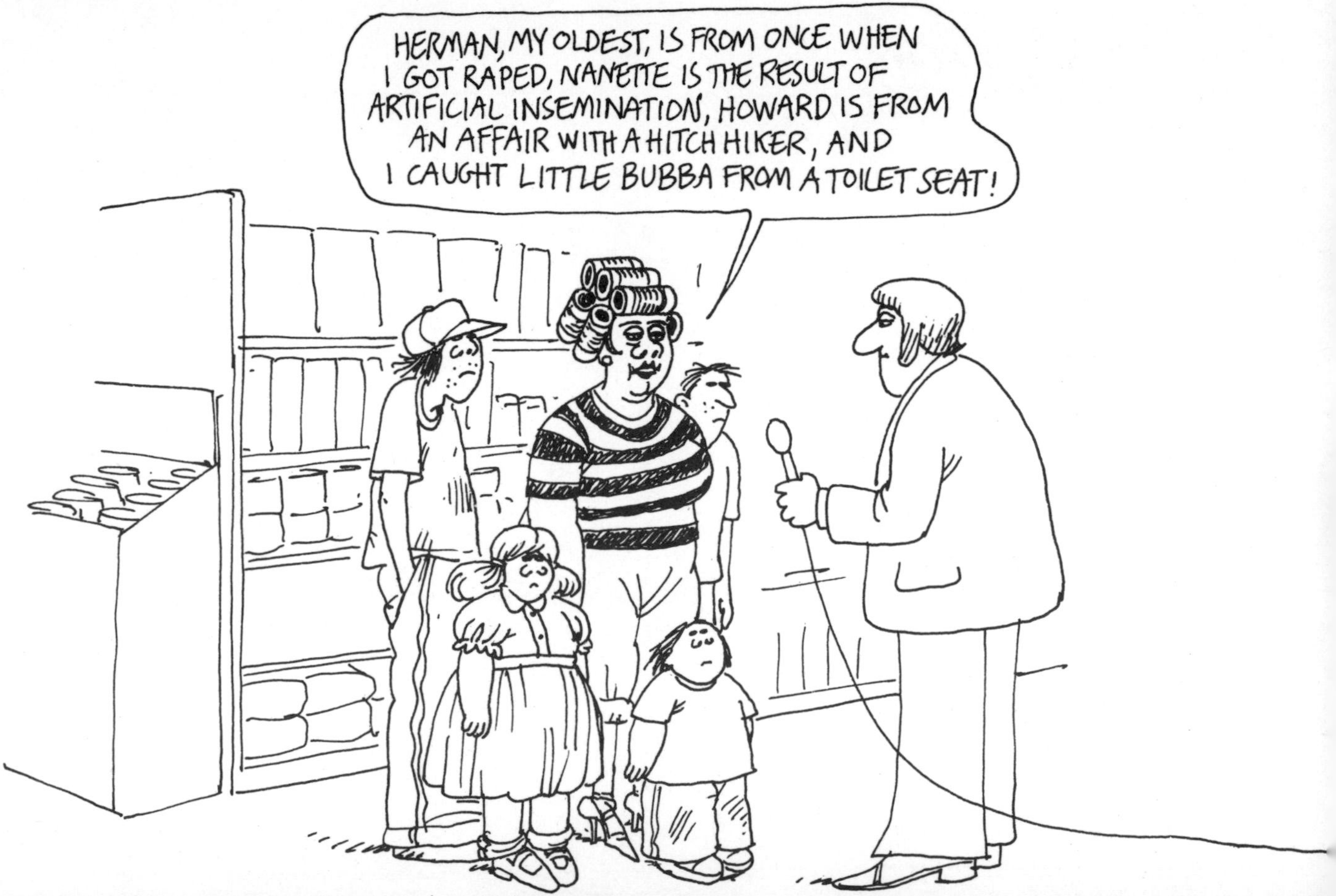
HERMAN, MY OLDEST, IS FROM ONCE WHEN I GOT RAPED, NANETTE IS THE RESULT OF ARTIFICIAL INSEMINATION, HOWARD IS FROM AN AFFAIR WITH A HITCH HIKER, AND I CAUGHT LITTLE BUBBA FROM A TOILET SEAT!

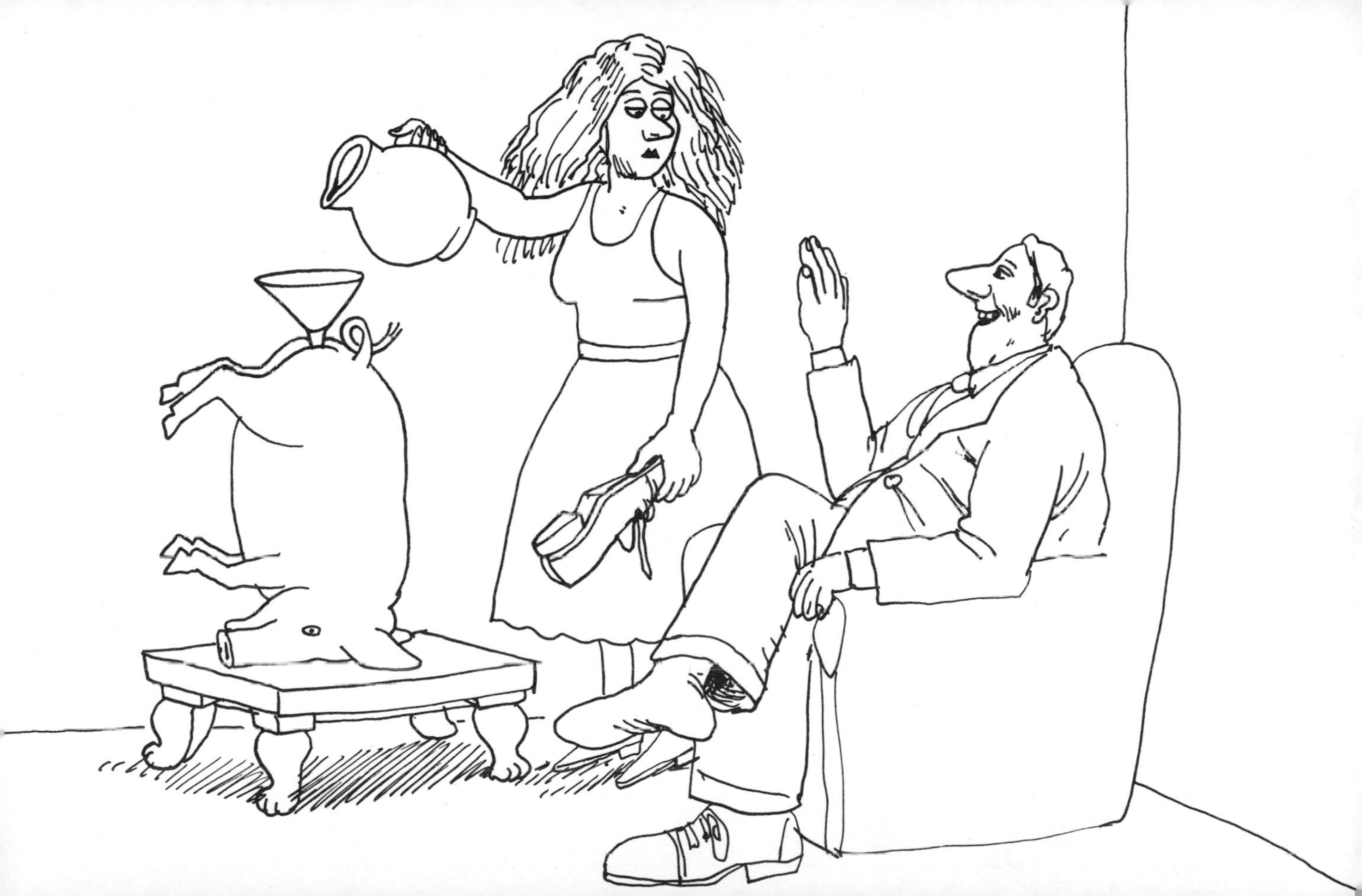

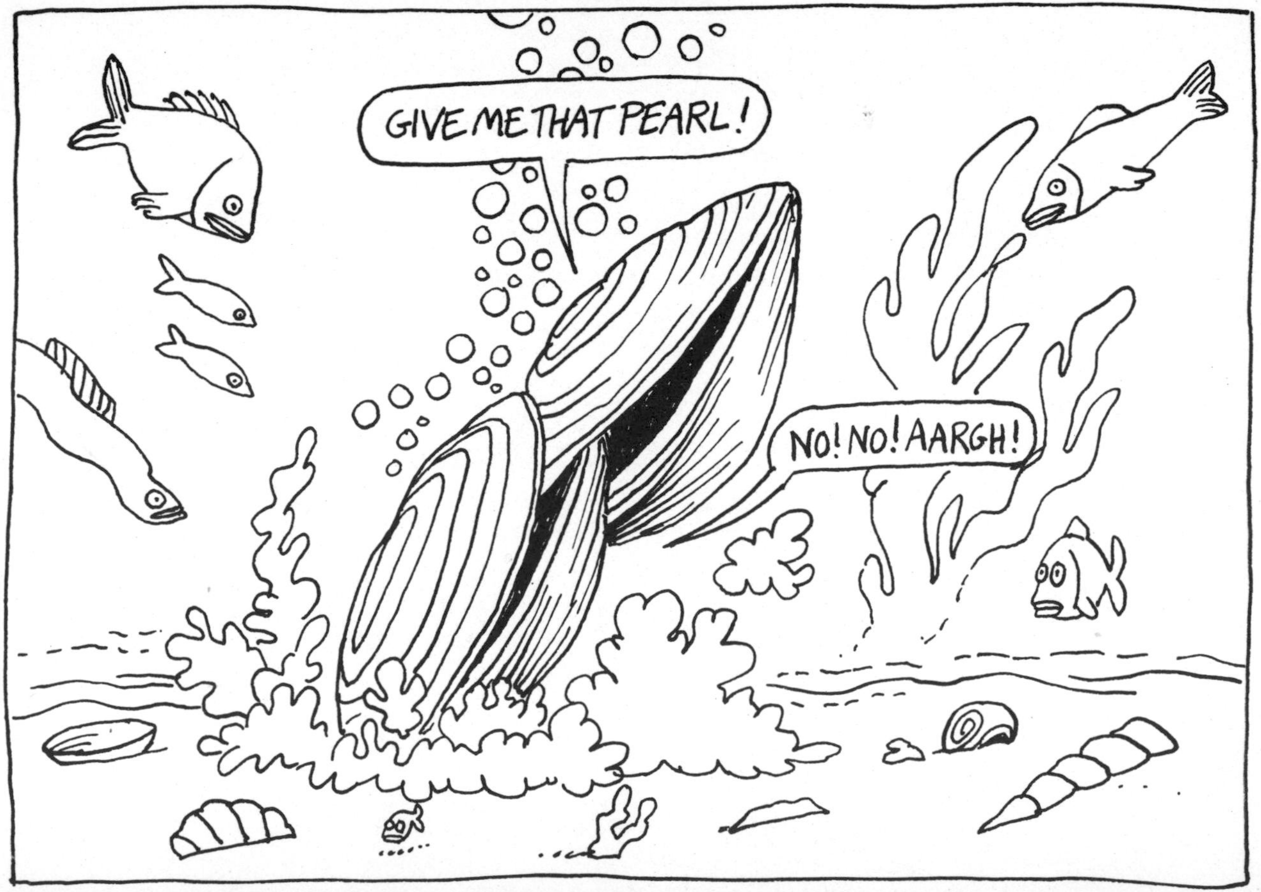
GIVE ME THAT PEARL!
NO! NO! AARGH!

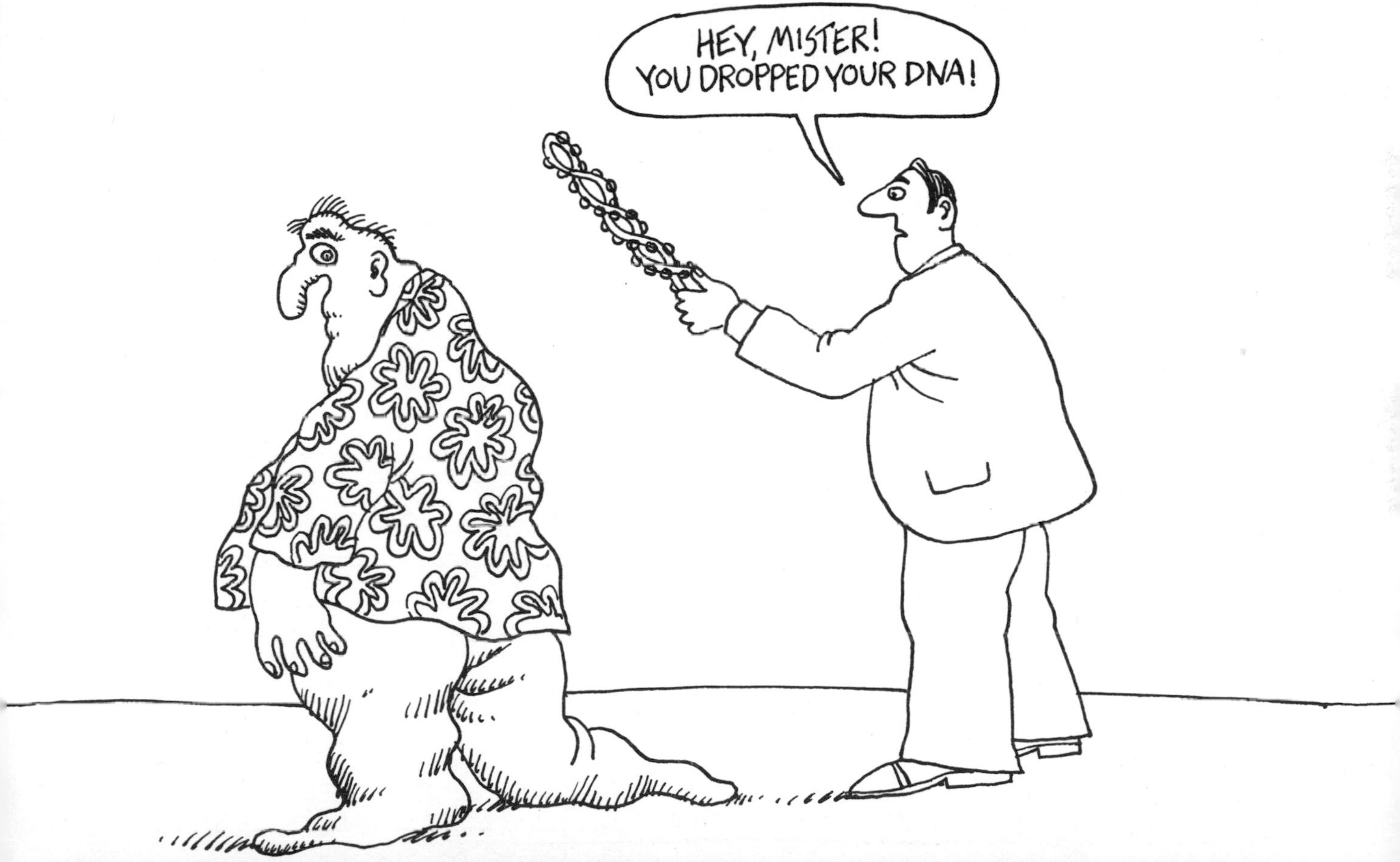
HEY, MISTER!
YOU DROPPED YOUR DNA!

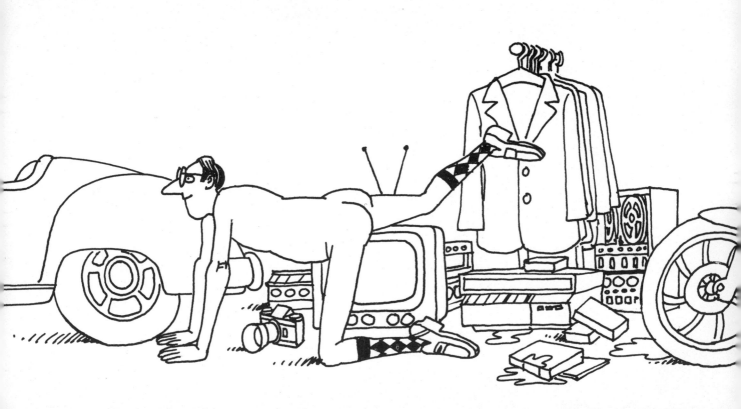

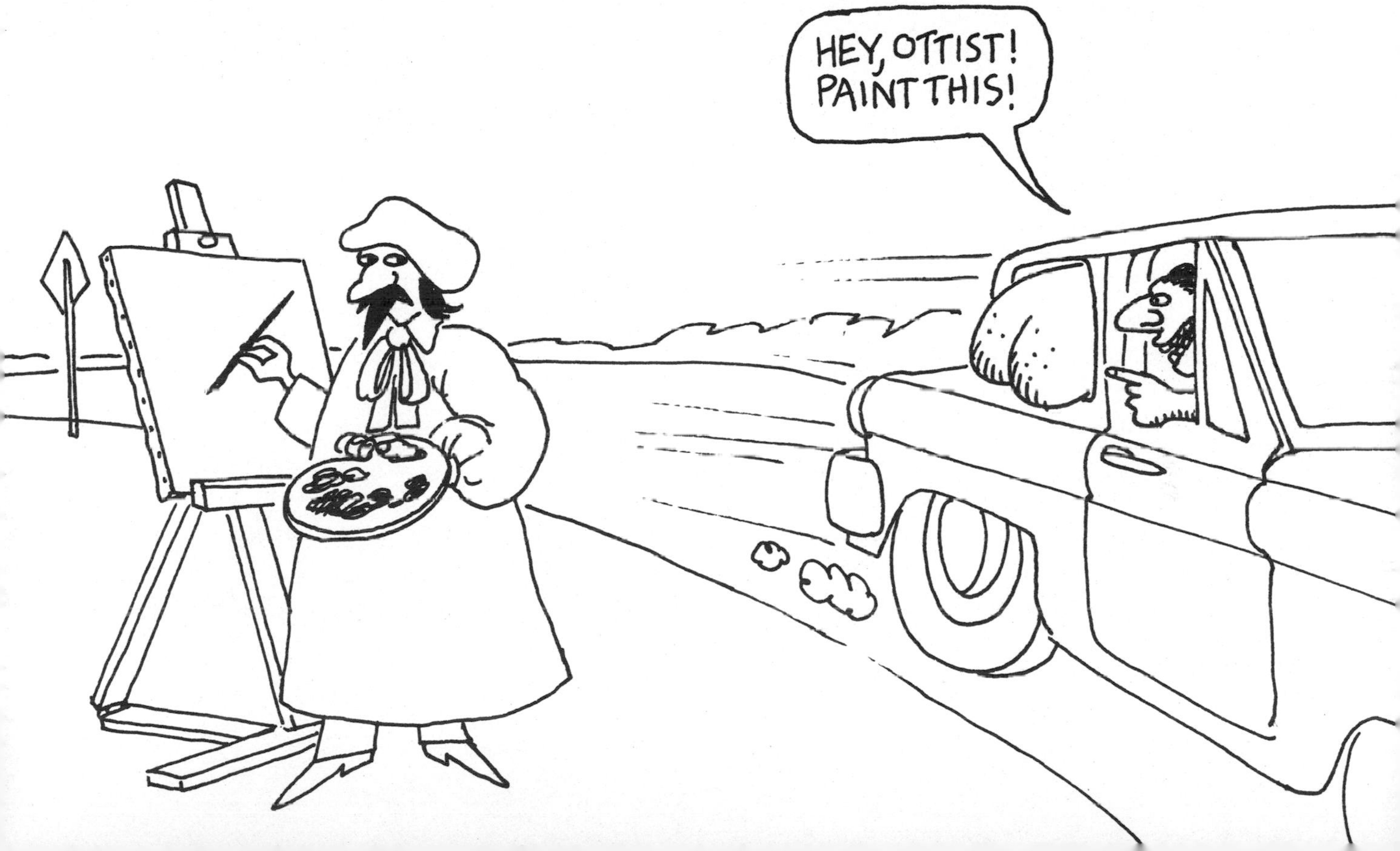
HEY, OTTIST! PAINT THIS!

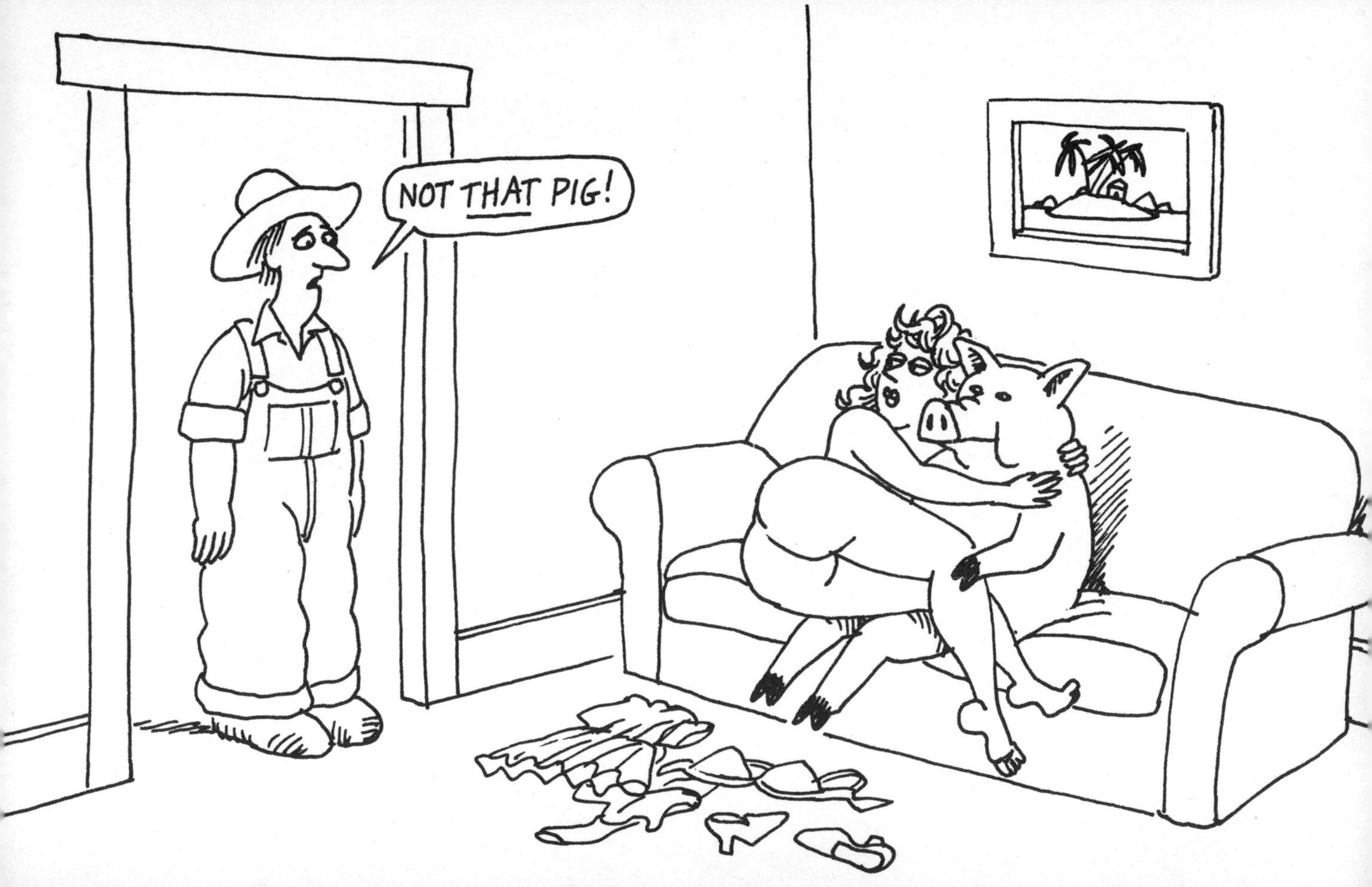
NOT THAT PIG!

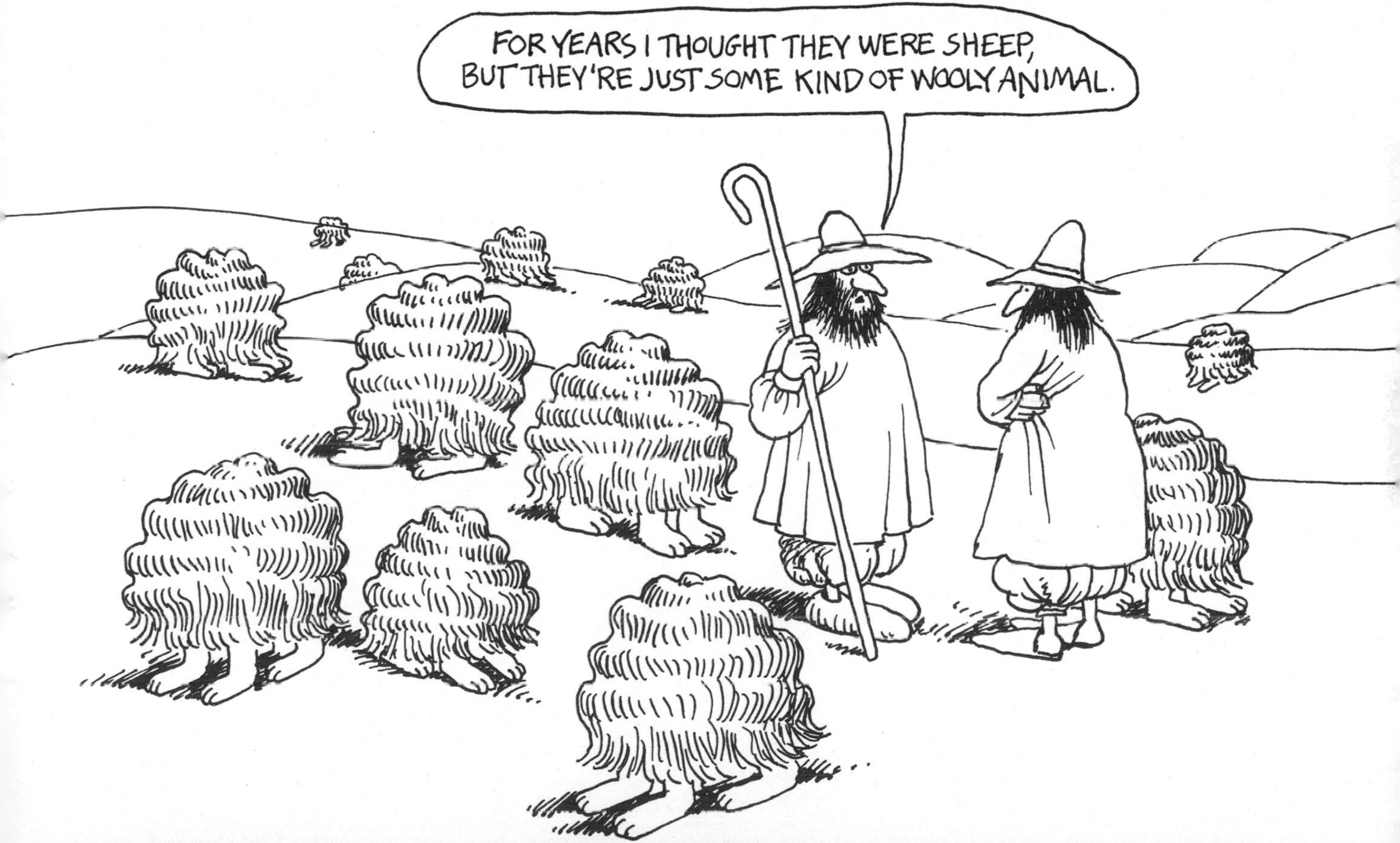
FOR YEARS I THOUGHT THEY WERE SHEEP, BUT THEY'RE JUST SOME KIND OF WOOLY ANIMAL.

Uncle Sid's Birthday Peek

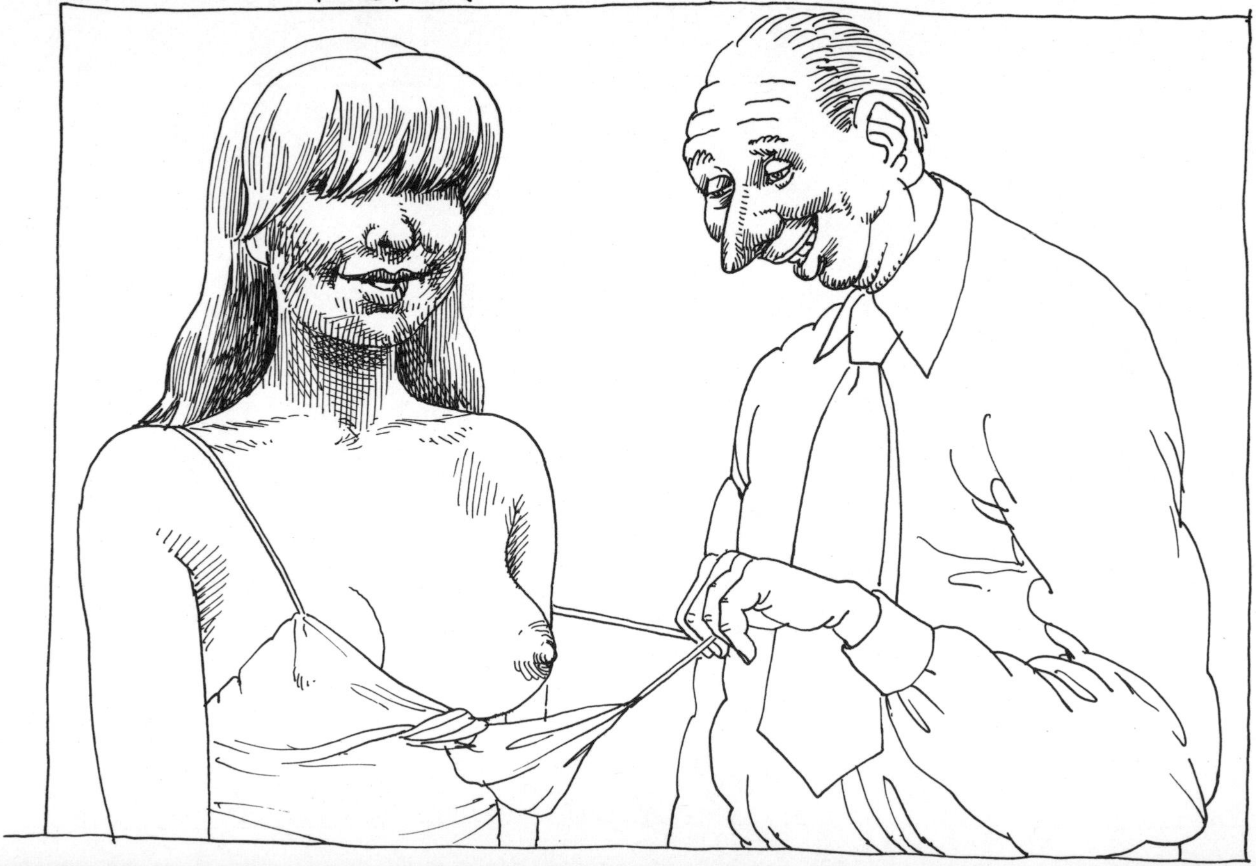

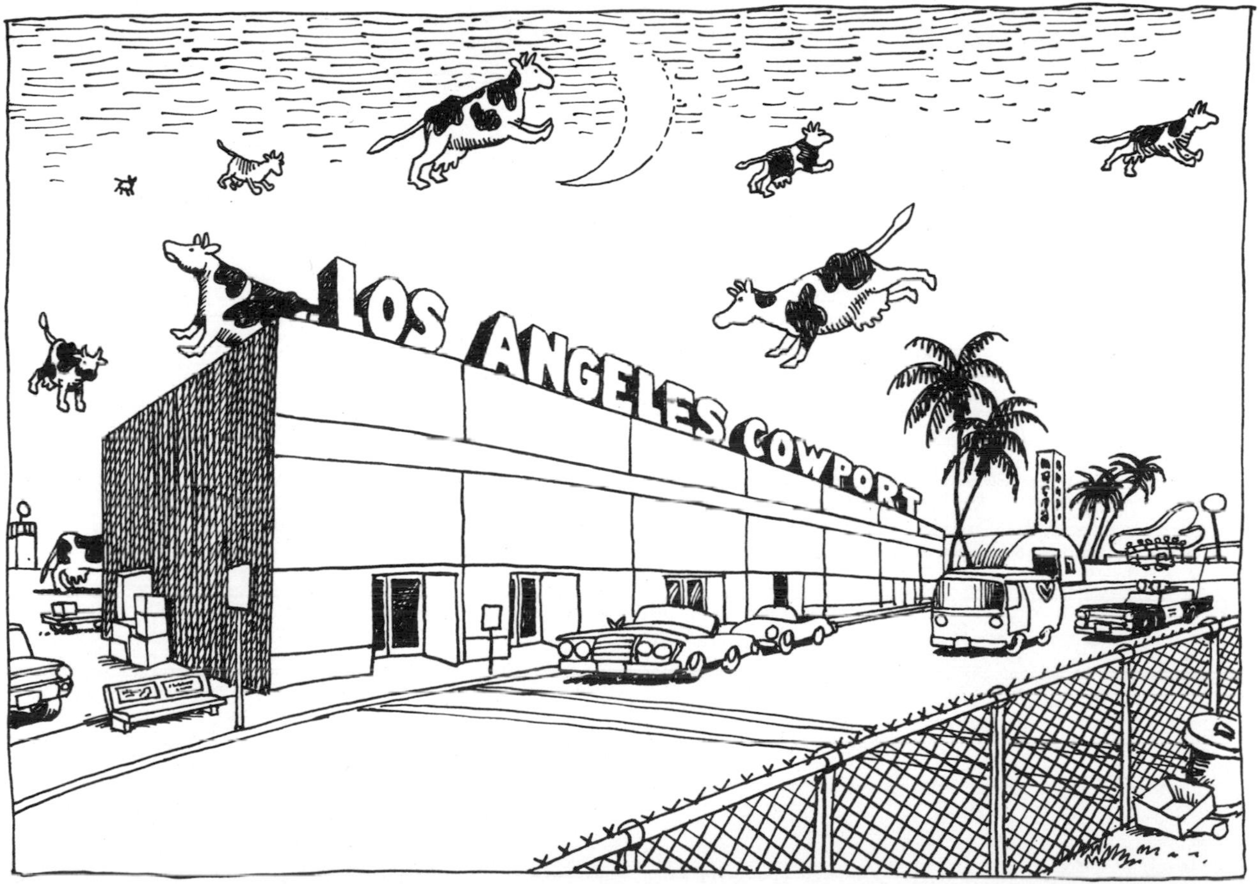
LOS ANGELES COWPORT

Tim and Sue see the All Meat Puppets

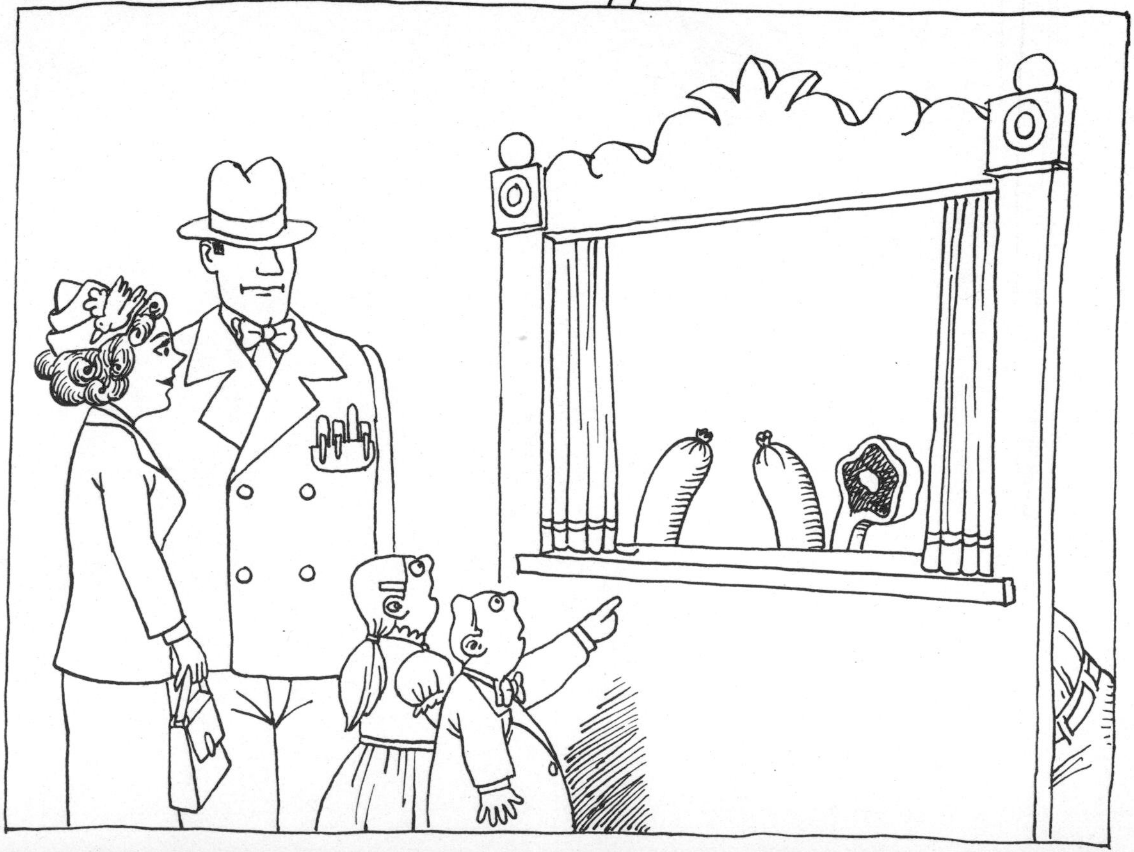

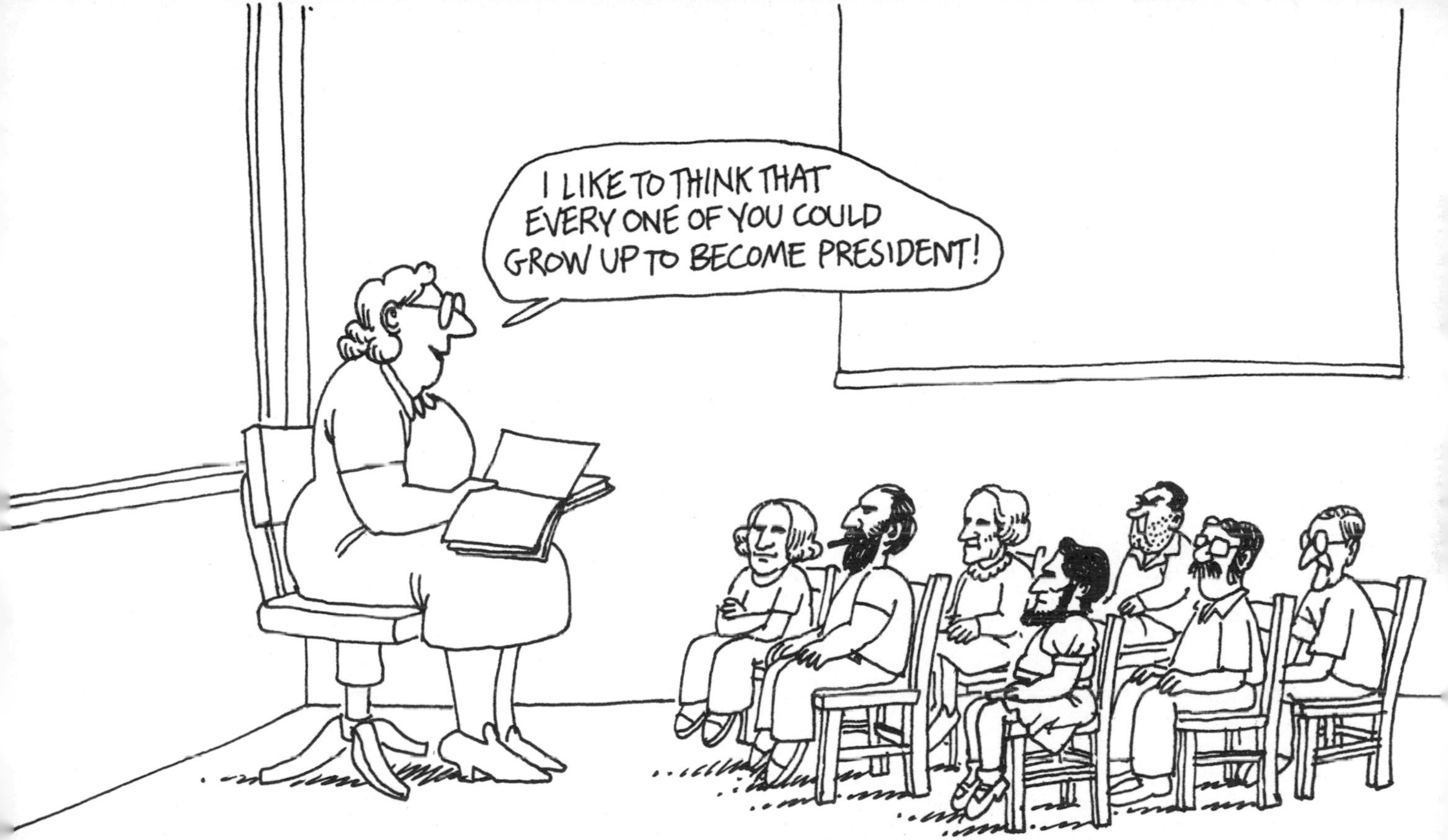
I LIKE TO THINK THAT EVERY ONE OF YOU COULD GROW UP TO BECOME PRESIDENT!

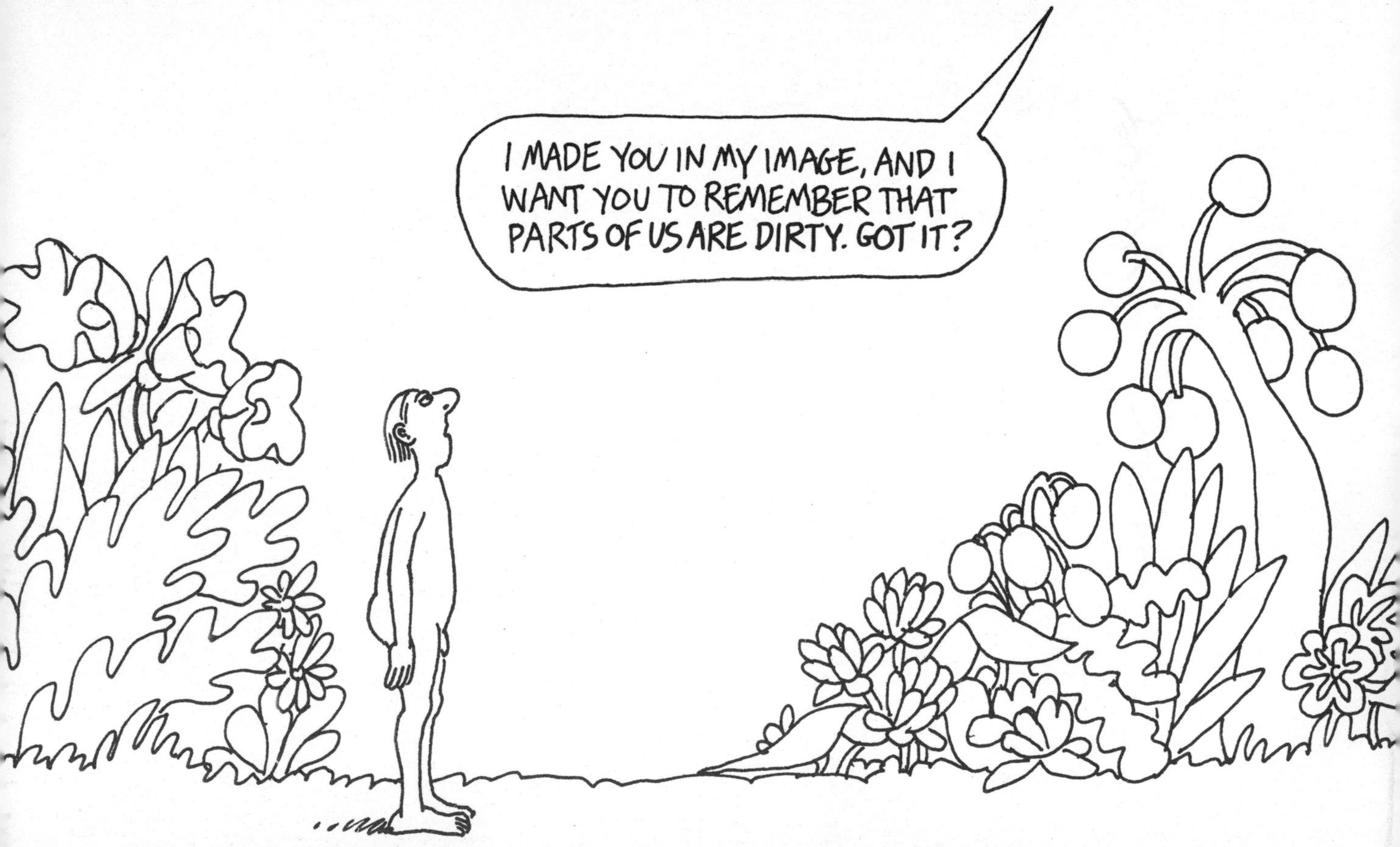
I MADE YOU IN MY IMAGE, AND I WANT YOU TO REMEMBER THAT PARTS OF US ARE DIRTY. GOT IT?

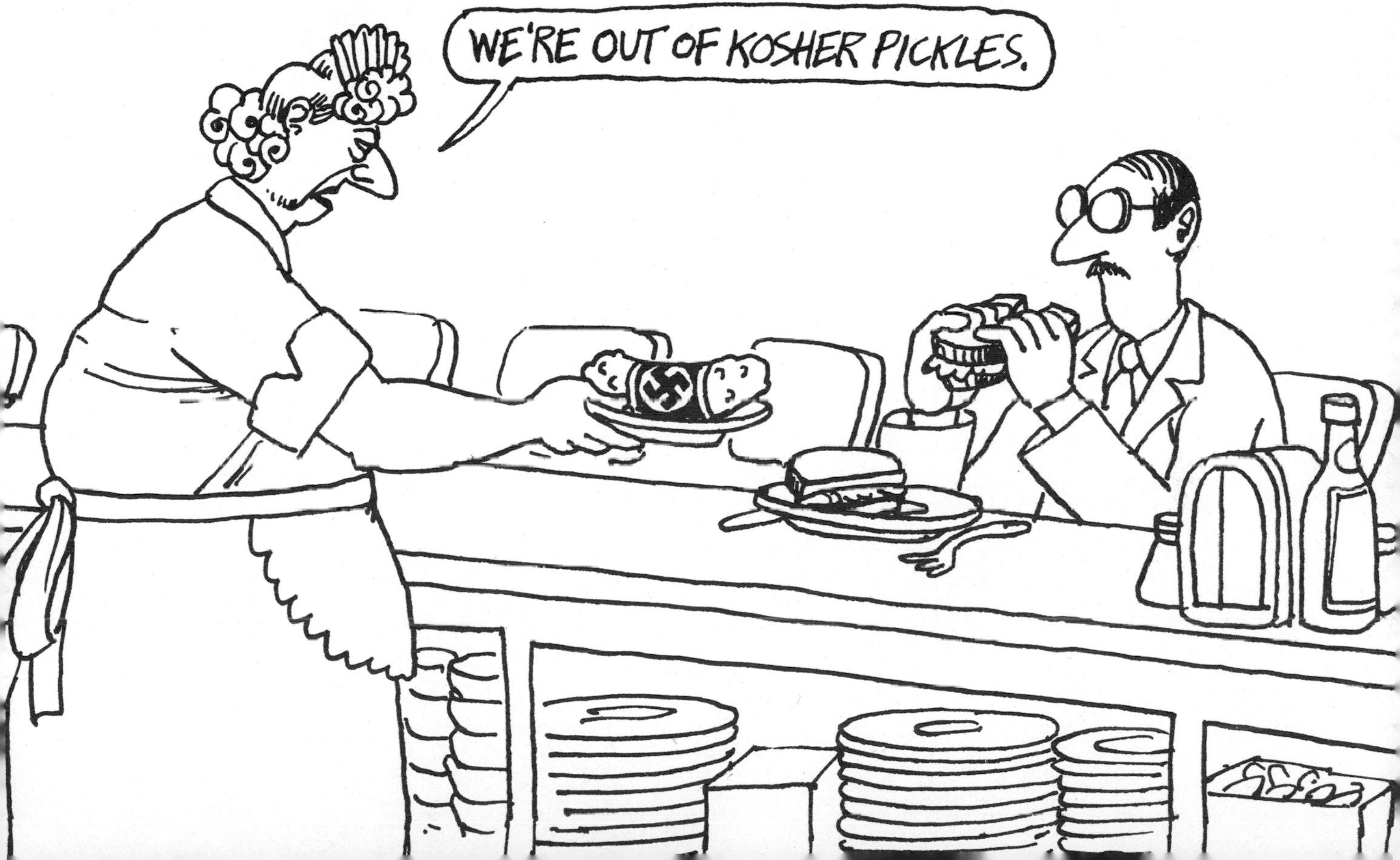
WE'RE OUT OF KOSHER PICKLES.

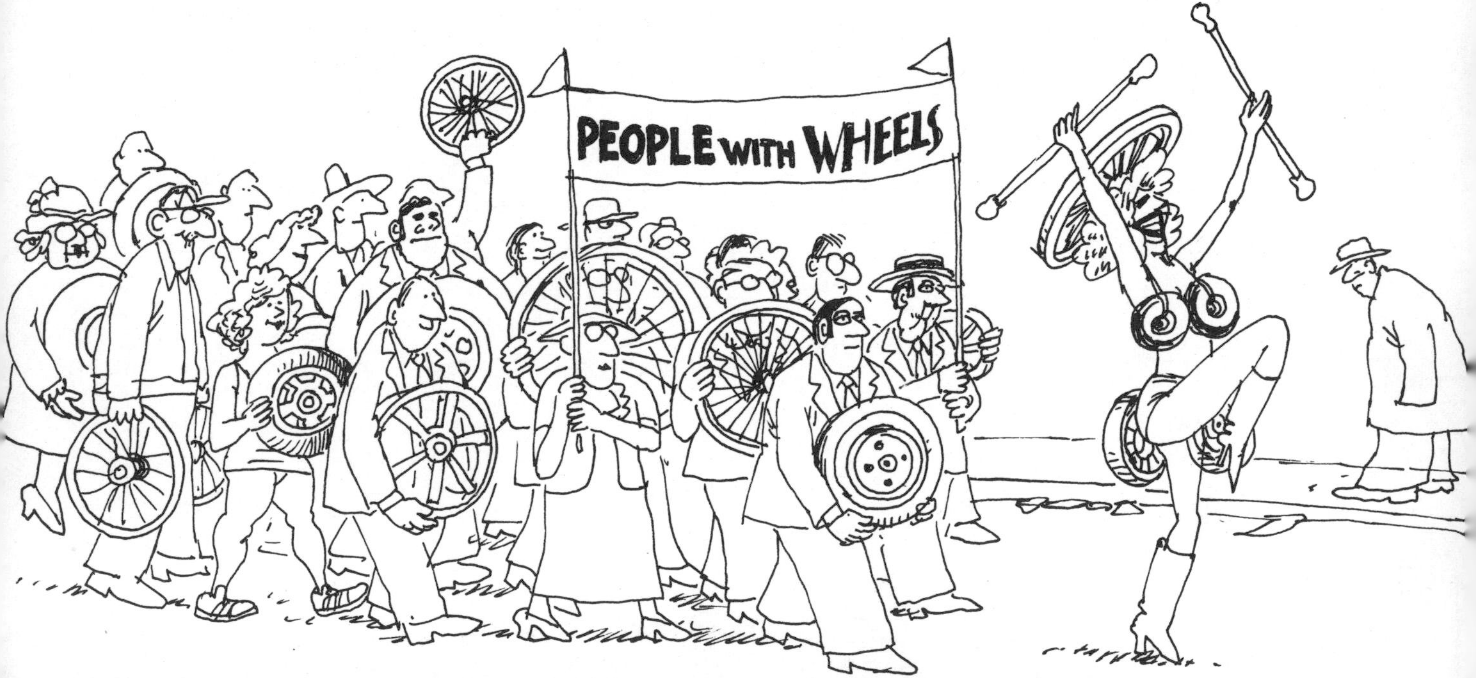
PEOPLE WITH WHEELS

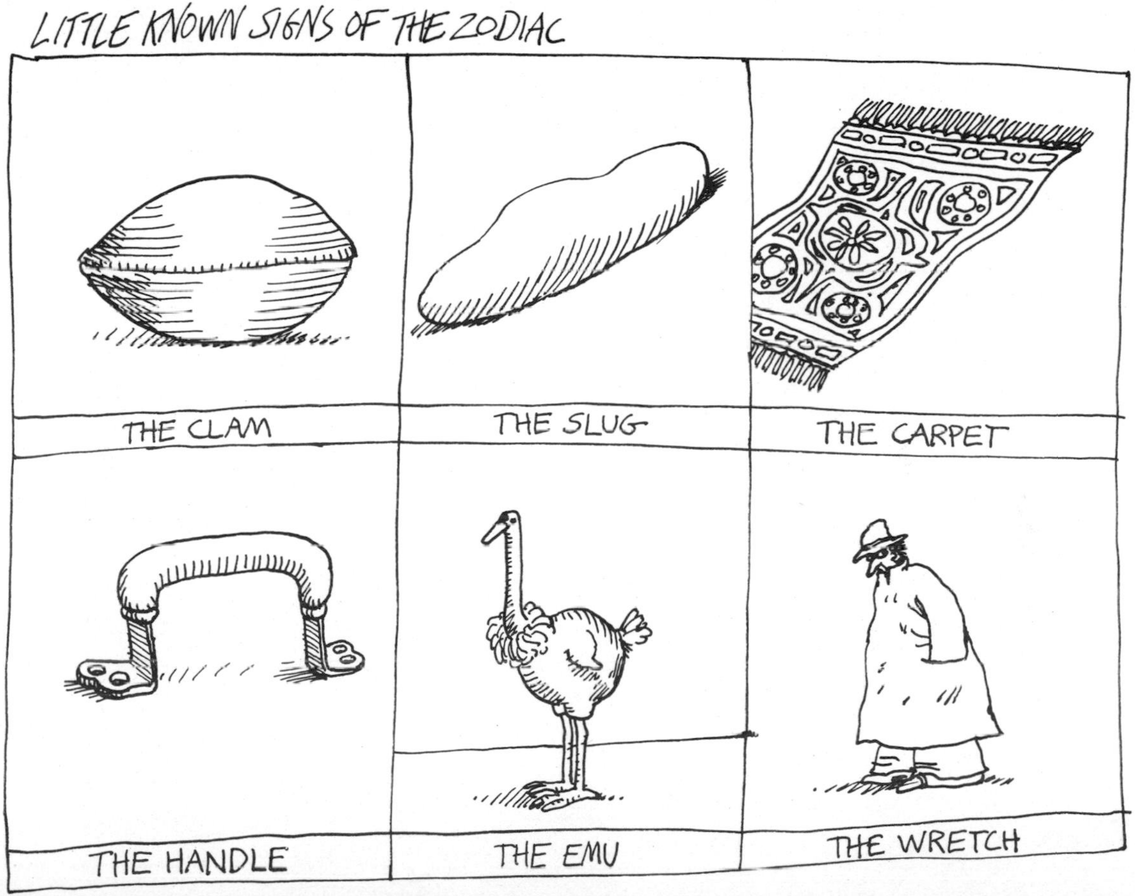
LITTLE KNOWN SIGNS OF THE ZODIAC
THE CLAM
THE SLUG
THE CARPET
THE HANDLE
THE EMU
THE WRETCH

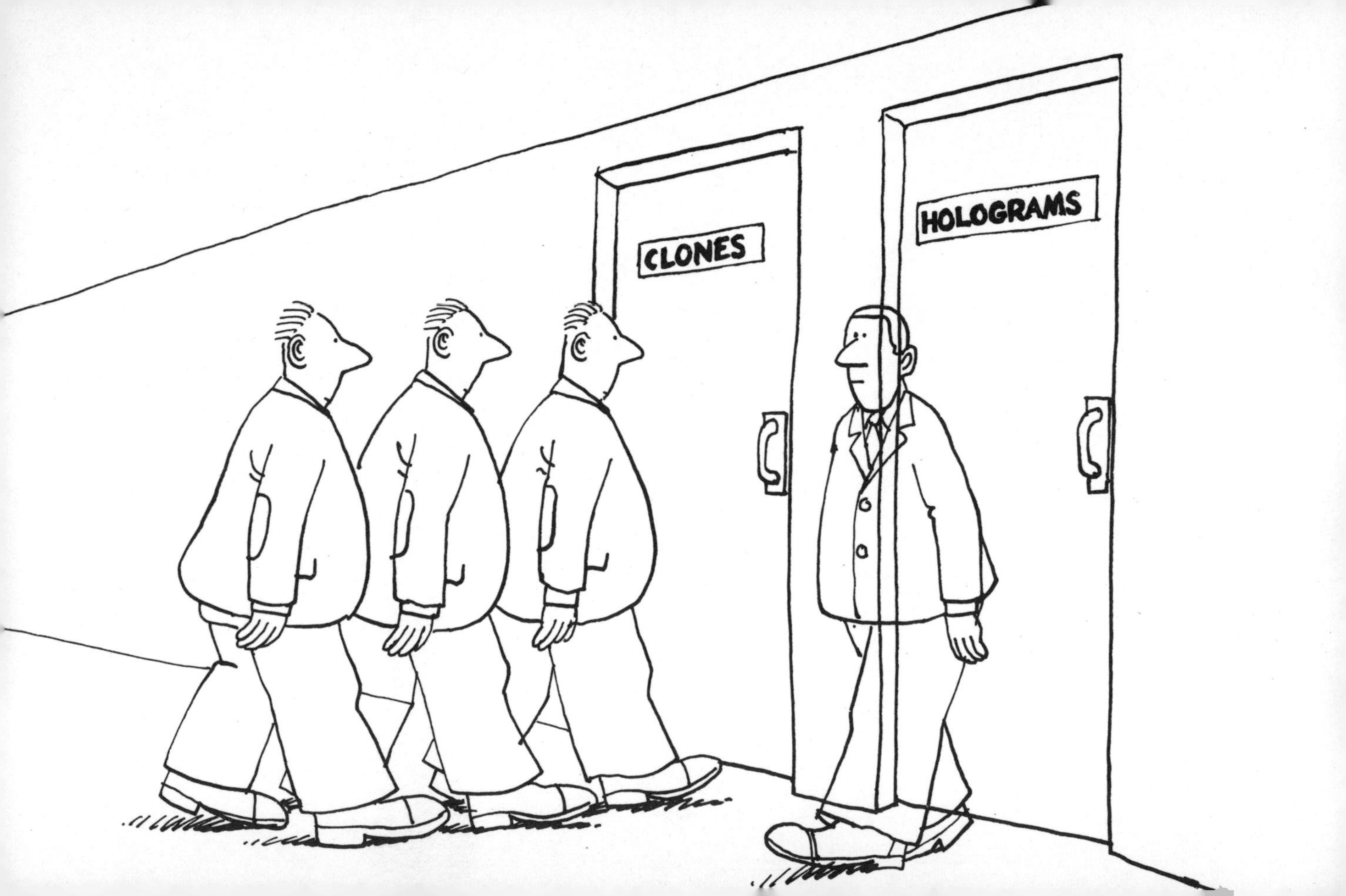
CLONES
HOLOGRAMS

## Chapter I.

NOBODY SAYS ANYTHING TO ANYBODY.

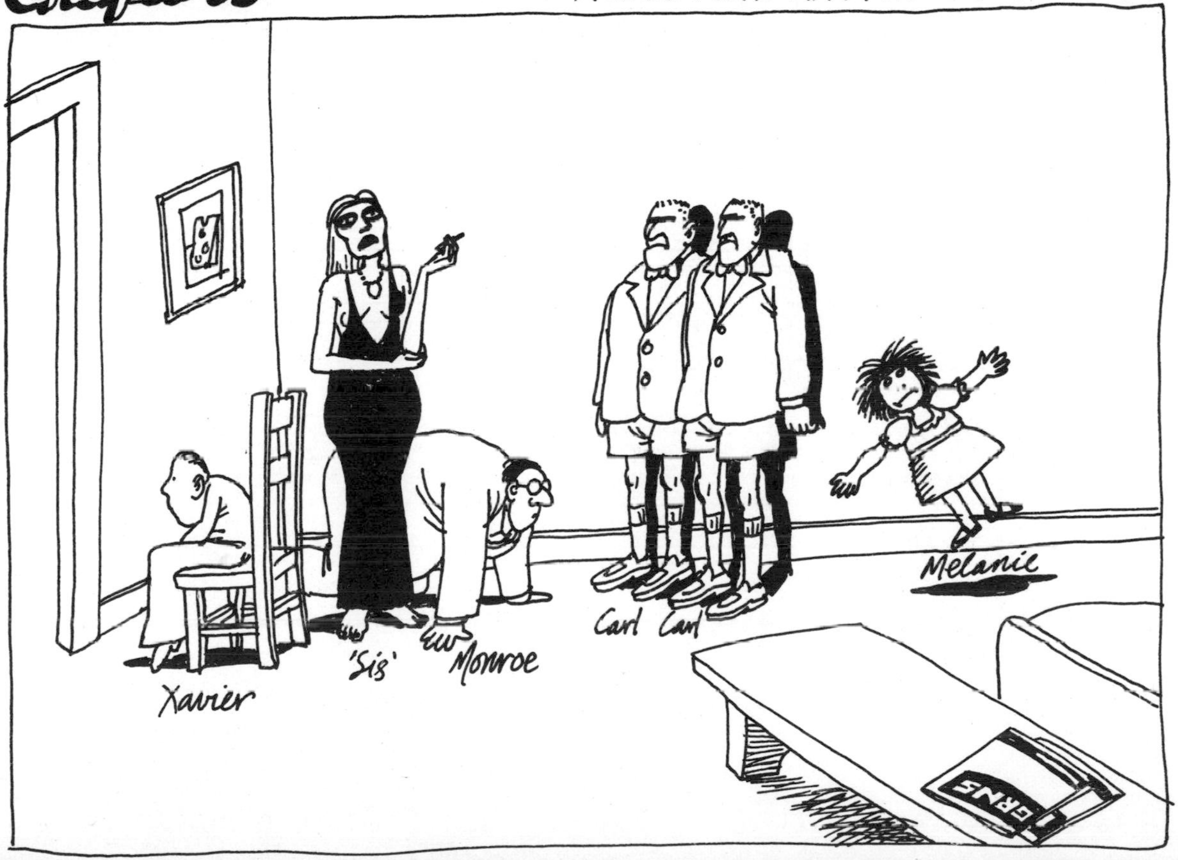
Xavier
'Sis'
Monroe
Carl
Carl
Melanie

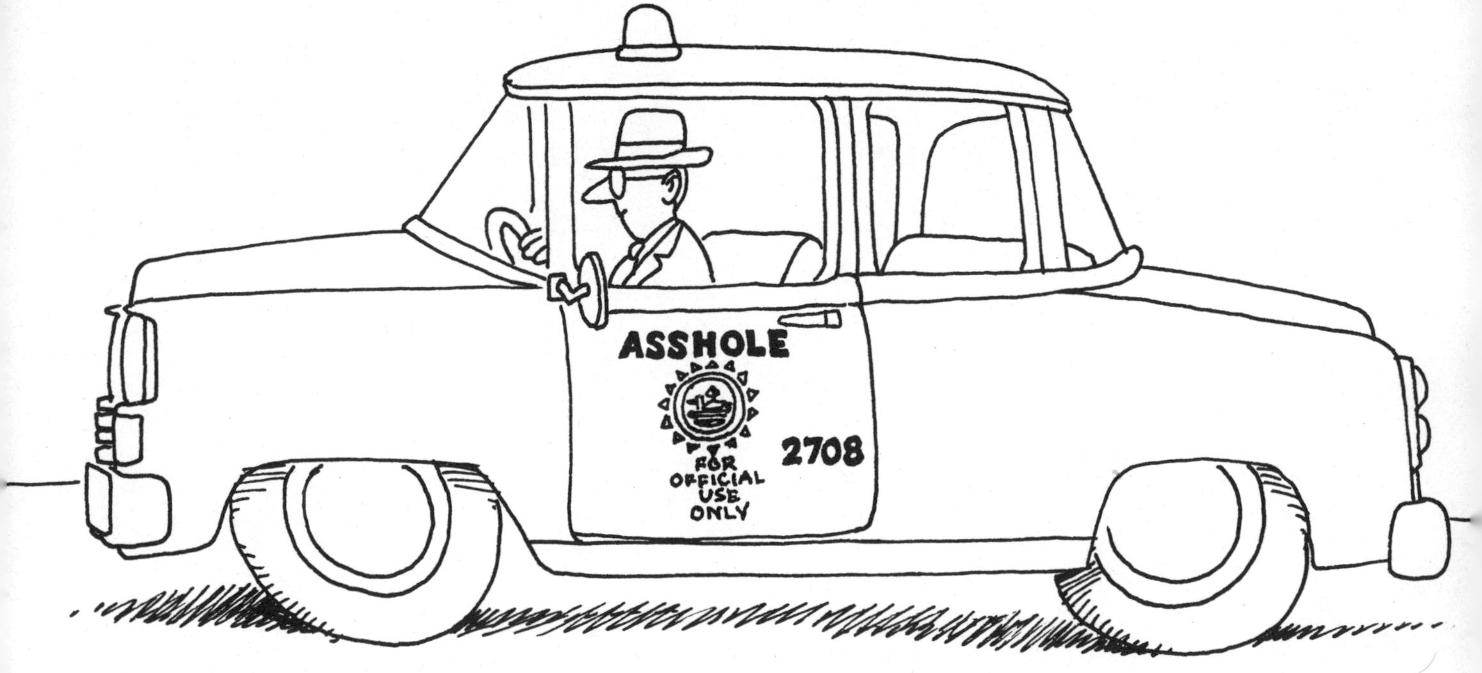
ASSHOLE
FOR
OFFICIAL
USE
ONLY
2708

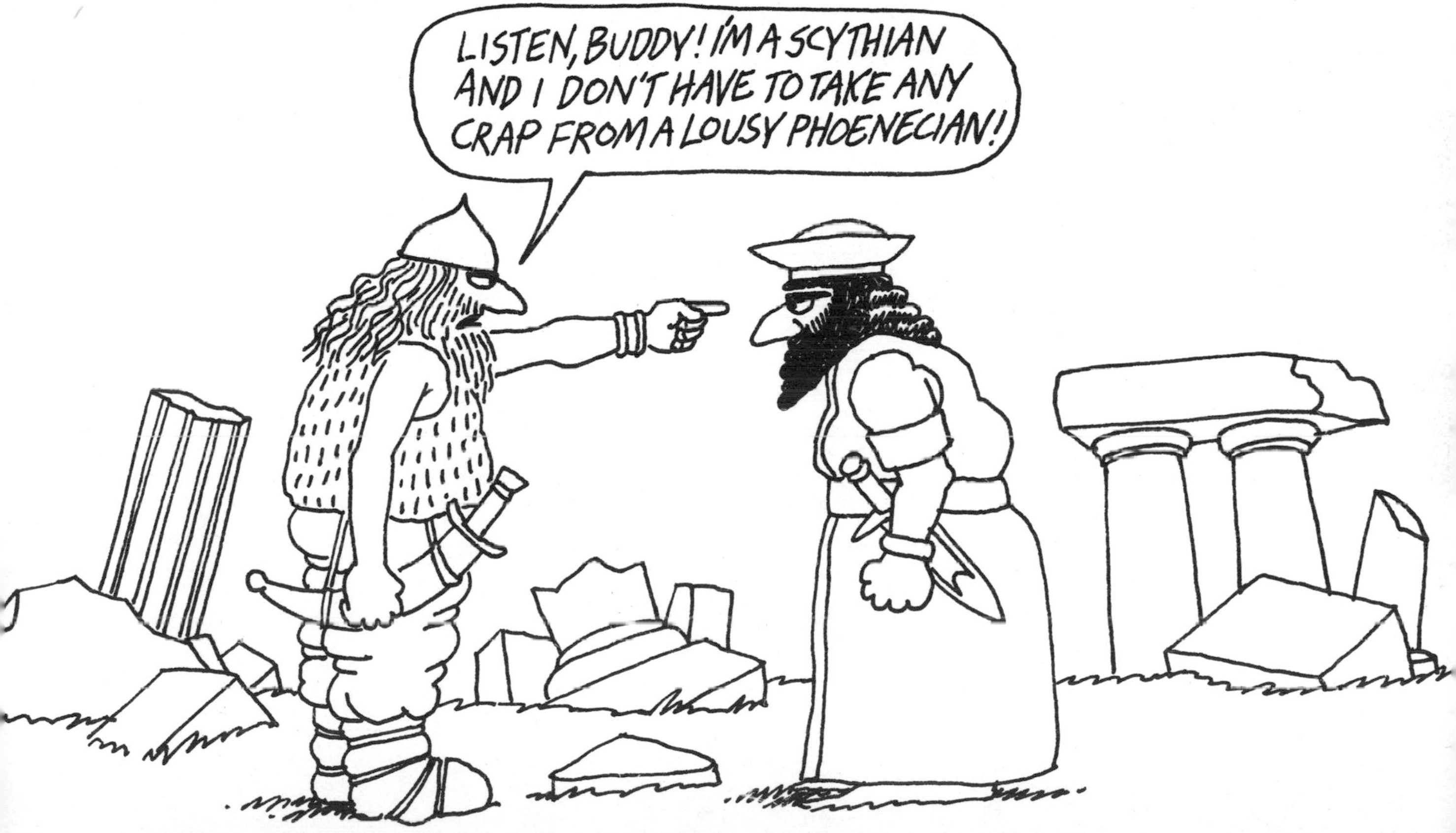
LISTEN, BUDDY! I'M A SCYTHIAN AND I DON'T HAVE TO TAKE ANY CRAP FROM A LOUSY PHOENECIAN!

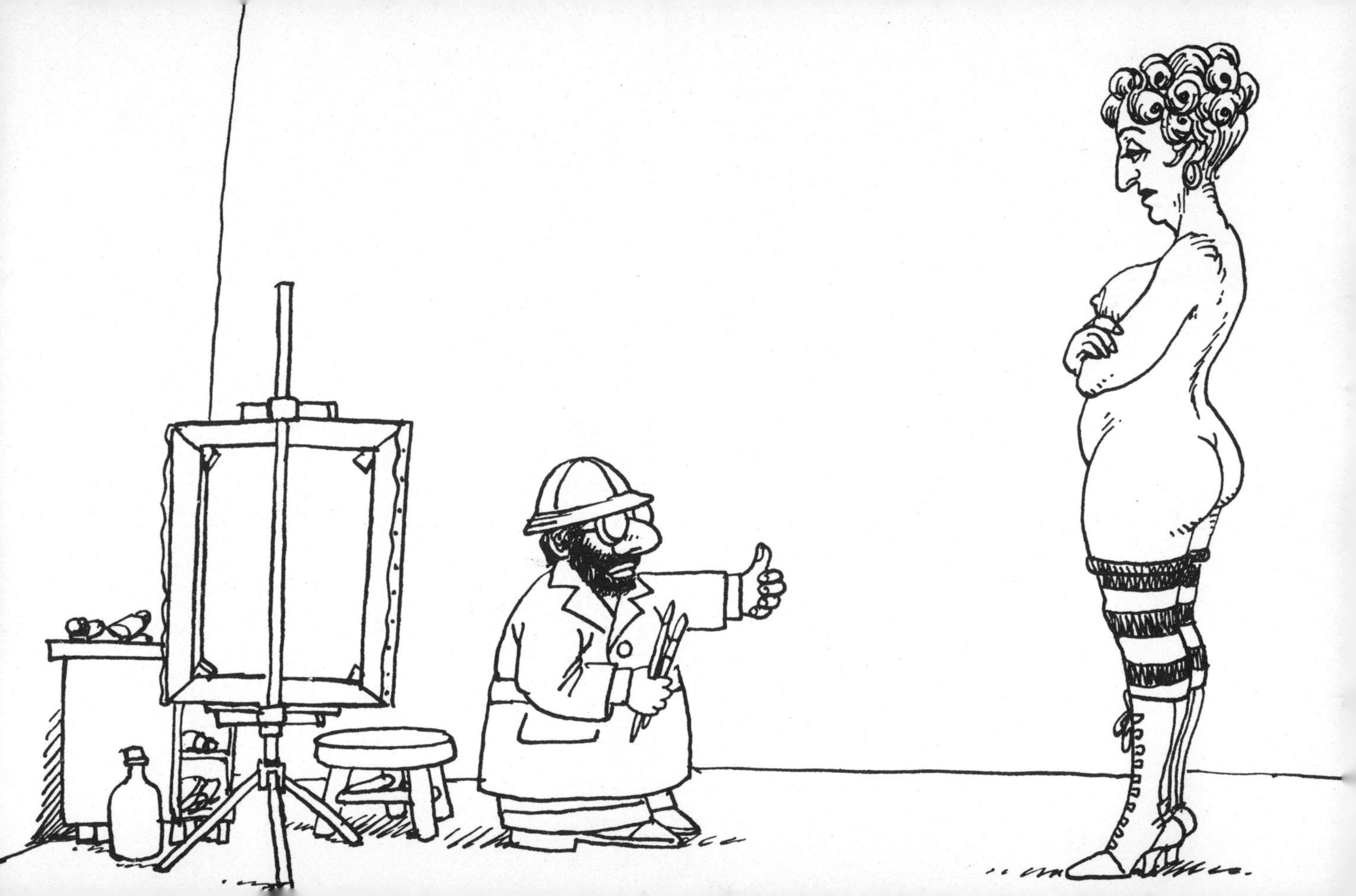

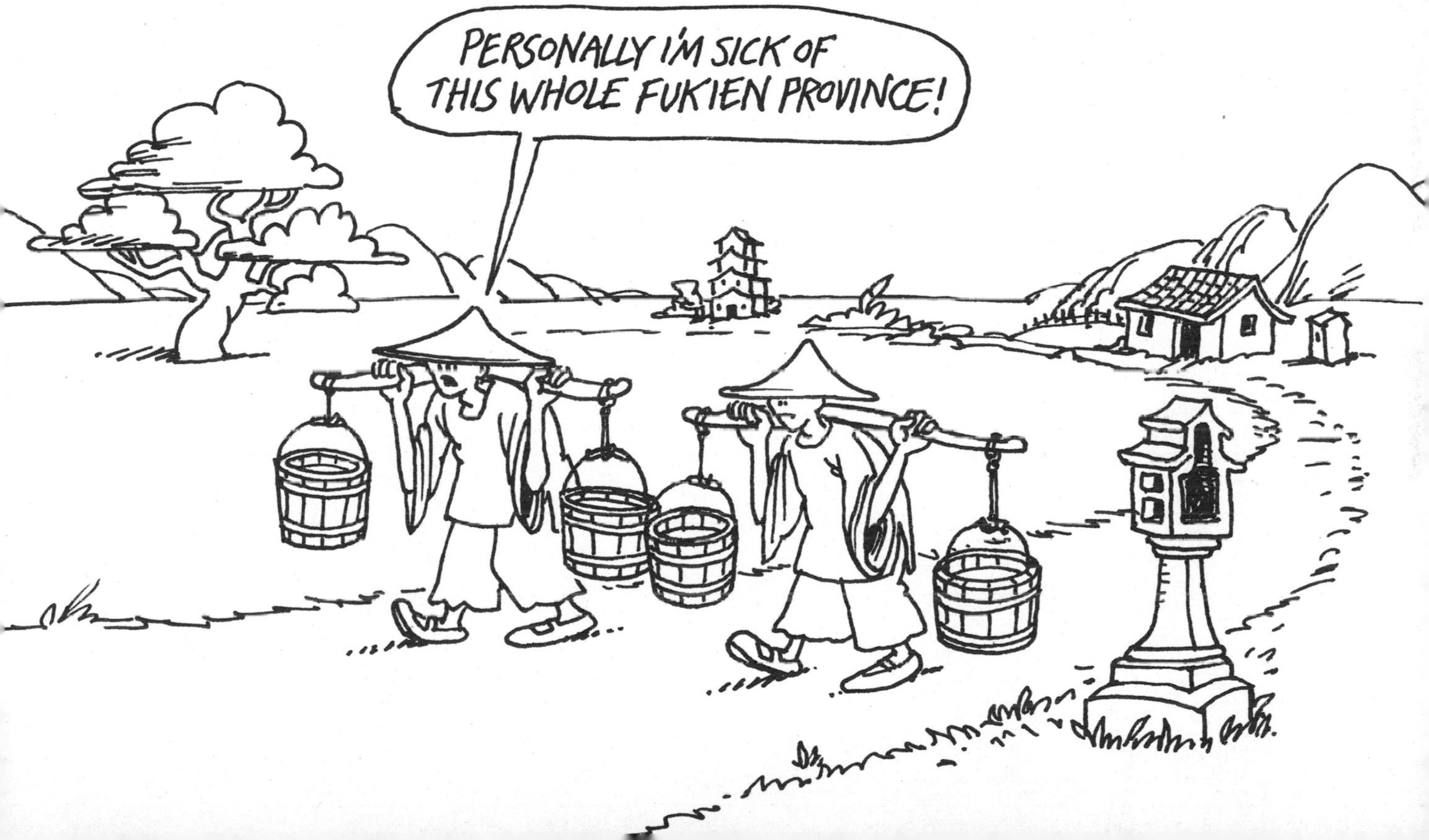
PERSONALLY I'M SICK OF
THIS WHOLE FUKIEN PROVINCE!

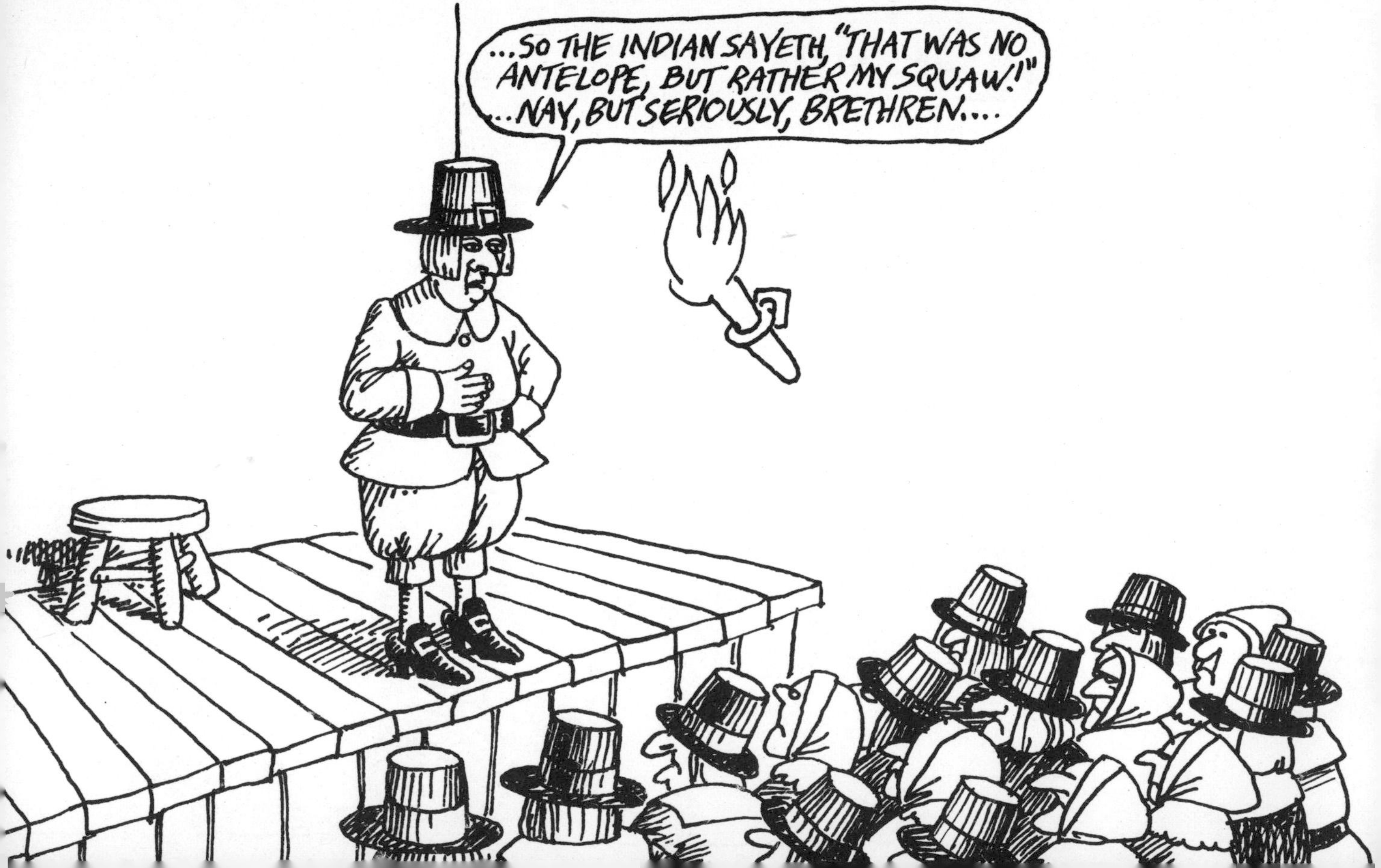
...SO THE INDIAN SAYETH, "THAT WAS NO ANTELOPE, BUT RATHER MY SQUAW!" ...NAY, BUT SERIOUSLY, BRETHREN....

# Bigotry in Action

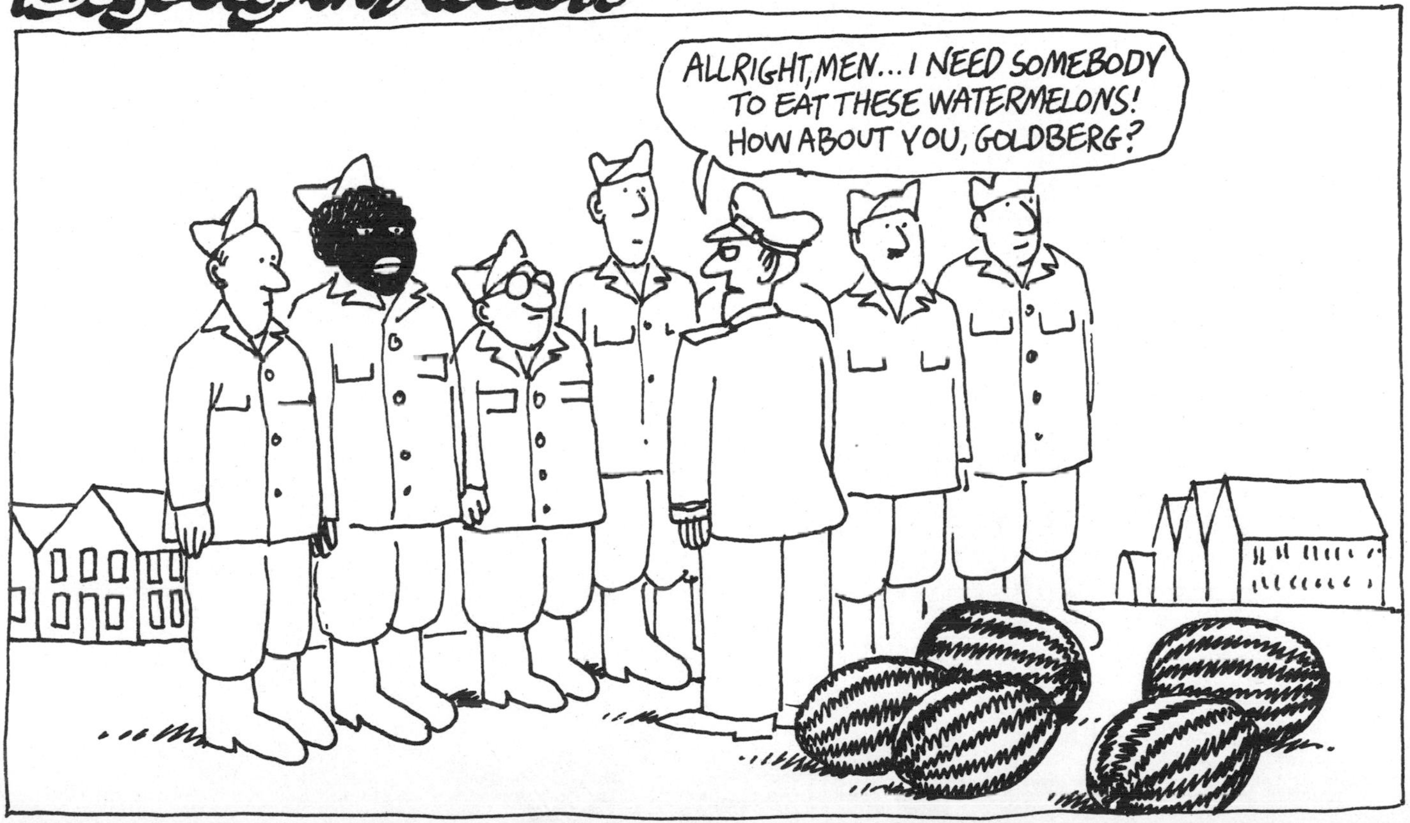
ALLRIGHT, MEN... I NEED SOMEBODY TO EAT THESE WATERMELONS! HOW ABOUT YOU, GOLDBERG?

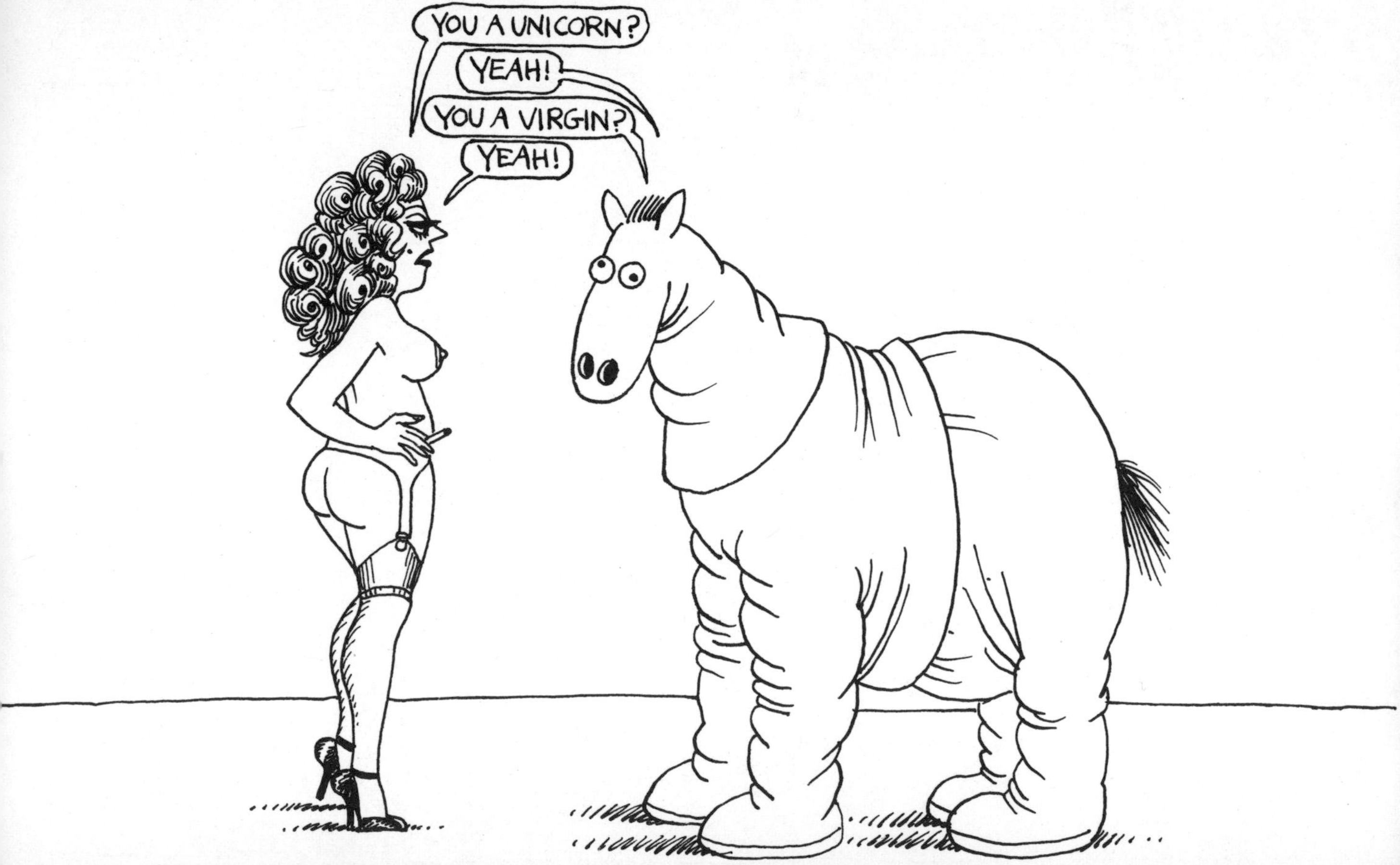
YOU A UNICORN?
YEAH!
YOU A VIRGIN?
YEAH!

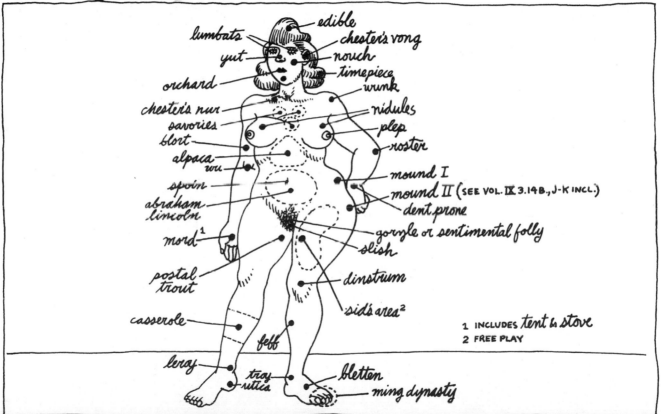

Know Your Bod

edible
lumbats
chester's vong
yut
nouch
orchard
timepiece
wrunk
chester's nur
nidules
savories
plep
blort
roster
alpaca
wu          lox
mound I
spoin
mound II (SEE VOL. IX 3.14 B., J-K INCL.)
abraham
lincoln
dent prone
mord.¹
gorzle or sentimental folly
slish
postal
trout
dinstrum
side's area²
casserole
feff
leraj
tray
utica
bletten
ming dynasty

1 INCLUDES tent & stove
2 FREE PLAY

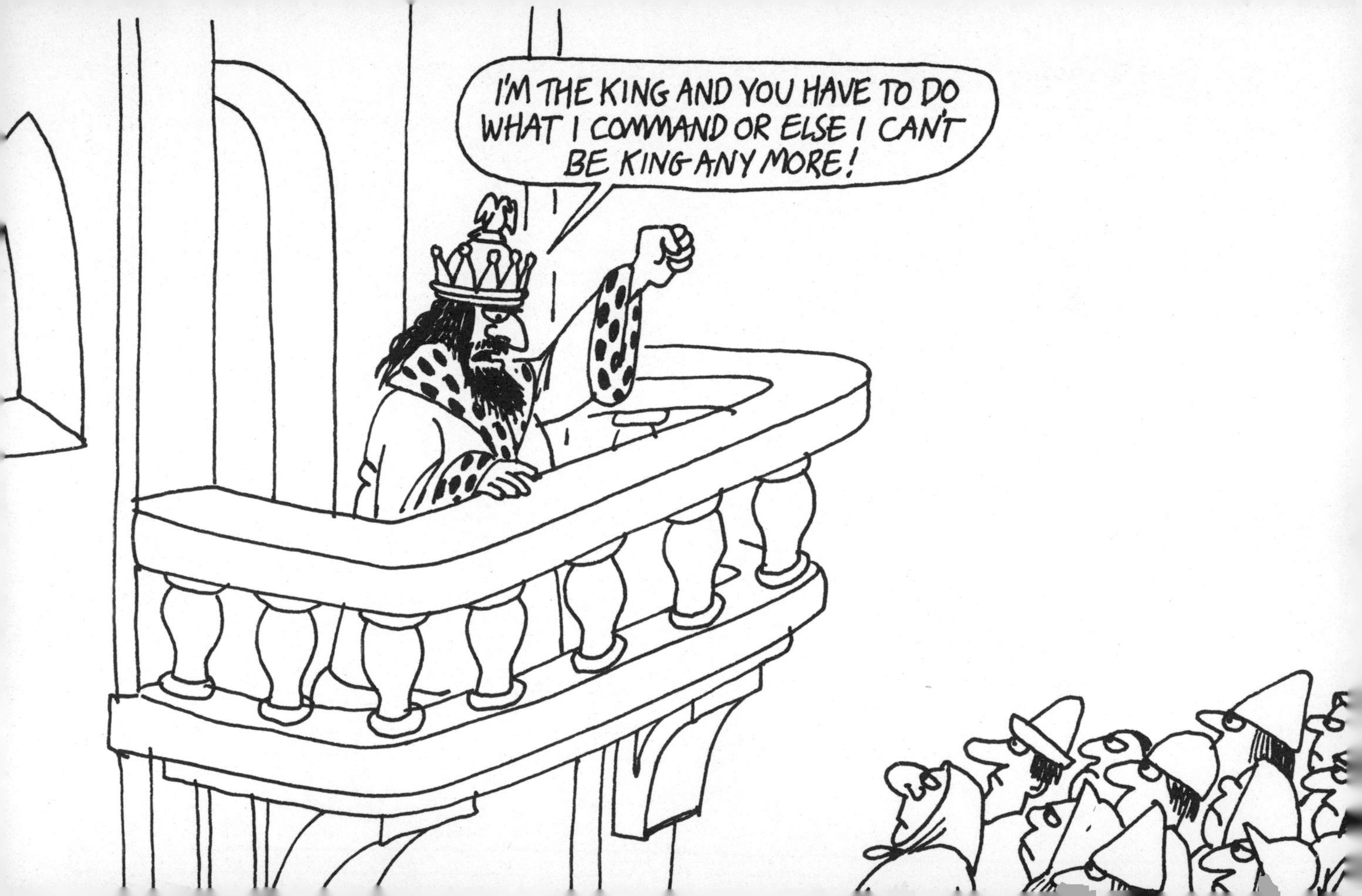
I'M THE KING AND YOU HAVE TO DO WHAT I COMMAND OR ELSE I CAN'T BE KING ANY MORE!

# Expressions of Joy in the Business Community

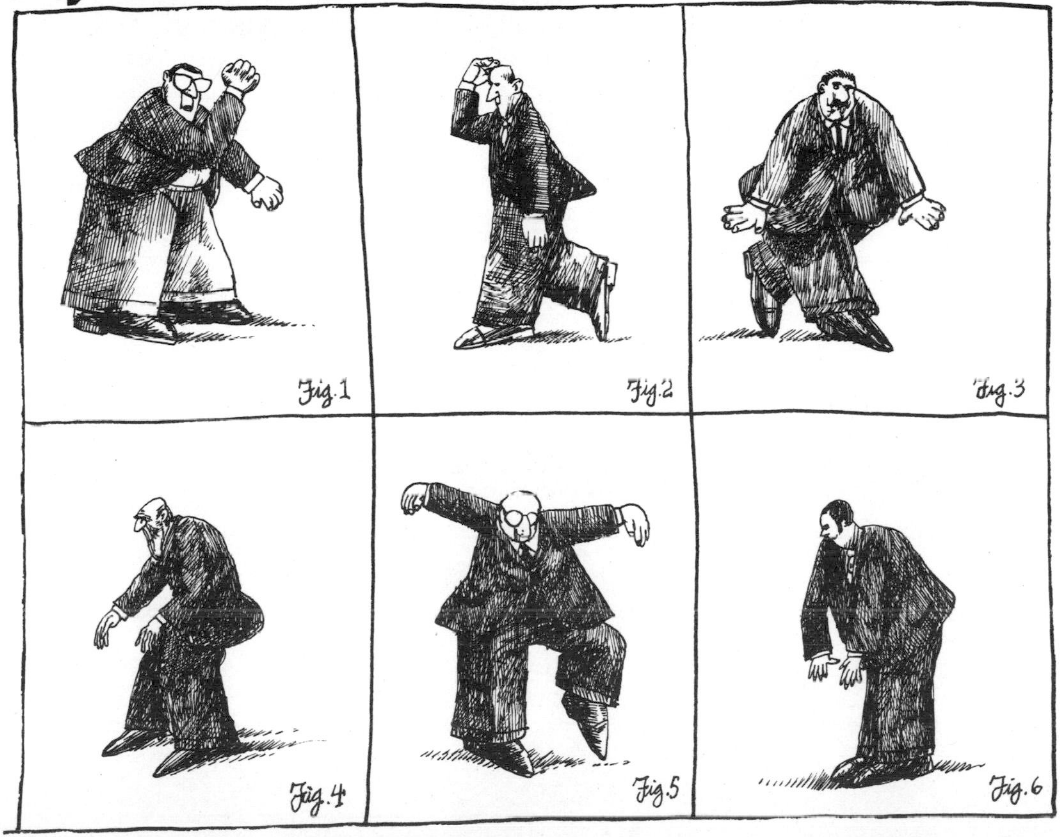
Fig. 1
Fig. 2
Fig. 3
Fig. 4
Fig. 5
Fig. 6

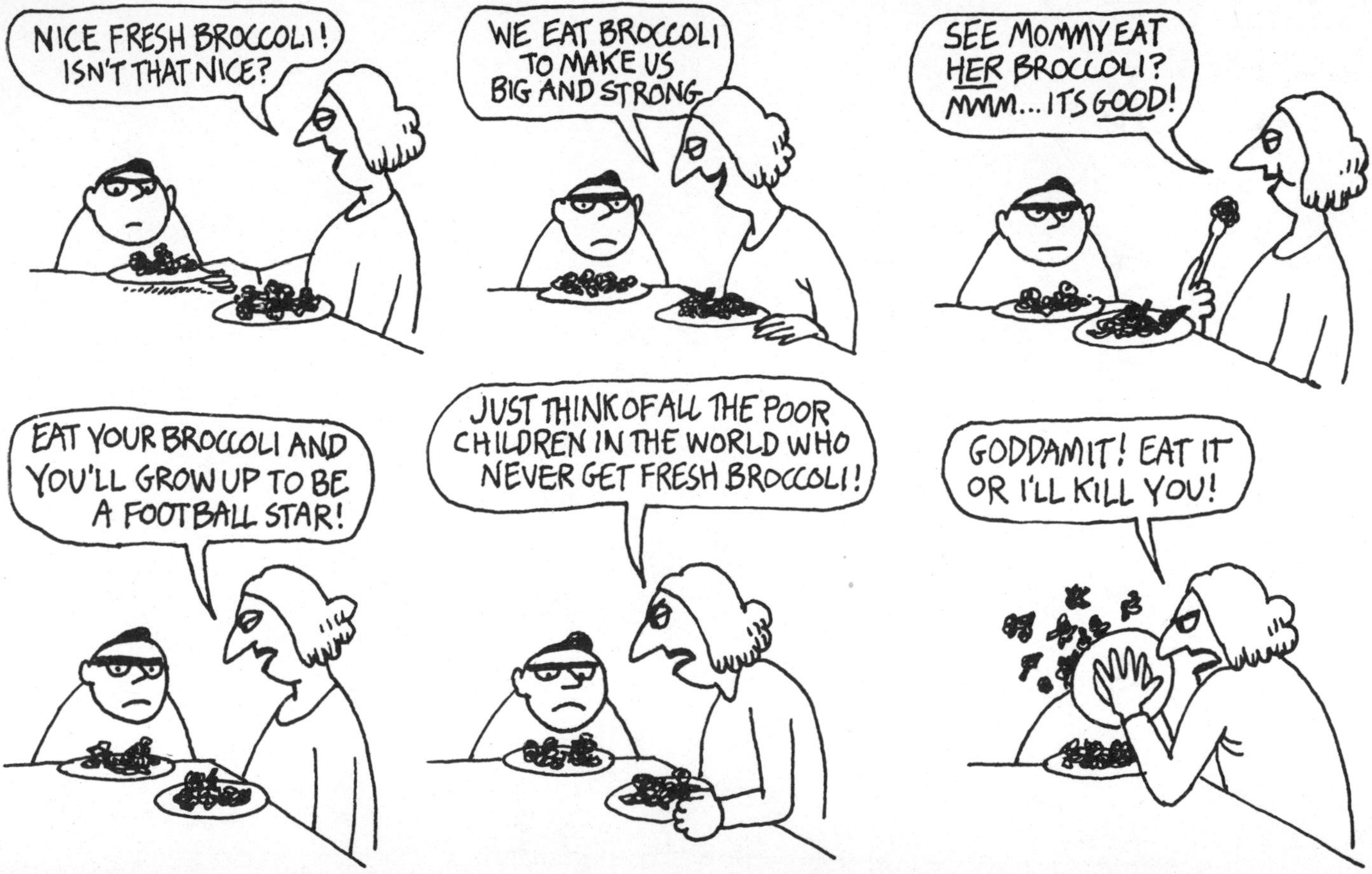
NICE FRESH BROCCOLI! ISN'T THAT NICE?
WE EAT BROCCOLI TO MAKE US BIG AND STRONG
SEE MOMMY EAT HER BROCCOLI? MMM... ITS GOOD!
EAT YOUR BROCCOLI AND YOU'LL GROW UP TO BE A FOOTBALL STAR!
JUST THINK OF ALL THE POOR CHILDREN IN THE WORLD WHO NEVER GET FRESH BROCCOLI!
GODDAMIT! EAT IT OR I'LL KILL YOU!

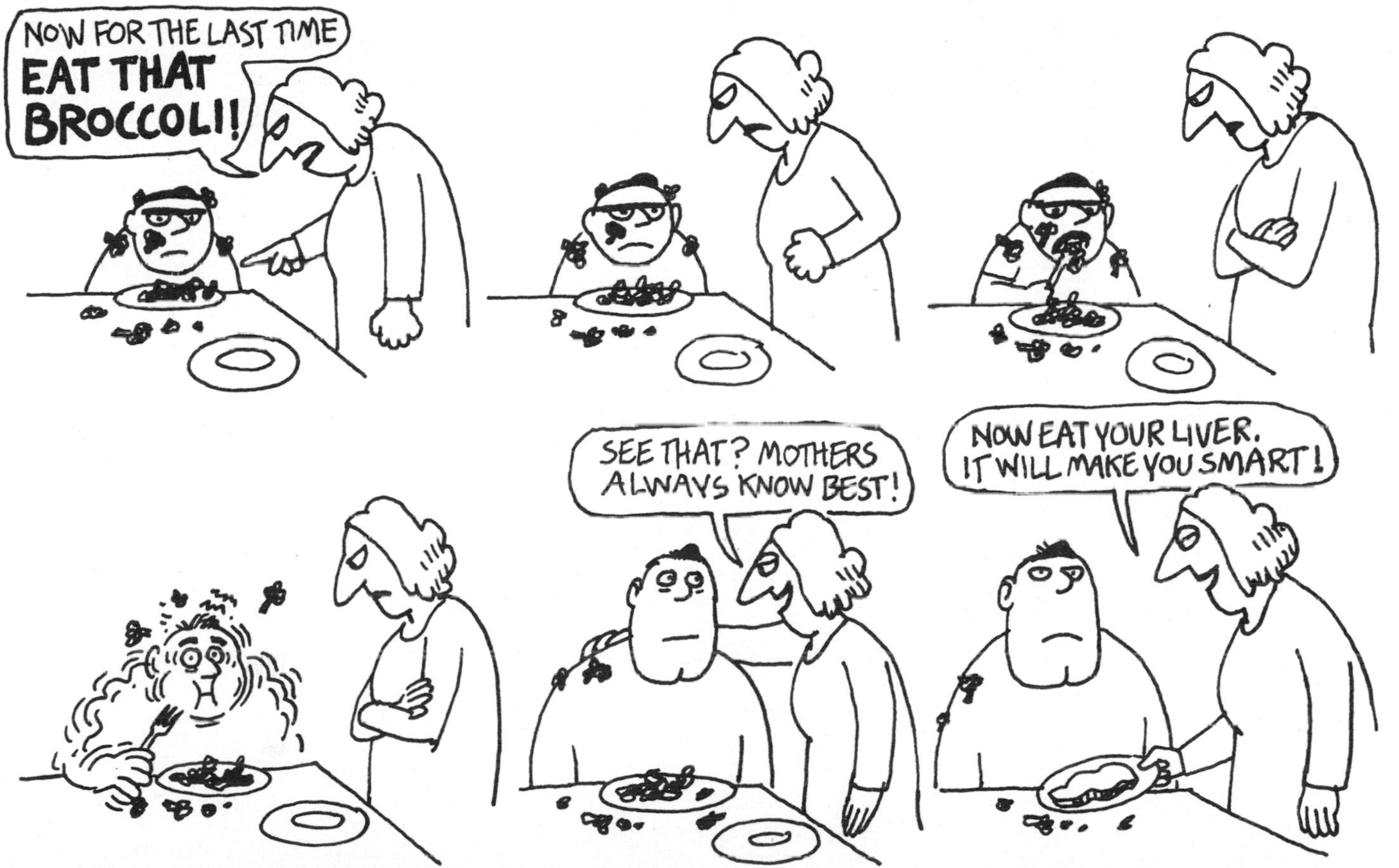
NOW FOR THE LAST TIME
EAT THAT BROCCOLI!
SEE THAT? MOTHERS ALWAYS KNOW BEST!
NOW EAT YOUR LIVER. IT WILL MAKE YOU SMART!

# Shambles

SAN RAFAEL · CALIFORNIA

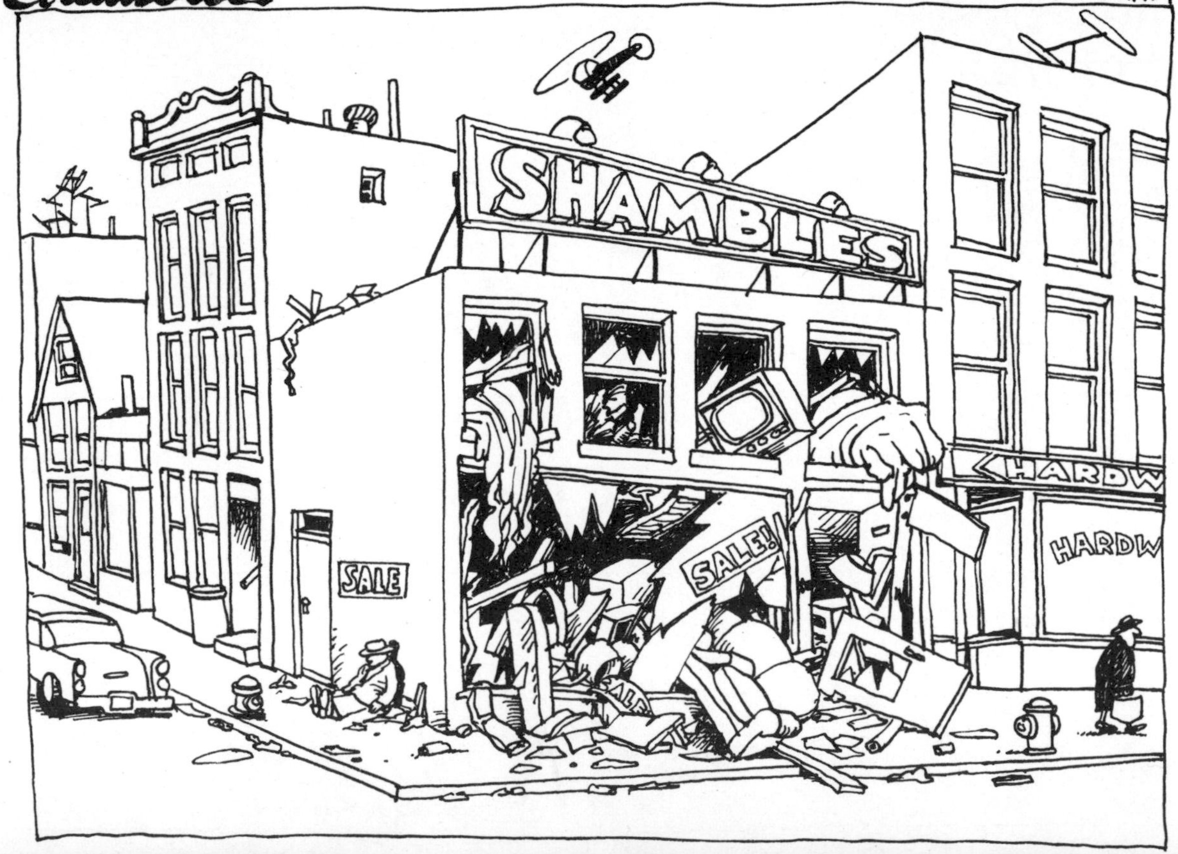

SHAMBLES
SALE
SALE!
HARDW
HARDW

KING MALCOLM IV WAS HAMSTERED ON THE STEPS OF PEWKSBURY CATHEDRAL, JUNE 11, 1058.

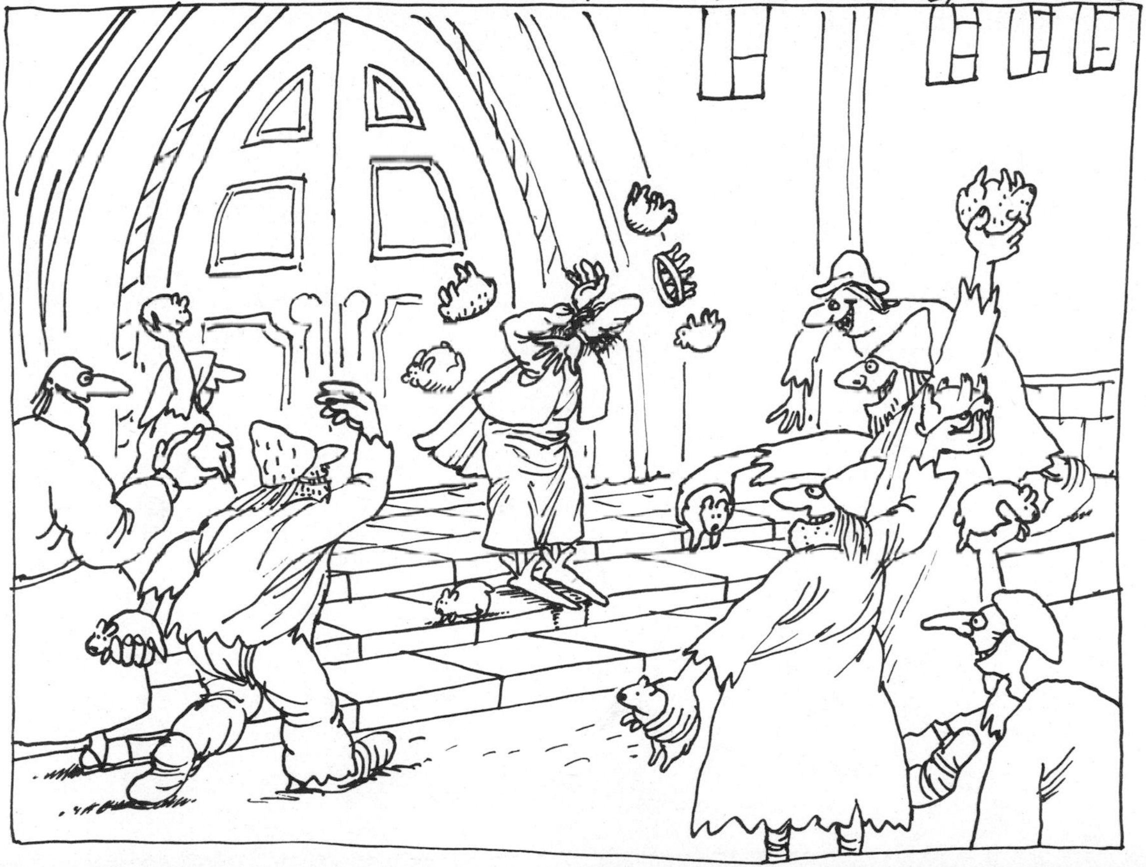

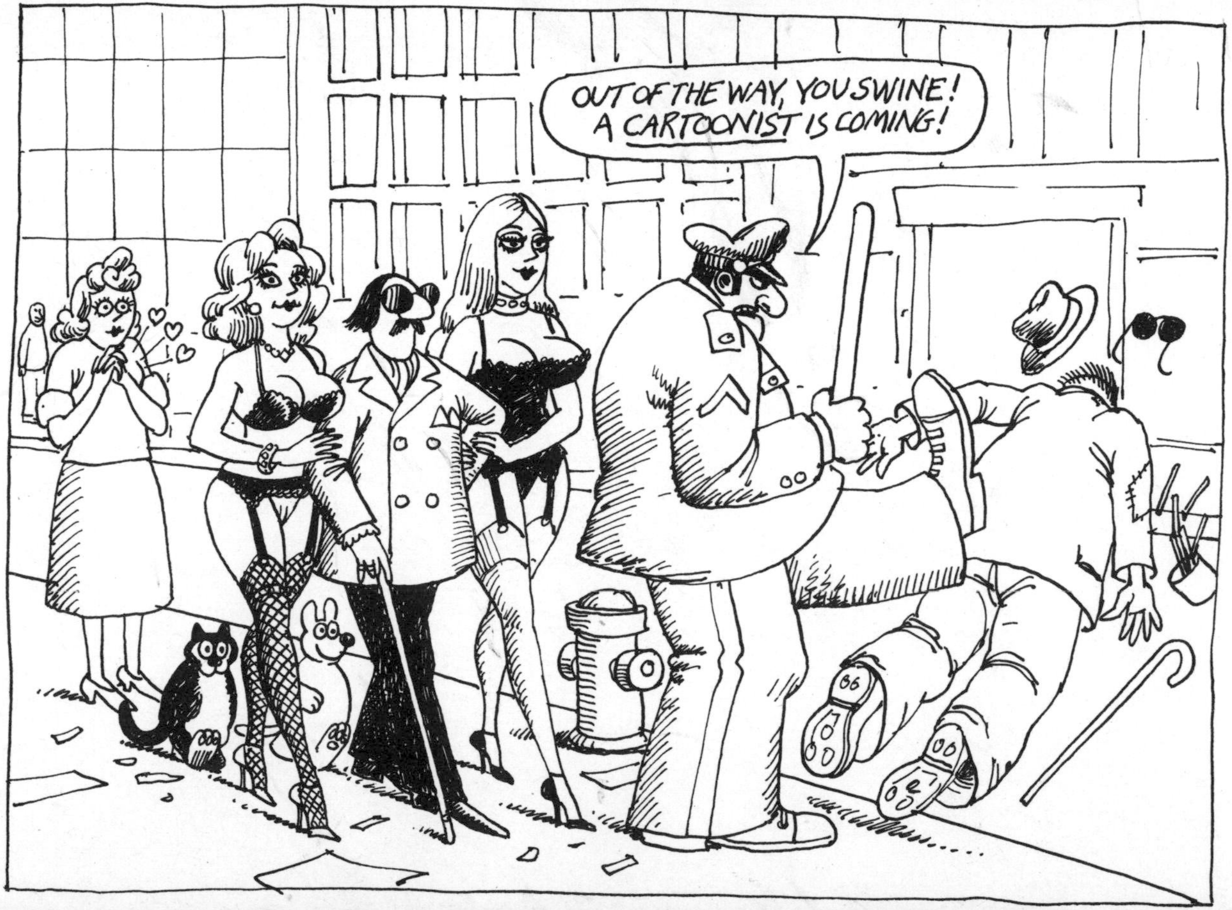
OUT OF THE WAY, YOU SWINE! A CARTOONIST IS COMING!